GLOBAL POLITICS OF WELSH PATAGONIA

SERIES EDITORS' PREFACE

In a rapidly changing world, how we understand nations, their formations and contexts is being transformed. Across a range of disciplines, the focus on race/ethnicity studies is growing. In recent decades, a considerable body of writing and research has been produced that details the place and reception of racial and ethnic minorities in Welsh society, speaking more broadly to Wales's global encounters past and present. These social, economic and cultural connections shape Wales today. This research and cultural output has great significance to the general understanding of *stori Cymru*, the telling of how Wales sees itself and how it relates to the wider world.

The series *Race, Ethnicity, Wales and the World* aims to consolidate attention to this existing work, and to stimulate new and emerging work in the field of study as part of more general trends in both the *globalising* and *decolonising* of Welsh studies. The series is an exploration of the ways in which Wales has been and is being reshaped and reimagined through its racial and ethnic diversity, showcasing and stimulating multi-disciplinary research, and providing accessible works to a broad public and available for cross national comparison and scholarship.

Charlotte Williams OBE and Dr Neil Evans

GLOBAL POLITICS OF WELSH PATAGONIA

Settler Colonialism from the Margins

Lucy Taylor

University of Wales Press
2025

www.uwp.co.uk

British Library Cataloguing-in-Publication Data

A catalogue record for this book is available from the British Library.

ISBN   978-1-83772-216-7

e-ISBN   978-1-83772-217-4

Cover image: Studio photograph taken in 1867 of Indigenous and Welsh contingents who travelled from Chubut Valley to Buenos Aires, both on government business: Kilcham, Yelulk and Wisel stand; Lewis Jones, centre; Cacique Francisco, Kitchkskum and Waisho in the front row. See David Williams, *Entretelones y Tolderias* (Buenos Aires: Editorial Jornada, 2010), pp. 84–97.

Typeset by Geethik Technologies

Printed by CPI Group (UK) Ltd, Croydon CR0 4YY

For GPSR enquiries please contact:
Easy Access System Europe Oü, 16879218
Mustamäe tee 50, 10621, Tallinn, Estonia. gpsr.requests@easproject.com

Contents

Acknowledgements

It has taken a long time to bring this book to fruition and count-less people have helped me along the way, for which I am sincerely grateful. I will begin by thanking the hugely helpful staff of the var-ious libraries and archives I have consulted, including the National Library of Wales, the University of Bangor Archive, the Museo Regional Trevelin (gracias a Alberto Williams and Jorge Fiori) and Museo Histórico Regional Gaiman (gracias Fabio Gonzales). With-out the care and curation of archivists we would not be able to 'hear' voices from the past. Thank you too to scholars Marcelo Gavirati, Guillermo Williams and the wider Welsh Patagonian community for their super-helpful hospitality. I also wish to thank the many Argen-tine scholars whose tireless work in piecing together the Indigenous archive and collecting the vital oral history has played such a piv-otal role in bringing to light Indigenous experience and struggle in Patagonia. I lean gratefully on their expertise, while accepting any mistakes as my own.

My research has enjoyed the support of many kind and knowl-edgeable colleagues. In Aber, I would particularly thank Elin Royles, who magicked up an utterly invaluable list of the Welsh Patagonia sources in the NLW, and all my Welsh colleagues at Aber who share their vast reserve of cultural and linguistic insights with great gener-osity – diolch o galon! I'd also like to thank my Directors of Research during the writing of this book: Mustapha Pasha, Anwen Elias, Ber-it Bliesemann de Guevara and Milja Kurki. It was Milja's energised enthusiasm at the start of this project that really made me believe that I could do something valuable, after so many years of self-doubt. I would also like to thank Aberystwyth University for granting me periods of study leave and small pots of money to fund research trips, as well as the HEFCW funding which enabled the publication of this book. Diolch Aber!

My work has also been shaped by many colleagues outside Aber, especially Geraldine and Laura. Geraldine (Lublin) has been my writing and organizing partner in recent years. Her knowledge, insight and team spirit make our intellectual exchanges and social outings a pleasure (even the tricky bits!). Laura (Brace) is the wisest person I know and my oldest academic friend. Our writing retreat jaunts are a source of inspiration without any doubt – fuelled by tea and cake.

Of course, I offer my sincere thanks to the team at University of Wales Press for their prompt and helpful guidance through the publishing process, and especially to Neil Evans and Charlotte Williams for accepting me into their book series. Thank you to the anonymous reviewers too for their valuable insights on the drafts and to Neil for his meticulous and encouraging notes.

Finally, I'd like to thank my family: my beloved sisters and the Taylor Clan, my teulu Cymraeg hyfryd and all my friends in Aber and Goginan. Most importantly, diolch i Arwyn, my patient, loving husband, and Efan our lovely son. Without you … well I'd be nothing, and this book would not exist. Diolch o galon, muchisimas gracias, my heartfelt thanks.

INTRODUCTION

Where the Welsh Are

The aim of this book is to reveal just how complicated settler colonial relationships can be. The focus of the study – the Welsh colony in Patagonia (established in 1865 and known as Y Wladfa) – is familiar to everyone in Wales but little known in wider academic circles such as settler colonial studies or Latin American studies. Yet it can tell us a great deal about not just settler-Indigenous relations in the colony but also the importance of origin countries and the complex interplay of ideologies, pragmatic aims and the desire for freedom which shapes people's actions in settler scenarios. What makes the case special is the ambiguous position of this particular Welsh settlement: the leaders were driven by an anti-colonial impulse that responded to colonization at home (as they saw it), yet their strategy entailed creating a colony on Indigenous land. That is, they were simultaneously colonized and colonizing. To help me untangle these complexities I deploy three conceptual tools which are equally, though differently, applicable to both the Indigenous and Welsh communities: possession, racialization/barbarization and assimilation.

The Welsh did not use physical violence during the settlement process and this has been a source of empowering pride in Wales when drawn in contrast to the use of physical force by 'English' and British imperial colonizers, and has often been celebrated and romanticized. As a result, Y Wladfa has not only been viewed as legitimate, it has been deployed as an asset, contributing to Welsh strategies for cultural resistance and social renewal back home. Yet Y Wladfa was also undeniably fundamental to Argentina's nation-building project which required that state authority be imposed across the whole territory on the map. The Welsh pioneer settlement might have had its own agenda, but it was also a key step in the dispossession of Indigenous lands, the assertion of sovereignty and capitalist modernity. The moment has come for a candid appraisal of this darker side of Y Wladfa. Now that Wales is maturing as a political nation (following over twenty-five years of devolution), its cultural confidence is growing and it is boldly adopting anti-racist policies, the time is ripe to revisit Wales's role in colonial projects and recognize that the nation might be dominated by England, but has also benefitted from colonial expansion. This book brings Y Wladfa to the centre of those discussions about identity and the future of Wales.

Ultimately, the book argues that, as both academics and citizens we should resist the poles of celebration and condemnation, and recognize the dilemmas and human stories in the vast and muddled middle ground. It is only by appreciating the complexity of human relationships in the past, I suggest, that we can build better relationships in the future. But this is not a level playing field: Welsh voices and concerns dominate the archives and literature. In order to shift this habit, I begin this introduction by bringing an Indigenous voice centre stage and plunging the reader into the Mapuche world of Katrülaf.

***

Sometime in the late 1870s or early 1880s a young man called Katrülaf went on a journey to Where the Welsh Are with his older brother and two friends. He left his family and the wider extended group that his family lived with – sometimes staying in one place, sometimes travelling – and took off on a young man's adventure. His brother had been before and they were well equipped with the life skills and landscape knowledge necessary to traverse the wide-open plains, mountains, rivers and windswept hillsides of Patagonia. They took with them rhea feathers and guanaco skins to trade, as did many Tehuelche, Pampa and Mapuche people during this time. In his memoir, Katrülaf recalls this 'life' and 'work' already framed by (settler) capitalism (to really 'hear' Katrülaf's voice, I suggest that the reader speak these quotes aloud):[1]

> The people just lived from ostriches [rheas], the people; the people could just live from guanacos. Ostriches exist, arma-

dillos exist, and from this the people lived, the people had all kinds of animals. Then also the people did work for the *wingka* [European descendants], they gathered ostrich feathers, all kinds of things they gathered. They made leather mantles called *waralka*, that is what the people collected together, three or four *waralka* they took to the foreign *wingka* (the Welsh). That's what the people did.

They gathered a hundred, two hundred feathers to take to the *pulpería* [trading post], that is what the poor people did. They travelled for three or four months, this is the only way that they worked on our lands, us, the people that we are [...]. Only with the ostriches were we wealthy people, the poor people. They call the men like this because they work to trap ostriches with *boleadoras* [hunting weapon of three balls on a lasso], trap the guanacos with *boleadoras*, that is what the people did. Also the women, when they grow up in our lands they work, they make the *waralka*, they make blankets called *pontro*, they made all kinds of woollen mantles called *lama*, they made *chamall* – men's clothing like a chiripá – this was the women's work, in this way the poor people worked, they called the women like that because they only worked in this.

So, they took this to the *pulpería*, and with it they obtained all kinds of things (clothes, tools) ... so people dressed in very good clothes. In this way they accumulated all kinds of animals, he who was busy [working] had cattle, had horses, had sheep, had mares, had goats ... So, people accumulated all kinds of things, people wore all kinds of ornamental silver ... At the time when I grew up, I was just a young man, there was nothing bad in our land, in this way I grew up.[2]

One of their trading destinations was the Welsh colony in the Chubut Valley (it was established in 1865 by around 160 Welsh settlers, mostly families, who we will meet throughout the book). The Welsh in turn traded these goods with merchants in Buenos Aires where the skins were fashioned into rugs for middle-class homes and the feathers would adorn the hats of fine ladies around the world. In this way, Katrülaf and his people were hooked into the nineteenth-century global market economy.

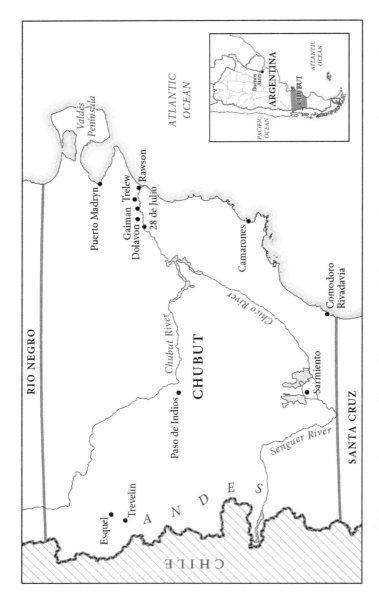

Figure 1 Welsh Patagonia. Source: Geraldine Lublin, *Memoir and Identity in Welsh Patagonia* (Cardiff: University of Wales Press, 2017), p. ii.

Previously, the various groups who lived in Patagonia south of the Rio Negro had traded with the Spanish-speaking Argentine merchants in towns like Patagones but the new Welsh settlement in the Chubut Valley was closer and easier to access. For this reason, just six months after the Welsh arrived Cacique Antonio wrote to Lewis Jones (leader of the colony), opening trade negotiations.[3] A little while later another Indigenous leader, Cacique Francisco, visited the settlement to make contact and began to trade. Soon he helped the Welsh learn how to hunt and thrive in the arid and windy conditions so unfamiliar to them, and thus established a favoured position as trader and intermediary.[4] The relatively peaceful and mutually profitable relationships that were established with a range of Indigenous groups enabled the Welsh colony to settle and thrive.

For the first ten years (1865–75) the Welsh enjoyed political and economic autonomy from the largely absent Argentine government, and developed a relationship with their Indigenous neighbours that the Welsh called 'friendship'. Their peaceability was appreciated by the Indigenous, as Katrülaf reports: 'At the same time the Welsh began to come in. "There's no problem at all with these people, they are all good" said the people at this time … they just had a few houses, they had a few *pulperos* [traders].'[5] However, this independence was gradually eroded during the following ten years (1875–84) as the Argentine state sent a *comisario*, a harbourmaster with militia, and eventually appointed a governor (Colonel Luis Fontana) to oversee the entire region in 1884.

Up until then, and even as late as 1870, the state only exercised sovereignty over half of the territory that it claimed on the map with the rest in the hands of a wide range of Indigenous groups. Most were nomadic and all were integrated within a network of trade, travel and shifting political alliances. These mobile societies were of different ethnicities, languages, spiritualities and kinship groups, but each was aware of the presence and territories of the other, and they frequently interacted. The Welsh colony in the Chubut Valley thus became just another point in this constellation of societies. Katrülaf remembered:

And at that time we always went to where the Welsh are, that is what the people did at that time. Us, we had no idea [yet] what was going to happen. Absolutely all of the people lived by their own rules. At that time I did not know the *wingka*. One time my brother said 'let's go to the *wingka*, let's visit the Welsh'. So we gathered ostrich feathers [and] leather mantles, we got it all together. We fattened up our horses to go and visit the *wingka* (Welsh). This is what the people that we are, did at that time.[6]

After a long journey they arrived Where the Welsh Are, galloping towards the end because they were eager to arrive and Katrülaf was excited. They camped near the settlement and his brother entered a conversation with the (anonymous) Welsh trader. Katrülaf says:

It was the very first time that I had seen a *wingka*, and I didn't even know how to speak the *wingka* language at that time, and in this way I entered Where the Welsh Are. In this place we were hosted, in this way we passed over our ostrich feathers that night. That is how we did it on that occasion.[7]

But the Welshman knew that the Argentine military were close by:

We ought to buy quickly, quickly. 'The soldiers are coming that is what my friend is saying now' said my brother, then. They spoke together, that *wingka* and my brother [...] We watched and we watched, but we didn't understand one jot of the way that he was talking to the *wingka*. [So] ... 'we will just be here for three days, in just three days we must go' this is what he said to him ... 'that's the way it is, you must go. If they discover that you are here, it would be my fault if they imprisoned you, and they could also imprison me. This *wingka* said to me' this is what my brother said at that time.[8]

They made their trades, purchasing 'all kinds of clothes, we looked for *chiripás* [cloth], mantles, shirts, pants, knives', as well as liquor and then went to say goodbye to the Welsh trader.[9] He gave them gifts: 'for each one he gave us a *bombacha* [gaucho trousers], shirt, pants and also cigarettes ... So "we have to go my good man" we said to the trader "when we come back, one day when we get here, when we return, we will meet again anyway".'[10]

It is not surprising that both the Welshman and Katrülaf's brother were concerned about the soldiers, given military activity to the north, above the Rio Negro. Katrülaf describes the time before the soldiers came south to the Chubut Valley with longing (*anhelo, hiraeth*) and a bitter nostalgia for their own trouble-free life, even in the face of terrible events elsewhere.

> We lived as if nothing troubled us, happy, happily we went around our place, we always played, we had horses and we galloped, we galloped, we ran and ran with the horses. We didn't know about anything bad, us, in our place. That is how I grew up. Then we heard about the misfortunes, this time. 'They punished Namunkura's people, the people of Kewpü, like dogs' they said at that time; 'they keep on killing his people, his young *kona* [aides]' they said at the time about Namunkura's people; 'they threw him out, they stripped him away and stole his lands' they said at that time. We listened, we did, and I believed that nothing would happen to me, that's how it was. I didn't think anything of it, not at all, I had everything. I had horses.
>
> I didn't lack for anything, my father was alive at that time, my mother, my brothers, my sisters, all were alive at that time. 'Something is going to happen' they said at the time, in our place. Slowly, slowly after a good long time the soldiers entered our lands. At first they arrived in Patagones, the *wingka* [military] grabbed hold of anyone who arrived there. This is what happened to the people of our lands. That's how the problems started.[11]

These problems entailed military violence which pushed the boundaries of the state into Indigenous land. The Argentine Republic had come into being in 1816 after throwing off the Spanish imperial crown. The following fifty years were taken up with settling border disputes in the La Plata region and bloody inter-elite battles to determine the political soul of the republic, its constitution, federal system and ideology.[12] The settlement of such issues and triumph of liberalism freed up government to focus on those regions as yet not under the control of Buenos Aires – and also to deal with the border with

Chile, along the Andes. This required state-building measures which took the form of military incursion and domination of Indigenous lands, known in Patagonia as the *Conquista del Desierto* – or Conquest of the Desert. Soldiers swept down from the north and east, pushing Indigenous communities – now refugees – before it, capturing prisoners and brutally combatting any resistance.

Katrülaf witnessed this brutality. On their return journey from Where the Welsh Are, his party of young men met a famous Indigenous leader called Saiweke and his group of followers ('he had an impressive number of people'[13]). There was much talk about the arrival of the military in Manzanamapu (to the north):

> It was now a fact that the *wingka* (military) were invading at this time. They arrived all over the territory, they brought everything to the Land of the Manzanas [apples], that is what they came to do … 'once the *wingka* are well established, that will be when they are going to imprison Saiweke "if you don't present yourself, we are going to make a *malón* [invasive war] on you; if you present yourself, then we won't do anything, my friend"' these were the *wingka*'s threats. This is the message that the *kurüwingka* (go-between) brought, again and again.
>
> At that time I knew everything. 'What are they going to do to us, the people?' people said to one another 'Are they by chance going to imprison us stealthily?' […] After a while: 'the soldiers are leaving in the direction of Where the Welsh Are, the soldiers will also arrive Where the Welsh Are' […] 'So what can I do?' said Saiweke at that time, 'the soldiers are coming from all directions to imprison me.'[14]

While he wasn't captured then, eventually, Katrülaf became entangled in this snare. After returning home for a while, he and his brother-in-law Kalpian went once more to Where the Welsh Are in the company of two famous Indigenous Mapuche leaders who had been displaced from their homelands and were travelling together: Foyel and Inakayal. Katrülaf recalls: '"The people are going to present themselves!" they said at that time … "I am going to present myself Where the Welsh Are, because I am a person of the south, so I am going to present myself in the place of the Wüllümapu" said Foyel and Inakayal.'[15] Presenting oneself was a requirement of the government in order to count and regulate the Indigenous inhabitants of Patagonia. This time it seems to have been engineered by the *kurüwingka*, the go-betweens – and to the advantage of the Argentine military. After many journeys and events they all arrive Where the Welsh Are, and Katrülaf and Kalpian tag along with Inakayal's people. He describes the situation:

> We arrived that day to the place where the soldiers were. We were in a great corral … The powerful *wingka* was a Commandant, it was he who ordered absolutely everything there, he ordered everything Where the Welsh Are, this *wingka* Commandant, at that time. Lasciar was the surname of this *wingka* Commandant. They were Where the Welsh Are, this is where we met this multitude of soldiers on this occasion. For me it was the first time that I had seen soldiers in this period, honestly I had never seen soldiers before, up to that point in my life, so it was the first time that I saw soldiers.[16]

A couple of weeks went by – people were ordered to gather their horses together and hand them over, and *raciones* (food and goods) were given out to Foyel and Inakayal's people. Some were hiding in the mountains, afraid to come down and present themselves, and the Caciques were ordered to go and bring them down.[17] Eventually, Foyel and Inakayal had a meeting with Commandant Lasciar who promised that when they leave, they are free to go and will have *raciones*. Katrülaf explains what happened next:

> So it was that Foyel and Inakayal were saying: 'We will go in the morning, my friends. They have everything to give to us, my beloved people. All kinds of things so that we can live they will continue to give us' this is what Foyel and Inakayal's captains were saying to us […]
> 'Wake up!' they said to us [the next] morning. So, we woke up with a start and sat up. 'But what is happening!' we said to each other at that moment. Then, 'Take your clothes

off, everything, hand in your knives, your *boleadoras*, all your
things, everything that we have given you, everything, bring
them here quickly!' this they said to everyone there, 'you
are all surrounded by soldiers', that is what they said in the
morning.

So, when we got up, the soldiers were all around, absolutely all of them were armed [...] Foyel and Inakayal were
imprisoned in the corral [...] This is how we lived Where the
Welsh Are. In this way they imprisoned poor Foyel. So, when
they did this to us, we all picked up our things, the soldiers
were herding us like animals. Then, when we went into the
corral ... we left our things in the corral, they had us grouped
in a circle, we were all now prisoners.

Four soldiers were guarding us, we were all crouching inside the corral ... in that place they had us all tied up that day,
this was supposed to be the day that we returned to our land,
that was the time. With this sort of trick they captured Foyel
and Inakayal. We truly couldn't talk because we were very
afraid of the *wingka*. "'If you talk, if you talk we will kill you!
You must not talk!" this is what they say' our translator told
us when they tied us up that time in Where the Welsh Are ...

At night they brought long ropes to tie us up, we were
tied up like sheep, by the feet, they had us tied by two feet
on a long leash, we were each besides the other. [...] We endured these things Where the Welsh Are, when they took us
all captive.[18]

Thereafter followed six years of subjugation for Katrülaf. He was
forced to march for weeks on end in the desert from military post to
military post and forced to wait and wait in prisons and corrals with
poor food and little shelter. Many died, discarded by the roadside.
Eventually he was taken to a barracks in Buenos Aires where he was
forced to serve as a soldier for six years. This was a common fate
for young male prisoners; others were sent to the sugar cane plantations and refineries in the north, while women and children were
sent as servants for the middle class in Buenos Aires.[19] Communities and families were torn apart, societies decimated, a social system
smashed – and the original people of Patagonia set to work for the

new nation state of Argentina.[20] Yet, Katrülaf survived and created a family, as the photograph (dated 1900–7) on the front of the book that contains his memoir attests. In the face of state brutality, Indigenous survival, endurance and rebuilding constitutes a powerful form of resistance, and in recent years has transformed into political activism, social regeneration and the assertion of rights.[21]

Why begin this book with Katrülaf's story?

It has been unsettling for some readers, I expect, to read a story in which the Welsh play a bit part in the Patagonian drama, but my aim is to surprise the reader's preconceptions about the place of Y Wladfa in history and to make visible, from the start, the presence, perspective and experiences of the original people already living there. There are several reasons why doing so is important, all of which help to explain the purpose and sensibility of this book and unsettle the 'usual story' of Welsh Patagonia.

First, the existing body of writing and knowledge about Welsh Patagonia is the history of Y Wladfa – that is, of the heroic mission to establish a Welsh-speaking and Welsh-governing homeland colony in Patagonia. The work of Bryn Williams and Glyn Williams, and more recently E. Wyn James and Bill Jones have played a vital role in exploring this important aspect of Welsh political activism and action (the historiography of Wales and colonialism more broadly will be explored in chapter three).[22] These works complement the fascinating memoirs by some of Y Wladfa's key protagonists, including: Lewis Jones, Abraham Matthews, Edwyn Roberts, John Daniel Evans and Thomas Jones.[23] Recent work has explored many aspects of the Welsh culture and society, from the advent of tourism,[24] musical culture[25] or Welsh-language education in Patagonia.[26] Each of these, however, have focused on Welsh experience, and tend to understand Argentina as the setting for a Welsh story. This is also true of valuable non-academic writing which emerged in 2015 during commemorations of the 150th anniversary of the Welsh arrival in Patagonia. These included John Gower's insightful book *Gwalia Patagonia*, Matthew Rhys's evocative book of photographs and text commemorating his journey in the footsteps of the Rifleros, and

Mererid Hopwood and Karen Owen's compelling volume of poetry.[27] This book takes a different tack: while it is about the Welsh and draws often on the Welsh archive, my research places these protagonists and events in a wider and deeper story of nineteenth-century global shifts, including colonialism, racism and resistance – both in Patagonia and in Wales.

Having started 'elsewhere' we have already looked through another's eyes to realize that, while the Welsh were the central protagonists in their own lives, for Katrülaf they were merely helpful but unintelligible traders – and also the people who lived near to a scene of social catastrophe. Interestingly, what was a pivotal moment for Katrülaf and the Indigenous communities caught up in Comandante Lasciar's trick barely registers in the archives of Y Wladfa. We can only speculate as to why: perhaps the initial camp, Corral Charmata near Campamiento Villegas, was further away than the name 'Where the Welsh Are' suggests; perhaps they felt horrified/ashamed/impotent and turned a blind eye; or perhaps it just wasn't a significant event in their lives, just as Welsh traumas did not penetrate Katrülaf's memory. Whatever the reason, drawing attention to this very different perspective on the Chubut Valley/Where the Welsh Are displaces the Welsh settlers from their central position, unsettles our preconceptions and pluralizes Patagonia, adding complexity and nuance to our understanding. More than this, though, it embeds Y Wladfa within the actions and ideologies of Argentine nation-building which reflect global trends also at work in Wales, racializing the place, people and language on the one hand, and urging settler migration on the other.

In addition, this book is inspired by a sensibility (and a theoretical approach) which demands that we take the experiences of colonized people seriously. Let me be clear: I am not condemning the Welsh for settling in Patagonia. Rather, I am arguing that the Welsh entered a complex social world and that the original inhabitants were key actors during the processes of colonization. More than that, focusing on a person like Katrülaf – and using his words to describe what happened – allows us to see beyond the caricature of 'the Indian', and to foreground human dignity, an essential step on the decolonial road to unpacking, recognizing and perhaps beginning to repair the deep damage inflicted by the colonizing army which stole his land and brutalized his society. Chapter two explores this theoretical approach, drawing on postcolonial, Indigenous and settler colonial studies to create a conceptual toolbox. Importantly, these ideas can help us to understand both Wales and Patagonia in the light of key processes: possession, racialization/barbarization and assimilation. After all, these are global processes which shape both societies, though very differently.

A further aim of this book, then, is to foreground the work of colonial and racial logics in empowering and elevating the worldviews of some and disempowering and disparaging the knowledge and way of life of others, and thus shaping global relationships. Importantly, the book bridges between two bodies of work that seldom engage with one another: migration/early settler histories, and settler colonial theory and Indigenous studies. The analysis of historical migration pays close attention to the push factors (usually poverty or discrimination) which led people to seek a better life elsewhere.[28] This is complemented by early settler histories which offer nuanced analysis of the complex human relationships of early encounters between Indigenous and settler people (including enmity, dependence, cultural cross-fertilization, miscomprehension and family love). Examples of the latter include Richard White's groundbreaking book *The Middle Ground* and Sophie White's *Wild Frenchmen and Frenchified Indians,* while Colin Calloway's *White People, Indians and Highlanders* draws thought-provoking connections between the persecution of Highlanders which impelled their migration, and the position of Native Americans.[29] My own work takes inspiration from these fields and champions the need to pay careful attention to the settlers' situation in their origin country (in chapter three), and focuses on the complex relations that develop between settler and original inhabitants as people (in chapters four, five and six). However, I approach this historiography from a decolonial perspective which understands settler colonialism as a process which is structurally oppressive of the Indigenous communities it encounters. Inspired by authors such as Walter Mignolo and Aníbal Quijano, I apply the 'coloniality of power' approach to develop a critical analysis of Y Wladfa within the thrust of nineteenth-century colonization and Argentine nation-building (explored in chapter two).[30] Yet this is not an 'us-and-them' story: indeed, I want to leave behind binary interpretations of the world (colonizer/colonized, white/Black, superior/inferior) and explore the ambiguities that Welsh subjectivity embodies. For the Welsh are not either/or, but rather *both* colonizer (in Patagonia) *and* colonized (in Wales); they are *both* whitened (in Patagonia) *and* 'blackened' or barbarized (in Wales); they are *both* superior (in Patagonia) *and* inferior (in Wales). Each of these positions is held simultaneously, and the resulting ambiguity offers a rich and complex site from which to think about how power works in settler colonial settings, as will be explored throughout the book. It is only possible to identify this complex situation, though, by paying close attention to their own subject position in their origin country, Wales, and their own oppression by the 'English' state, examined in chapter three.

This book contributes to wider theoretical debates, then. It is not a provincial study of a minor settlement, but a sharply focused analysis of messy and multi-angled colonial relations of far wider reach. The story of Katrülaf helps us to remember that colonization affects real people's lives – people with a past and a future that was set on a wildly different course from its expected pathway by the interjection of *force majeure*. It also reminds us that, even when not exercised, violence underpins colonialism, and that survival 'to tell the tale' also constitutes resistance. Moreover, it proves that witnesses to colonial violence, like the Welsh, are implicated in that violence too.

Sources and research

This book is built on a wide range of sources. Primary sources have been gleaned from the invaluable archives here in Wales at the Bangor University Library and Aberystwyth's treasure house – the National Library of Wales. I also benefitted from the wisdom and insights of archivists in Patagonia's Museo Regional Gaiman in the Chubut Valley and the Museo Regional Trevelin in the Andes. My sincere thanks go to all of the librarians who guard these voices from the past and help researchers in the present.

Importantly, the book also draws on sources which will be new to many readers: articles and books written in Spanish and published with Argentine presses or in Argentine journals. This nuanced and specialist scholarship is what embeds the current book within the wider sweep of Argentine society and history, both its nation-building project and

Indigenous experiences. Indeed, this is the first time, I believe, that Katrülaf's story has been revealed in an English-language publication and many sources that are new to the historiography of Y Wladfa will be drawn upon here. I have not undertaken this primary analysis, though: this requires specialist archival and anthropological skills which are beyond the scope of my research. Here I thank the tireless work of expert Argentine anthropologists and historians such as Claudia Briones, Walter Del Rio and Ana Ramos who, among many others, have led the effort, in the last twenty years or so, to uncover, interpret and share long-buried histories of Indigenous oppression – and resistance.

As you can tell, I enjoy allowing the protagonists of the archive to speak for themselves by sharing long quotations. For me this makes history compelling, and I find Katrülaf's seemingly simple memoir powerful – but are these really 'his own words'? In a way they are not, because they have been translated and reinterpreted many times. Indeed, the story of this text tells us a lot about how knowledge is shaped by global relations of power.

Katrülaf was interviewed in October and November 1902 by a German anthropologist called Robert Lehmann-Nitsche who was working at the Research Institute in the Museum of La Plata, Buenos Aires.[31] He spoke to a number of Indigenous people and took copious notes, as well as recording songs on wax cylinders. These languished in the archives of the Ibero-Amerikanisches Institut in Berlin until 2008 when the two Mapuche academics who edited the book tracked them down. The process of transcribing and translating the words written in Mapuzungun (the Mapuche language) was long and difficult but they brought these archival treasures into public view in 2013.[32] Eventually, they were printed in a large book (complete with pictures of the notebooks, the wax cylinders and many photographs) in which the text is arranged (using Lehmann-Nitsche's format) into two columns – the Indigenous language on the left, and the Spanish translation on the right. Now, let us count the moments of slippage between Katrülaf's account and the words in this page before you.

Slippage 1: Katrülaf words are written in Mapuzungun – he may have written them himself or a scribe may have noted down his words. Moreover, Mapuzungun was originally an oral, not written language, so the marks on paper borrow their shape, linkage to sound and syntax from other languages. Despite care, then, the text will always fail to capture Katrülaf's nuance of enunciation and the habitual practices of oral expression.

Slippage 2: Robert Lehmann-Nitsche's natal tongue was German. While he seems to have understood Mapuzungun and was fluent in Spanish, how did his Prussian-German tongue shape the archive? More than that, given his powerful position as a white, male, educated European, it was he who chose to commission, discard or keep items in the archive, to silence or make-speak the Indigenous people who had survived the Conquest of the Desert.

Slippage 3: Margarita Canio Llanquinao and Gabriel Pozo Menares transcribed and then translated the written archive and the much-degraded wax cylinder recordings into Spanish. Sometimes the meaning was unclear, so they consulted other Mapuche speakers to help derive meanings from blurred sounds or faint pencil marks. A further layer of distance was necessary in order to make the script 'legible' to a Spanish-speaking audience when the researchers adapted the original writing to the Spanish alphabet.[33] Even though they carefully note the changes, and there is no doubting the integrity of their work, once more, Katrülaf's words must be adapted to fit the dominant script.

Slippage 4: I have translated the Spanish text into English, both in my head as a reader, and on the page as a writer, in order to convey Katrülaf's experiences to you, the reader. While I am not a trained translator, my fluent Spanish language skills, plus my long-standing and relatively deep knowledge of Argentine history – and a sensibility which approaches the text with the dignity it merits – all make me reasonably well placed to translate this text. For, as anyone who has tried it knows, translation is not just a question of transposing words but of interpreting meaning. At each moment of slippage, though, there is a good chance that meaning is lost or distorted, and Katrülaf's words – his experiences and views – become more and more distanced from the original ideas and recollections in his mind.

In contrast, the Welsh archive is written by the protagonists themselves, using their own language (Welsh or English), cadences, expressions and linguistic habits. The thinker of thoughts and conveyor of memories was in charge of their own interpretation, and given that the Welsh-speaking preachers (who made up the bulk of the archives' authors) were fluent in English, they also retained control over translation into the dominant tongue. This lies in stark contrast to Katrülaf who had little control over the annotation of his memories and their subsequent journey to Berlin. Indeed, even though they were on good terms and corresponded together,[34] the interviews were conducted under coercive conditions: Lehmann-Nitsche was backed by the power of a state that had just stripped Katrülaf of his homeland, society and way of life, under pain of violent coercion, abduction and forced work in the army. While my role as a reader (of Welsh, English and Spanish) and writer always intervenes in the process of selecting material from the archives, I can get much closer to the voices and sources of the Welsh archive than I can of the Indigenous whose voices are more distant and muffled.

Moreover, colonialism and racial thinking actively skew practices in the archive. The words of Welsh settlers in Patagonia were celebrated at the time in newspapers and lecture tours, and today are cherished in the National Library – conserved, monitored and kept cool and dry. They spoke without fear and (as middle-class, male preachers) expected to be heard. Today, their words are often digitized and accessible. By contrast, the Indigenous archive in Argentina has not, until recently, been curated with care. One article by Pilar Pérez, which details the fate of those imprisoned in Valcheta (a major camp near the Rio Negro where Katrülaf also went), describes the difficulty of even gathering the 'shattered archive'.[35] It took years to find loose papers, fragments of reports and documents in provincial, national and municipal offices, damp basement record rooms, dusty cupboards in local museums and even inside a file labelled 'Useless Documents'. Such was the scant value placed on Indigenous life. Indeed, Peréz argues that this carelessness and chaos is a bureaucratic technique which purposefully reinforces and legitimates state oppression of Indigenous people. As we will see in chapter two, this attitude to Indigenous people, as people, contrasts shockingly to the meticulous cataloguing *at the same time* of Indigenous skeletons which filled the anthropology section at the Museo de La Plata. Thus, in the late nineteenth and early twentieth century, Indigenous people were valued only as scientific bodies – as objects – of service to the state and its 'experts'.[36]

The attitude of the Argentine state reflects a colonialist and racialized mindset, common throughout the world at this time, which celebrated European understandings of the world, mimicked its actions and thereby hoped to attain European status. Branding Indigenous people as barbaric and consigning them to the past was a key move, not only to take control over their lands but also to 'perform' white civilization in a global milieu dominated by the celebration of empire. This global context also shaped the Welsh archive too, and it was surprising how many sources, including personal diaries, were written in English rather than Welsh. Llwyd ap Iwan for example (son of Y Wladfa's architect, Michael D. Jones) wrote both daily diaries and longer journals in English as he had trained as a surveyor in English, and thus conducted his daily work and public life in that language. The nineteenth-century Welsh archive also betrays other inequalities too. Almost half of the settlers were women, but they left behind not one contemporary source from those early days of the settlement to tell of their anxieties, struggles and joys – let alone the experience of both losing a child and giving birth in the middle of the Atlantic, as one of the *Mimosa*'s passengers, Rachel Jenkins, did.[37] Nor do we hear the voices of the many working-class men who arrived on the *Mimosa*. Rather, stories are recounted by the middle-class and literate men – preachers mostly – who had the time, skills and confidence to put pen to paper and convey their impressions of Y Wladfa.

There is one final contrast to note. While it is true that the past is 'a different country' no matter whose voice is found in the archive, the Welsh sources are more intelligible to those of us who have a knowledge and intuitive understanding of Welsh culture and worldview because we live and work here – or indeed to readers whose range of everyday thought and intellectual schooling is shaped by the liberal, Western European tradition of thought. However, Katrülaf speaks to us not only from a distance in place and time, but also from a very different worldview, one built on foundations beyond my experience and imagining. The original peoples of a land mass that we now call the Americas were (and are) as widely varied as those in Europe and their thinking is founded on fundamentally different understandings of what it means to be a human.[38] For example, Indigenous thinking in the Americas knows no distinction between humans and nature (nature is not 'outside' humans), all things (including rocks) are part of mother earth and therefore have life essence, and the spirit world (ancestors, gods) are not somehow beyond everyday human life but exist alongside people.

Moreover, as an oral culture, 'history' combines both facts and sensations and the mode of recounting events is distinctive. The telling of histories entails collaboration; it is understood not as a one-way instructive exercise but as the collective sharing of a common story. As Ana Ramos's perceptive work indicates, Katrülaf's history is not meant to be conveyed by and for one person at a time (which is what happens when it is written down in a book), but rather to be the vehicle for a collective oral and aural experience in which the look of the eye, the shake of the head, the sorrowful glance, plays as much of a role as the words spoken. This form of narration is called *nütram* in which 'the validity and performative force of these painful experiences are embodied by narrators and audience through silences or what is being presupposed or implied'.[39] All of this is not available to Western scholars who miss so much. For example, on first sight of Katrülaf's testimony, I searched the text for adjectives or similes, for explanations and descriptions, but found the script dry and repetitive. I read the words 'we were tied up like sheep' and thought: 'is that all he has to say?' I came to understand that for Katrülaf this says it all. It was only when I read it out loud that it began to come to life, yet still his story remains unintelligible to me at the deepest of levels, no matter how careful the translation.

The organization and significance of the book

As is now clear, this book explores far more than a fascinating colonial quirk, located at the western margins of Europe and a remote corner of South America – it is a highly unusual settler scenario which, precisely because of its marginality, tests the limits and capabilities of settler colonial theories. The Welsh colonizers are positioned in an ambiguous and contradictory position, being both colonizing and colonized at the same time, and in two locations, which challenges the easy binaries of settler colonial theory. Indeed, this case requires that experiences in the origin country – Wales – be fully integrated into analysis of the colony's origins, the actions of the settlers and the settlement's legacy today. Drawing the origin country into the analysis enriches our understanding of colonialism and points towards a fruitful dimension of study largely ignored up until now.

Overall, I argue that while the romanticized stories of Y Wladfa have great emotional value, they portray its protagonists (both Welsh and Indigenous) as stereotypes, rendering them invisible as people even while they appear as caricatures. This is especially damaging for Indigenous people, whose supposed disappearance has been used by the Argentine state as a technique of violent erasure, in plain sight. Getting closer to a truth, therefore, requires a return to the archive, to the people, and the messy, ambiguous, contradictory stuff of life, and requires analysis using a decolonial sensibility in order to address, and not reiterate, colonial injustice.

Organization

I approach this story of a settler colony conscious that this is also a story of Indigenous dispossession. For this reason, the introduction has focused on the life and experiences of a person on the receiving end of the colonial juggernaut: Katrülaf. This shift in perspective is vital, not only to step towards doing justice to Indigenous histories of this colony but to shake and uproot the certainties of Welsh satisfaction with the colonial effort in Patagonia. As Welsh identity becomes stronger in the post-devolution era, it is time to question the nature and consequences of its most famous colonial enterprise. Chapter two provides the intellectual tools which I have used to do so. Here I explain 'coloniality of power' approaches and demonstrate their usefulness in setting the intellectual agenda of decolonial research. I then create a conceptual toolkit of three dynamics which I deploy throughout the book: possession, racialization/barbarization and assimilation. I begin my study by analysing how the Argentine state used these processes to achieve subjugation of Indigenous people in Patagonia.

Chapter three turns to focus on Wales and colonialism, beginning by exploring its relationship with its dominant neighbour to the east, England, which has been the source of its subjugation since the Norman period over 900 years ago. However, I quickly pivot to look west, a move which reveals the role of Welsh people in colonial enterprises, including the original colonization of Ireland and later colonial ventures in the Americas. While often coerced and sometimes escaping oppression, Welsh people's colonization of societies to the west also presented opportunities which benefitted them. The status as both colonized and colonizing is, I argue, a long-standing and perhaps constitutive condition of Welshness. This theme is developed in the concluding section of the chapter which explores the conditions that propelled the Welsh Patagonian enterprise. These included experiences of racialization/barbarization and assimilation by the English state, but also domination in anglophone USA.

Chapters four, five and six shift the focus to Welsh Patagonia itself. Chapter four maps out the early years of the colony under the theme of possession; chapter five examines the heyday of the Welsh colony and its much-celebrated 'friendship' with Indigenous people, exploring the theme of racialization/barbarization; chapter six deploys the lens of assimilation to chart Y Wladfa's incorporation within the Argentine state from 1875 onwards and examines the consequences of Argentine nation-building. These chapters draw on original archives and unsettle some of the well-worn stories which play an iconic role in Y Wladfa's narrative pantheon to challenge the reassuring heroic account of the Welsh Patagonian venture. If Wales is to contribute towards a decolonial future in Patagonia, we need to strip back the rhetoric and re-find the complex, ordinary people whose ingenuity and courage deserves to be celebrated, alongside a critique of their role within the wider colonial enterprise.

Indeed, chapter seven brings the book back to the present day, enquiring into the significance of Welsh Patagonia for contemporary Welsh identity. This unique research explores its depiction in popular culture, especially television, film and books for children, including school materials. It concludes that Y Wladfa played a key role in the mid-twentieth century through bolstering the campaigns for Welsh-language rights and cultural dignity by providing proof that Welshness could endure and flourish, even in adverse conditions on the other side of the world. It argues, though, that the romantic stories created a caricature of Welsh Patagonia, pivoting around the

Welsh-Indigenous 'friendship', which is still repeated in classrooms today. As a result, while Wales has taken great strides towards tackling racial assumptions in relation to slavery and migrant communities, racial caricatures persist when it comes to Welsh Patagonia. The conclusion takes up this theme and suggests ways in which the Welsh government today might take responsibility as an origin country and develop practical actions to start embedding a genuine friendship between Indigenous Patagonians and Wales.

Significance

This book makes significant contributions to two increasingly influential academic fields – Indigenous/settler colonial studies and the study of Wales – precisely by generating dialogue between them. That is, Wales and Y Wladfa test the assumptions which underpin Indigenous/settler colonial theory, while Indigenous/settler colonial studies provide much-needed conceptual tools to help us understand the Welsh condition. Welsh Patagonia may be obscure, but its ambiguity is instructive.

Indigenous/settler colonial studies is dominated by important and iconic cases linked to anglophone settlement, especially the USA, Canada and Australia. While other cases from around the world are increasingly studied, this book serves to broaden and deepen the field by breaking the mould in three ways: first, it brings to English-speaking audiences the largely unknown case of Indigenous Patagonia; secondly, it applies settler colonial concepts to a country never before analysed using this frame – Wales; thirdly, as a result, it shows the importance of unpacking the social and political context of the origin country to recognize the settlers as complex social and political actors, entangled in the march of modernity, capitalism and colonialism, even before they arrive. The dominance of anglophone scholarship in this field means that the experiences of people like Katrülaf go unremarked.[40] The invisibility of Tehuelche and Mapuche peoples in the settler colonial scholarship in particular perpetuates the genocidal logic of the Conquest of the Desert, and a core aim of this book is simply to bring their experience to light in order to enrich understanding and drive decolonial efforts. This analysis also breaks with the colonizer/colonized binary typical of settler colonial theory by bringing two 'colonized' communities together and examining what happens. The resulting interplay of hierarchy and affinity, enmeshed in global capitalist and racialized relations, is complex yet sustains a kind of coherent ambiguity.

Another significant contribution of this book is that it demonstrates the importance of looking back to the origin country to understand not only the motives behind the settlement, but the complex structures of unequal power which condition the colonial enterprise, both home and away. Settler colonial studies focus almost entirely on the actions of settlers in the colony and treats them as if they just appear from over the horizon. As a result, settlers are often caricatured and their own background, motivations and cultural complexities are left to migration scholars to explore. However, the latter seldom adopt a postcolonial or decolonial approach, nor do they follow the settlers much beyond arrival down through the years to the present day. This book, by contrast, takes the context of the origin country seriously, it follows the 'migrants' through to their settler colony, observes the process of embedment and assimilation, and then turns to assess the colonial relationships today, not only in Patagonia but also in Wales where the settlement continues to condition Welsh identity. That is, it follows the enterprise full circle and asks what the role of the origin country might be in promoting decolonization.

More than that, the book considers Wales through the same theoretical lens, applying theories developed in settler situations to a European context which is seldom considered a site of settler colonialism but which fits the bill in many ways. It tests the applicability and flexibility of concepts like possession and assimilation, and finds that they can indeed shed light on unequal relationships between core (England/ Britain) and marginal nations (Wales) within European states. It probes the usefulness of racialization to Welshness and proposes that a sideways step (inspired by Latin American decolonial thinking) towards barbarization offers a way to express similar experiences of prejudice whilst also acknowledging that Cymrophobia and racism are hugely different, especially in the force of their impact on real people's lives. Overall, the book challenges the image of a homogeneous privileged Europe, so often assumed by subaltern theories, by identifying and exploring those subjected to similar processes of subordination within it.

The study of Wales itself has focused on historical and also literary analysis, more than other disciplines, largely because Wales has only had a government and public policy arena of its own for the last twenty years or so. Wales's growing cultural and institutional confidence, though, has not been accompanied by theorization of the Welsh position as a country. As a result, Wales is described and traits are identified but it could be more robustly conceptualized. This is an enormous task, but the analytical framework used here – possession, barbarization and assimilation – might offer a starting point for analysis of Welsh subordination and disparagement. I hope that engagement with this theoretical framework might generate a more conceptual approach to understanding the Welsh condition. This in turn could prove important in both combatting anti-Welsh prejudice and promoting a decolonial agenda in Wales.

Also important is the book's insistence on seeing Wales from a global perspective, and one which focuses its gaze to the west and colonial activity, rather than the dominant trope of colonization from the east (England). This enables the development of a new argument: that from the moment of colonization, Welsh people have been drawn into colonial opportunities from which they have benefitted, as subordinates. The theme of Welsh empowerment through its colonial relations underpins analysis of the contemporary cultural products which celebrate Y Wladfa – the first analysis of its kind – and the problematization of this issue is what drives the public policy proposals set out in the conclusion. It introduces brand new archives and arguments into contemporary debates about race in Wales which have yet to contemplate the Welsh Patagonian legacy: the book inserts the colonial relations into that debate and expands the field for action.

The Welsh Patagonian case should be regarded as much more than a colonial quirk, then. Y Wladfa exposes the unstitched edges which muddle neat categories of colonizer/colonized and shows us the real human beings caught up in colonialism, how they resist and succumb to its pull. Yet Y Wladfa continues to play a role in Welsh resistance to political domination, economic marginalization and the thinly veiled Cymrophobia which persists. As a result, this touchstone for Welsh empowerment must be disrupted critically but with care. Nevertheless, a reassessment of Y Wladfa could be a mark of our growing maturity as a nation embedded in a complex way within a complex world.

Notes

1 This memoir was recorded orally in 1902 by a German anthropologist; I will discuss its origins and the politics of knowledge which surround it shortly. Please note that round brackets appear in the original while square brackets enclose notes providing essential knowledge and translations for the reader. It is published in Mapudungun and translated into Spanish, which I have translated into English. All translations throughout the book are mine, unless otherwise stated.

2 Margarita Canio Llanquinao and Gabriel Pozo Menares (eds), *Historia y Conocimiento Oral Mapuche: Sobrevivientes de la 'Campaña del Desierto' y 'Ocupación de la Araucanía' (1899–1926)* (Santiago: Ediciones LOM, 2013), p. 345. The word *wingka* is used to denote a range of different 'foreigners' in this testimony.

3 Glyn Williams, 'Welsh Settlers and Native Americans in Patagonia', *Journal of Latin American Studies*, 11/1 (1979), 41–66.

4 Lucy Taylor, 'Welsh-Indigenous Relationships in Nineteenth Century Patagonia: "Friendship" and the Coloniality of Power', *Journal of Latin American Studies*, 49 (2017), 143–68.

5 Canio and Pozo (eds), *Historia y Conocimiento*, p. 363.

6 Canio and Pozo (eds), *Historia y Conocimiento*, p. 375.

7 Canio and Pozo (eds), *Historia y Conocimiento*, p. 384.

8 Canio and Pozo (eds), *Historia y Conocimiento*, p. 384.

9 Canio and Pozo (eds), *Historia y Conocimiento*, p. 385.

10 Canio and Pozo (eds), *Historia y Conocimiento*, p. 386.

11 Canio and Pozo (eds), *Historia y Conocimiento*, pp. 371–2.

12 David Rock, *Argentina 1516–1987: From Spanish Colonization to the Falklands War and Alfonsín* (London: IB Taurus, 1985), pp. 118–61.

13 Canio and Pozo (eds), *Historia y Conocimiento*, p. 391.

14 Canio and Pozo (eds), *Historia y Conocimiento*, p. 392.

15 Canio and Pozo (eds), *Historia y Conocimiento*, p. 394.

16 Canio and Pozo (eds), *Historia y Conocimiento*, p. 398.

17 Canio and Pozo (eds), *Historia y Conocimiento*, p. 400.

18 Canio and Pozo (eds), *Historia y Conocimiento*, pp. 402–4.

19 Alexis Papazian and Mariano Nagy, 'Prácticas de Disciplinamiento Indígena en la Isla Martín García hacia Fines del Siglo XIX', *Revista TEFROS*, 8 (December 2010).

20 Walter Delrio, *Memorias de Expropriación: Sometimiento e Incorporación Indígena en la Patagonia, 1872–1943* (Buenos Aires: Universidad Nacional de Quilmes, 2005).

21 Sebastián Valverde, 'De la Invisibilización a la Construcción como Sujetos Sociales: el Pueblo Indígena Mapuche y sus Movimientos en Patagonia, Argentina', *Anuário Antropológico*, 1 (2012–13), 139–66.

22 R. Bryn Williams, *Y Wladfa* (Caerdydd: Gwasg Prifysgol Cymru, 1962); Glyn Williams, *The Desert and the Dream: A Study of Welsh Colonization in Chubut, 1986–1915* (Cardiff: University of Wales Press, 1975); E. Wyn James and Bill Jones, *Michael D. Jones a'i Wladfa Gymreig* (Llanrwst: Gwasg Carreg Walch, 2019).

23 Lewis Jones, *Hanes y Wladfa Gymreig* (Caerdydd: Gwasg Genedlaethol Gymraeg, 1898); Abraham Matthews, *Hanes y Wladfa Gymreig yn Patagonia* (Aberdâr: Mills ac Evans, 1894); Edwyn Roberts, *Hanes Dechreuad y Wladfa Gymreig yn Mhatagonia* (Bethesda: J. F. Williams, 1893); Clery Evans (ed.), *John Daniel Evans, el Molinero: una Historia entre Gales y la Colonia 16 de Octubre* (Esquel: Gráfica Alfa, 1994); Thomas Jones, *Historia de los Comienzos de la Colonia en la Patagonia* (Trelew: Biblioteca Popular 'Agustín Alvarez', [1924] 2000).

24 Geraldine Lublin, 'The War of the Tea Houses, or How Welsh Heritage in Patagonia became a Valuable Commodity', *e-Keltoi*, 1/1 (2009), 69–92.

25 Lucy Trotter, 'Performing Welshness in the Chubut Province of Patagonia, Argentina' (PhD thesis, The London School of Economics and Political Science, 2020).

26 British Council, 'Welsh Language Project', *https://wales.britishcouncil.org/en/programmes/education/welsh-language-project* (accessed 11 July 2023).

27 John Gower, *Gwalia Patagonia* (Llandysul: Gwasg Gomer, 2015); Matthew Rhys, *Patagonia: Crossing the Plain/Croesi'r Paith* (Llandysul: Gwasg Gomer, 2010); Mererid Hopwood and Karen Owen, *Glaniad: Cerddi Dwy wrth Groesi Paith Patagonia* (Llanrwst: Gwasg Carreg Gwalch, 2015).

28 For example, Marjory Harper and Stephen Constantine, *Migration and Empire* (Oxford: Oxford University Press, 2010); Anne Kelly Knowles, *Calvinists Incorporated: Welsh immigrants on Ohio's Industrial Frontier* (Chicago: University of Chicago Press, 1996).

29 Richard White, *The Middle Ground: Indians, Empires and Republics in the Great Lakes Region, 1650–1815* (Cambridge: Cambridge University Press, 1991); Sophie White, *Wild Frenchmen and Frenchified Indians: Material Culture and Race in Colonial Louisiana* (Philadelphia: University of Pennsylvania Press, 2014); Colin Calloway, *White People, Indians and Highlanders: Tribal Peoples and Colonial Encounters in Scotland and America* (Oxford: Oxford University Press, 2008).

30 Walter Mignolo, *The Darker Side of Western Modernity* (Durham: Duke University Press, 2011); Aníbal Quijano, 'Coloniality of Power and Eurocentrism in Latin America', *International Sociology*, 15/2 (2000), 215–32.

31 Canio and Pozo (eds), *Historia y Conocimiento*, p. 26.

32 Canio and Pozo (eds), *Historia y Conocimiento*, p. 23.

33 Canio and Pozo (eds), *Historia y Conocimiento*, pp. 35–8.

34 See images of letters, Canio and Pozo (eds), *Historia y Conocimiento*, pp. 660–3.

35 Pilar Pérez, 'Futuros y Fuentes: las Listas de Indígenas Presos en el Campo de Concentración de Valcheta, Rio Negro (1887)', *Nuevo Mundo Mundos Nuevos* (2015), *https://journals.openedition.org/nuevomundo/68751* (accessed 17 November 2023).

36 Carolyn Larson, *Our Indigenous Ancestors: A Cultural History of Museums, Science and Identity in Argentina, 1877–1943* (Pennsylvania: Penn State University Press, 2015), pp. 51–92.

37 Nadine Laporte, 'Gamechangers: the Women who made Y Wladfa Possible' conference paper, Y Wladfa Gymreig Patagonia, 1865–2015, Cardiff University, 6–7 July 2015, https://www.youtube.com/watch?v=583wI-1BjNk&list=PLPxx37uA8RSKxlcgaGyBHbM3thMDz1bdu&index=4 (accessed 25 September 2024).

38 Among a vast literature, see Amaya Querejazu, 'Water Governance', *New Perspectives*, 30/2 (2021), 180–8.

39 Ana Ramos, 'Senses of Painful Experience: Memory of the Mapuche People in Violent Times', in Carolyn Larson (ed.), *The Conquest of the Desert: Argentina's Indigenous Peoples and the Battle for History* (Albuquerque: University of Notre Dame Press, 2020), p. 198.

40 Important exceptions linked to Latin America include the essays collected in *American Quarterly*, 69/4 (2017), and the special issue of *Settler Colonial Studies*, 11/3 (2021), edited by Geraldine Lublin and Lucy Taylor.

CHAPTER 2

Theorizing Y Wladfa

The aim of this chapter is to examine theories which can help us to understand the power relations at work in Y Wladfa. Its purpose is to provide a series of conceptual tools which could prove useful in analysing the colonial condition, not only in Patagonia but also in Wales. These are complex because they entail interactions between the Indigenous and Argentine, the Indigenous and Welsh, the Welsh and English/British, the Welsh and Argentine, with the whole enveloped and shaped by global relations of power.

First, the chapter will set out the main approach to understanding the colonial condition: the coloniality of power, or coloniality/modernity paradigm. It then examines three core processes which create and sustain settler powerfulness: possession; racialization/barbarization; and assimilation. I show how each of these processes is at work, first by applying them to Indigenous experience in the Patagonian context: I go on to explore their impact on Welsh experiences of domination in Wales in the following chapter.

I have borrowed from an eclectic mix of theoretical fields and have particularly drawn on theories built from the Latin American experience, as well as settler colonial and Indigenous studies. While on the surface these approaches seem more obvious for Indigenous Patagonia than Wales, I demonstrate that they offer a fresh and revealing framework for theorizing Welsh colonial relationships, as well as anti-Welsh prejudice, both of which are usually described but are seldom theorized. Thus, a key contribution of this theoretical chapter is to provide a starting point for a more sustained theorization of how power works in the relationship between Wales and its looming neighbour, England.

Approaching Welsh Patagonia and Wales

For most of the twentieth century the paradigms of modernism dominated our understanding of development and justified the hierarchal relationship between wealthy 'First World' countries and developing or 'Third World' states. The idea that places like Patagonia and Wales were somehow lacking served to naturalize inequalities of wealth, powerfulness and also knowledge (who 'knew' and who 'knew best'). In the 1980s, those certainties were destabilized by postcolonial thinking which made a number of key contributions. Ranajit Guha shifted the focus of colonial history to the poor and oppressed and mounted a sharp critique of colonialism.[1] Ashis Nandy exposed colonialism's distorting impact on the outlook of both the colonized and the colonizer.[2] Edward Said revealed how European colonial thought used stereotype to configure 'The Orient' as both dangerous and desirable.[3] Dipesh Chakrabarty exposed the cultural particularity of Western knowledge and decimated its claim to be universally applicable.[4] Gayatri Spivak showed how gender and colonialism intersect to silence people, famously asking 'Can the Subaltern Speak?'[5] While the authors of these early interventions were not without their own advantages, their profound contribution was to expose three new topics of critique: the history of colonialism from below; the dimensions and systematic impact of the colonial imaginary; the politics of knowledge from 'elsewhere'. These topics form the foundation of my approach and research sensibility which takes the side of the colonized, understands colonialism to shape most social relations, and cherishes non-dominant knowledge.

Postcolonial scholarship had an early and profound impact on literature studies and some Welsh scholars in this field deployed postcolonial theory to make sense of anglophone writing in Wales.[6] Jane Aaron, for example, was inspired to edit a collection of essays with Chris Williams on *Postcolonial Wales*, while Kirsti Bohata's book *Postcolonialism Revisited* developed a nuanced adaptation of postcolonial analysis to discuss the inherently ambiguous and in-between subject position of English-language Welsh writers.[7] Yet postcolonialism as a theory has found little purchase for analysts of Wales's social world and power relations, perhaps because they do not fit Welsh reality. Postcolonial scholarship is rooted in critiques of the British

Empire and emerged in countries that now enjoy formal independence. Neither of these is true for Wales – a territory colonized over 900 years ago, formally assimilated into 'England-and-Wales' in the 1530s and now a subordinate partner within the United Kingdom. I suggest that postcolonial theories lack explanatory power in Wales because societies shaped by British imperialism and those subject to long-term settler colonialism are very different. I propose to look elsewhere for conceptual inspiration, and Latin America seems to be an appropriate choice for both pragmatic and intellectual reasons. This book studies Welsh settlement in Patagonia, thus Latin American approaches seem apt. Moreover, my own academic trajectory began with studying democratization and social movements in Argentina and Chile so I naturally think through these experiences and the theories they generate. Of course, Welsh colonial experience is distinctive: different colonizer, different epoch, different method and ideology. Yet both Patagonia and Wales are locations where the 'settler came to stay' and both have experienced its key characteristics: sovereign domination; territorial dispossession; social assimilation; and cultural prejudice. For this reason, I believe that a focus on settler colonial theory, embedded in Latin American understandings of global power, offers a potentially useful way to approach thinking about Wales and colonialism, as well as (Welsh) Patagonia.

Coloniality of power

A key concept to emerge from Latin American thinking is the coloniality of power. This term is not an adjective – the colonial-ness of power. Rather, coloniality is the twin counterpart of modernity, its hidden, oppressive underbelly which requires the subordination of all that is not 'modern'. As Argentine scholar Walter Mignolo explains: 'the rhetoric of modernity is the rhetoric of salvation (by conversion yesterday, by development today), but in order to implement what the rhetoric preaches, it is necessary to marginalize or destroy whatever gets in the way of modernity'.[8] This implies a very strong linkage to capitalism, liberal democracy and the hyper-elevation of Eurocentric culture and language, as well as ways of thinking and acting. Indeed, starting with Peruvian Aníbal Quijano, coloniality scholarship understands the 'encounter of the Americas' between Indigenous people, Europeans and Africans to be the birth-moment of contemporary capitalism and the modern world order of knowledge.[9]

Quijano argues that the conquest and colonization of the Americas entailed the creation of two pivotal elements which order global relationships today: 'a new, original single structure of relations of production ... world capitalism', and 'the idea of race', a hierarchy of global reach which structured people and societies.[10] These two combined to create a racial system of labour which mapped onto a racial hierarchy of status and power. Thus race and capital were 'structurally associated and mutually reinforcing'.[11] Importantly, the term 'coloniality' imagines power to be a relationship, not a specific sort of regime and takes a long view, focusing on colonialism prior to the British imperial project. Echoing Said, Quijano explains that 'Europe' as an idea and identity was created when it experienced rapid ascendancy and became the global seat of capital, power and imperial expansion. The creation of this hub was justified (and reinforced) by its comparison to the Americas, utilising racial tropes to legitimate the subordination of Indigenous people and captured Africans.[12] This racial distribution of power had a global reach. However, the glossy whiteness and Eurocentrism of modernity hides the territorial, cultural and existential oppressions necessary to fulfil its destiny (coloniality), which must remain hidden to enable the celebration and naturalization of capitalist modernity. Here we see the 'coloniality of power' at work in perpetuating patterns of subordination and also of dominance.

In broad terms, a focus on the coloniality of power underpins my own approach to interpreting the social world. Most importantly, it foregrounds the impact of colonialism on those on its receiving end, and takes seriously their lives and experiences, whilst at the same time framing this within logics and processes that have a global reach. It links indigeneity/race and class to early capitalism – indeed it assumes that capitalism, modernity and 'modern' colonialism are co-constitutive and inextricably entwined. For example, it helps us to comprehend that even though Katrülaf (who we met in the introduction) was not yet personally 'colonized' at the start, his social world was subject to colonial land-grab and racism, he was oppressed by

Argentina's desire to emulate European modernity, and was engaged in capitalism, even before he went to Where the Welsh Are.

This approach also enables fresh thinking about Wales's colonial situation. It shifts the focus from the British imperial period (which inspired postcolonial theory) and moves back in time to 1492. It reminds us that the incorporation of Wales into English sovereignty and law through the Acts of Union in 1536 and 1542 was not prior to but broadly contemporaneous with the arrival of Cortéz in what was to become Mexico in 1519, and the triumph of Pizarro over Atahualpa in Peru in 1532. Of course, this is contextualized closer to home by the colonization of Ireland from 1536. Looking towards the Atlantic world in the long sixteenth century, and from Wales, offers a distinctive and complicating perspective, and opens different analytical pathways that might shed fresh light on well-worn concerns. It invites us to think about how Europe – and England, and England-and-Wales – was made and imagined in this turbulent, hyper-productive period, and to look for resonances between sites. Seeing Europe as a place in flux (with Spain being reinvented by the 'expulsion of the Moors', the persecution of the Jews, colonization of the southern Americas and religious/political struggles;[13] and England embarking on colonization in Ireland and northern Americas) frames Welsh subordination very differently than if we begin our thinking from British Imperial experience and South Asian postcolonial scholarship. Doing so also has the potential to enrich coloniality/modernity scholarship which has a major limitation: it treats Europe as a caricatured and homogeneous whole. Thinking back to the Americas from a marginal position in Europe adds much-needed nuance to a theory which portrays European states and nations as unitary, powerful and unproblematic, and pays no attention to existing prejudices and hierarchies in European society.

Coloniality and Patagonia
When the Welsh arrived in 1865, Patagonia was not formally a colonial setting but (at least on paper) part of an established nation state. This does not stop us from thinking about colonial logics, though, as the coloniality of power approach foregrounds relationships of power. Rather than focusing on forms of government (colonial or republican), it looks at colonial continuities in social relations and

identifies how changing practices of governance adapt in order to reiterate colonial patterns of power and wealth.

Officially, colonialism came to an end in Spanish-speaking Latin America in the period 1810–20 when *criollos* (European-heritage elites born in Latin America) led independence movements against the Crown. Quijano (and many others) argued that this entailed 'independence' for settlers only and that the role of colonizer passed fluently to the white elites.[14] For those on the receiving end of domination, little changed in terms of subjugation, disdain and exploitation. Nations were built which perpetuated – indeed institutionalized – colonial-era logics and practices, though skilfully adapting them to the new emblems and categories of rule, such as republic, state and citizen.

In Argentina, this discourse of inclusion and equality before the law was combined with aggressive, colonizing policies which brought land still controlled by Indigenous people within the possession of the new nation, its boundaries and bureaucracy.[15] We see this forcefully at work in Patagonia which was, as Katrülaf testified, under the control of leaders such as Foyel and Inakayal. Here, fifty years or so after 'independence' from Spain, physical colonization was used by the national government to 'close the frontier' (much like the push west in the United States). Katrülaf witnessed his people's territories being taken by armed force, his society subjugated, his culture derided, his social group decimated and the political power of his leaders stripped away – all in the name of Argentina. The seeming Europeanness and whiteness of Argentina thus hides a history of Indigenous oppression, invisiblization and disavowal in order to sustain its image as a place where capitalist development and liberal political culture have been embedded.[16] This is the basis of its claim to global status and power.

Coloniality and Wales
The coloniality of power approach also opens a way to think about colonialism and Wales. Importantly, it suggests that colonial relationships should be viewed as socially embedded and as having adapted to different modes of governance over the 900+ years of English settlement. Moreover, it suggests the intimate linkage between race and capitalism, and explicitly connects Wales's particular experience of industrialization with the global movements of ideas, capital and

power.[17] Yet to talk of colonialism and Wales is a risky topic: even to ask 'is Wales colonized?' is highly contentious. In the opening chapter of *Postcolonial Wales*, Chris Williams argued forcefully that Wales cannot be viewed as postcolonial. While he was willing to accept that Wales was colonized by the English, especially from 1282 onwards, he argues that 'for all intents and purposes the Acts of Union abolished the distinction between Wales and England: Wales was no longer a colony, but part of an expanded England or Greater Britain'.[18] This view is based on seeing colonialism as a specific mode of governance. However, a relational approach allows us to identify not only pivot-points of change, but also continuities in social and political relations. Most of the other contributors to the *Postcolonial Wales* volume implicitly accepted a relational and ongoing view of 'the colonial', yet the essays are notable for their uncertain theorization of colonialism and indeed few scholars have pursued a conceptual understanding of Welsh colonialism since.[19]

As suggested earlier, colonialism in Wales has often been misdiagnosed through being compared to British imperial experiences, but there the colonizer did not, for the most part, intend to stay. By contrast Wales, like Argentina and the whole of the Americas, was (perhaps is) a settler colony. Thus, colonial dynamics associated with settler/Indigenous experience can, I believe, resonate in the Welsh context. Of course, each settler scenario is unique, with its own history and cultural, political and economic relations with the colonizing society – Wales is not Argentina, nor is it Australia. However, other examples can point us towards common social dynamics, helping us to think systematically about the nature of domination where the colonizer comes to stay by focusing on the relationship, not the mode of governance, which makes it colonial. This entails the activation of (at least) three processes which perpetuate those colonial relations: possession, racialization/barbarization and assimilation. It is to these processes that we now turn.

Process one: possession

Settler colonial studies has emerged as the response of settler-heritage scholars who began to reflect on their own position and complicity in the ongoing subjugation of Native American, First Nations and Aboriginal peoples.[20] Their work is helpful because it analyses the logics and practices of colonizers who 'come to stay' in Patrick Wolfe's memorable phrase.[21] This policy element is lacking in the coloniality of power scholarship which foregrounds the complexity of Indigenous lives and the big picture of capitalist modernity, but pays far less attention to the institutions and everyday actions of how the process of settling works. There are several areas of common ground between coloniality/modernity approaches and settler colonial theory which suggest their compatibility.[22] Both understand that colonial logics and practices shape settler societies even after such states achieve formal independence: they identify continuities over time. Moreover, both see colonialism as a global phenomenon that conditions both colonizing and colonized societies: they identify its global reach.[23] As such, there is potential for each theoretical approach to complement the other, though so far this has been seldom operationalized.

The central commodity of settler colonialism is land: as Patrick Wolfe puts it: 'territoriality is settler colonialism's specific irreducible element.'[24] Land is central to the colonial struggle, for both settler and Indigenous people: it is a physical space to be governed (politics/sovereignty); it is the place where group identity is imagined and history/spirituality is embedded (belonging/nation); and it is the stage on which competing worldviews are played out (knowing and being). Thus, the struggle over land is multi-layered and plays a prominent role in the social imaginary. Following Wolfe, settling itself entails two interlocking phases: staking a claim over a territory and announcing sovereignty (conquest); then, continuously reiterating the legitimacy of that claim in the face of continued Indigenous presence (consolidation).

A recent book by Aboriginal (Goenpul) Australian Aileen Moreton-Robinson explores this settler logic as 'possession', an idea that her Gami (uncle), Dennis Benjamin Moreton, put succinctly: 'The problem with white people is they think and behave like they own everything.'[25] She defines 'possessive logics' as being 'a mode of rationalization ... that is underpinned by an excessive desire to invest in reproducing and reaffirming the nation-state's ownership, control and domination.'[26] Of course, settler possession entails Indigenous dispossession and 'the logics of white possession and the disavowal of Indigenous sovereignty are materially and discursively linked'.[27] Her book charts the way that institutional frameworks, laws and economic systems, as well as everyday habits, assumptions and visual cues, all work to reinforce the central claim to legitimate possession of the land. More than that, she explores the possessive sensibility – the 'will and desire to possess' which creates 'sets of meanings about ownership of the nation, as part of common-sense knowledge, decision-making and socially produced conventions'.[28]

As in all settler scenarios, possession in Australia began with a physical act when Captain Cook landed on an island that he (astonishingly) named 'Possession', fired a gun, planted a flag and claimed the territory for King George III on the basis of European law.[29] Importantly, these royal 'rights' and legal justifications already assumed the colonizability of lands and peoples marked as barbaric in the European imaginary.[30] This is a key point: possession requires the presence of a worldview which assumes the rightful supremacy of the colonizer and the subjugate-ability of Other lands and peoples in order to create a 'right to possession'. This then justifies the use of violent military action in order to fulfil the logic of rightful domination over a people already imagined as savage.

A key justification for settler colonialism is *terra nullius*, or conceptualizing Indigenous land as being empty and belonging to no one. If land can be considered to have no owner, then taking that land cannot be considered stealing and colonial acts of possession appear to be legitimate. Yet in order to make theories of *terra nullius* stick, fundamental acts of disavowal are necessary: Indigenous people must not be recognized as 'people', a sense of belonging not recognized as 'ownership', governance not recognized as 'sovereignty', and ways of life must be marked as too primitive to be a proper 'society'.[31] Settlers thus assert dominance over spatial territories, and also over concepts, such as 'owning' and 'being human'. Jodi Byrd (Chickasaw) explains that this turns Indigenous persons into *homo nullius*.[32] Once this deep dehumanization is achieved, all other forms of domination become viable: military, political, cultural, linguistic, racial, etc.

Carole Pateman explains that *terra nullius* emerged when Enlightenment theorists in the Protestant tradition (Hobbes, Grotius, Locke, etc.) tried to make sense of the conquest in the northern Americas, and the idea became hardened though encounters in Australia.[33] As such, *terra nullius* was entangled with the development of capitalism and early liberal thinking, and constituted the starting point for Locke's theory of value and property.[34] For him, land was an asset to be valued not in and of itself but in relation to the resources it provides in terms of food, minerals, fuel, etc. Its value remained latent to the extent that crops were not grown, iron not mined, or wood not turned into charcoal. For Locke, the taking of 'waste land' by those who could turn it into 'productive land' was justified because of the greater utility and happiness that could be garnered, not only for individuals and families, but for wider society. We can see here that property, a concept that underpins both liberal individualism and capitalism, thus constitutes personhood (a person is someone who can possess), which in turn is the basis for claims to sovereignty.

This logic is reinforced by another foundational Eurocentric assumption derived from Descartes: the binary separation between culture (humans) and nature, whereby humans are not part of nature but walk over it, controlling and utilising it.[35] This relationship is hierarchal, then, as nature is Man's servant to be used – or preserved – at His will. In turn this empowers and civilizes those who dominate nature and barbarizes those who do not tame it. Those associated with dominating nature are marked as 'human' and those who do not are understood to be part of nature themselves, and therefore are both sub-human and the legitimate objects of domination.[36]

While Pateman's analysis of *terra nullius* helps us to understand the initial claim to territory, Moreton-Robinson's work charts the everyday possessive processes which embed the 'white possessive' each day, yet which are always incomplete because of enduring Aboriginal presence. For example, she analyses the beach as a location of possessive practice, marked as owned by the performance of white masculinity in the form of surf-lifesavers and surfers themselves.[37] She charts how Hawaiian 'soul-surfing' (riding the flow of the waves) gave way to macho competitive surfing, laced with sex and parties, marking the beach as 'sovereign ground' of a certain sort of white masculinity. It is also a key site for Aboriginal protesters to enact re-possession, exposing the racialization of the beach and its central role in the colonial – and decolonial – enterprise.

Her analysis helps us to understand possession as not just material control but also as the feeling of sovereignty – a sense of rightful powerfulness over a specific place and everything within it. Understanding sovereignty – and indeed colonialism – to be fuelled by this feeling is a route into understanding what is at stake in settler identity-construction, based on pioneering, building and defending a settler nation. Importantly, though, she notes that while for settlers the settler world is banal:

> for Indigenous people, white possession is not unmarked, unnamed or invisible; it is hypervisible. In our quotidian encounters … every building and every street [signifies] that this land is now possessed by others … the omnipresence of Indigenous sovereignties exists here too, but it is disavowed by the materiality of these significations, which are perceived as evidence of ownership.[38]

Possession is a fact of domination and a feeling of rightful sovereignty; dispossession has huge material consequences and generates profound psychological trauma; repossession entails both a material and cultural claiming-back of sovereignty and dignity.

Process two: racialization/barbarization

A core process within colonialism is the establishment and maintenance of a social hierarchy between the colonizer and the colonized, whereby a somehow-identifiable, subordinated group becomes the subject of prejudice: this process is often called racialization. The analysis of race and racialization has been pioneered by critical race and intersectionality theorists, drawing primarily on the experiences of African Americans.[39] This excellent and important work examines the logics of prejudice that emanate from the experience of slavery and the desire to keep different races separate that characterizes US society.[40] However, whilst such work is inspiring, it builds its theories from this archetype which is specific to a particular regime of race. This raises questions about its translate-ability to other groups.

These tensions emerge in discussions about racialization, the process whereby a group of people are labelled pejoratively and discriminated against simply because they belong to that group. The most

commonly used definition comes from Michael Omi and Howard
Winant who describe racialization as 'the extension of racial meaning to a previously racially unclassified relationship, social practice,
or group'.[41] Tensions emerge because this definition starts its thinking
about race from American Blackness and expands the racialization of
people and things outwards from that position. As such, it has difficulty embracing the particularities of anti-Indigenous racism, for example, which is founded not on plantation slavery but on the dispossession of land and sovereignty.[42] To complicate things further, in Latin
America racism is associated with anti-Indigenous rather than anti-
Black discrimination.[43] Moreover, the struggle against inequality in
Latin America is understood through poverty, which filters Blackness
and Indigeneity through the lens of economic exploitation or social
exclusion, and racial distinctions are often replaced by class commonalities.[44] This reflects the region's huge wealth disparities, but also its
history of racial mixing (known as *mestizaje*), including widespread
mixing between people of African and Indigenous heritage. The specificity associated with American Black experience as a foundation for
theorizing race is not necessarily useful in Latin America, then.

A broader approach to racialization has been sought by scholars
studying non-Black racisms. For example, a recent issue of *Ethnic and
Racial Studies* edited by Bianca Gonzalez-Sobrino and Devon Goss
collected articles on anti-Polish or anti-Traveller racisms, and Steve
Garner and Saher Selod's special issue of *Critical Sociology* focused
on Islamophobia.[45] In their thought-provoking introduction, Garner
and Selod open up the category 'race' and identify three essential elements: a general *ideology* in society that utilises race (not necessarily
Blackness) as a way to categorize people based on phenotype and/or
cultural characteristics; a historical *power relationship* based on the
idea that negative traits are 'natural and innate to each member of the
group'; and *motifs and practices* of discrimination that follow from
this prejudice.[46] Crucially, they argue that group-ness can be constituted culturally and that a shared phenotype characteristic is not necessary to constitute racism. This opens space to consider anti-Welsh
prejudice which has a linguistic, not phenotype, marker. What is important for racialization is that negative traits are imagined as being
innate, including culture or spirituality traits. That is, the heritability
that is supposedly made obvious when people 'look Black' is also im-

agined when people share a religion or language, even where these are purposefully chosen. Of course, none of this negative 'heritability' (neither phenotype nor language) is borne out in reality – it is the fruit of prejudicial thinking.

How does racial prejudice work? It seems to follow a number of key, simultaneous and mutually reinforcing moves which are operationalized by the dominant group. The empowered group identifies the out-group as sharing an innate, and negative, characteristic (dehumanization); it denotes membership through distinguishing features, such as phenotype, language, clothing, place of residence, spiritual beliefs (homogenization); it defines them as external objects (objectification); it announces and explains the Other's inferiority and their own superiority (hierarchal othering); it reiterates their inferiority by repeating prejudicial motifs and ideas (stereotyping); and it blocks the prosperity and well-being of the group through institutional, cultural, political and economic obstruction (discrimination, sometimes violent). What makes this racial and not just prejudicial is the ascription (no matter how unscientific) of group uniformity based on a shared heritable essence. This is on display when we hear someone say 'Mapuche Indians are stupid' or 'you can't trust the Welsh'.

Can this discussion help us to understand Cymrophobia? The situation is complex. On the one hand, there is a strong association between Welshness and phenotypical whiteness, and indeed most Welsh people do benefit from racial privilege. Yet on the other, Welsh culture and language has been systematically identified as the target of prejudice and discrimination since the medieval period, as we will see in the next chapter. The term 'racialization' fits awkwardly with anti-Welsh prejudice, then, because it takes as its starting point the idea of race, which itself is deeply associated with the body. Moreover, because Welshness can be acquired (through residence, self-identity and language learning), people of all racial and religious backgrounds can become the target of Cymrophobia.

One alternative is to shift focus to a wider, more general realm of preference and prejudice based on ideas of 'civilization' and 'barbarism' – an ontological hierarchy. Here, those who wield cultural and moral capital (usually backed by wealth and military might) can announce their superiority by claiming to be civilized, and in turn denounce the barbaric lives of Others.[47] A focus on culture and lifeways highlights the existential essence of a person or group and measures their relative desirability according to their position on the spectrum of civilization/barbarism. It is the powerful who set the criteria by which people are judged and its purpose is to aggrandize the Self, as civilized, and mark the Other as barbaric. Although generally overlooked, the concept of barbarism – and therefore civilization – is fundamental to the Western philosophical tradition. Yongjin Zhang traces its evolution from Greek encounters with Persians who were marked as barbarians whose language (like Welsh) was deemed 'incomprehensible'.[48] The portrayal of Europeans as civilized, and the division of humanity into 'civilized' and 'barbarian' groups has continued to frame inter-community relationships and remains a key motif of international relations today.[49]

The civilization/barbarism motif is a more capacious and general framework, then, which can encompass prejudice beyond and including race, such as Islamophobia, xenophobia, anti-Welsh bigotry and anti-Indigenous prejudice – and many others. It broadens the focus too to encompass a whole range of human actions, moral values, sexual norms and cultural practices but also ontological matters such as individual-community and human-nature relations.

The inspiration for this approach comes from Walter Mignolo's approach to understanding race in the sixteenth-century Americas. In *Idea of Latin America*, Mignolo defined race broadly as 'categorizing individuals according to their level of similarity/proximity to an assumed model of ideal humanity'.[50] Mignolo's theories have their root in his research on the intellectual meeting between Spanish and Indigenous scholars during the very early colonial collision. In particular, he charts the Spanish consternation, disdain and rejection of Indigenous modes of annotating knowledge, such as Mayan pictograms; the Andean Quipu (a system of coloured knots and strings used by Inca bureaucrats which 'produced meaning ... by tracing figures in space'[51]); and the use of memory, oral recitation and repetition as authoritative sources. Mignolo reflects that: 'Spaniards stressed reading the word rather than reading the world and made the letter the anchor of knowledge and understanding.'[52] The ensuing destruction of Indigenous knowledge archives expressed claims of Spanish civilization and Indigenous barbarism fixed not on the body but on a profound disjuncture of intellects and ways of knowing.

Mignolo points to the writings of Bartolomé de las Casas, a key ideologue of the Spanish court to help explain what barbarism (and therefore civilization) is. For las Casas, the social and cultural world is understood as the outward expression of an inner life, and if it does not match that of the dominant, naming group, it is labelled as barbaric. In his treatise *Apologética historia sumaria* of 1552, he classified five types of barbarian. The first is the most familiar: those who demonstrated '*strange or ferocious behaviour* and [had] a degenerate sense of justice, reason, manners and/or human generosity'.[53] That is, they combined violence with a lack of moral reason to underpin their action. The second is related to language (once more): las Casas identified as barbaric 'all those people who *lacked a "literal locution that responds to their language* in the same way that our locution responds to the Latin language"'.[54] For him, Latin is the only proper language because others 'lacked the proper words to name God' and used the only proper alphabet.[55] The third sort of barbarians were 'those who *lacked basic forms of governmentality*' such as the law and the state.[56] Fourthly, barbarism was attributed by las Casas to everyone who '*lacked true religion* and Christian faith', even when they were 'sage and prudent philosophers and politicians'.[57] Las Casas's final category was *barbarie contraria* which 'identified all those who (like today's 'terrorists') actively worked to undermine Christianity'.[58] Civilization is defined, therefore, as the way of life of the dominant actor, while barbarism is defined by deviation from this norm. Racism is founded, Mignolo argues, not on disgust of the body, but disdain for the lifeway of the Other.[59] The Indigenous or Black body acts as a biological marker of the human lack within, signalling the 'barbaric' essence, or indeed essential 'civilization', of different Peoples. The dehumanization of the Black and Indigenous, and the hyper-humanization and hyper-valuation of the European, is anchored therefore in lifeways and knowledge which is classed as 'barbaric' or 'civilized'.

A shift to the broader category of barbarization creates an intellectual space that both Indigenous Patagonians and the Welsh can inhabit. This is not to say that their experiences are equivalent: clearly the stakes for the Welsh were and are much lower than that of Katrülaf and his descendants, and their position on the grim hierarchy of oppression is much more comfortable. Yet this does not shield them and their language from being the object of derision and prejudice. It is because 'barbarization' is a broader category than 'racialization' that we can draw in other forms of prejudice and envisage more complex tensions and hierarchies within the category of the barbarized. Using barbarization in place of racialization might open space for us to hold both (relative) privilege and prejudice in our minds together and develop a complex analysis of Welsh-Indigenous relations in Patagonia.

Process three: assimilation

As we have seen, what makes settler colonial regimes distinctive is their intention to stay and embed a new society. Accompanying the desire to possess land, and enabled by ontological and racial hierarchies, then, is the logic of Indigenous elimination. In order to utterly possess a place, the 'inferior' former way of life must be erased and replaced, a project that is ongoing while Indigenous people remain. For this reason, in Wolfe's famous phrase 'invasion is a structure, not an event' and Indigenous peoples around the world explain that their existence is fundamental to their resistance.[60]

Patrick Wolfe has explored the dynamics of elimination in his work on genocide. Drawing on case studies from Aboriginal Australia and Native American/First Nations' experience, Wolfe identified genocide to be at work in two ways. The first is violent physical erasure through direct attack, for example massacres or mass sterilization programmes. In the introduction, we witnessed Katrülaf's testimony to the violence employed by the Argentine military in Patagonia, and certainly massacres took place during the Conquest of the Desert.[61] Even after conquest is 'settled', though, the threat of violence never goes away, and for many Indigenous people being killed is an ever-present threat, especially if they get in the way of big business.[62] Physical violence is therefore active during all phases of settling in a very real sense.

Equally important, though, is assimilation. Often, assimilation is framed as 'integration' within the dominant (superior) order and appears reasonable as it entails economic development and social uplift, on settler terms. Turning 'Indians' into 'members of the nation' is a common aim of settler states once they are conquered and holds out the liberal ideal of equal rights and opportunities: citizenship.[63] 'Civilizing' policies are thus essential to eliminate barbaric behaviour, beliefs and ways of life, entailing ontological violence which can turn physical if the 'generous gesture' of citizenship is rejected.[64] For Wolfe, this too is genocide: 'Here, in essence, is assimilation's Faustian bargain – have our settler world, but lose your Indigenous soul. Beyond any doubt this is a kind of death.'[65] Yet those marked as barbaric cannot be full citizens because their existence, and therefore essential savagery, remains. Thus they become second class, 'barbarized' citizens who bear the responsibilities of citizenship (such as conscription) but can only patchily access its rights. These 'second-class citizens' are not a vestige of early settler colonialism but an essential structural component: it is their 'barbarism' that showcases settler 'civilization.'[66]

Wolfe's argument is important because it emphasizes the ontological and cultural aspects of human existence for both colonizer and colonized, both as a source of meaning and community identity and as a foundational terrain of political struggle. He is right, too, that the stakes are genocidal. Yet his apocalyptic analysis, while useful as an argumentative strategy, is problematic for two key reasons, both linked to assimilation. First, it denies Indigenous agency and overlooks cultural adaptation. Wolfe's analysis (and often settler colonial theory more generally) portrays Indigenous people and their cultures as victims who are at the mercy of an all-powerful, corrosive state. Without denying the atrocities committed in the name of policy (such as child abduction and forced assimilation in Australia), this significantly undermines the agency of Original Peoples.[67] Despite the onslaught, Indigenous societies resist cultural erasure and sustain their ways of knowing, speaking, living and being in the world in their families and at the margins of the settler regime. For example, the Huarpe people of northern Argentina have recently demanded recognition and rebuilt their language anew, despite being declared 'extinct' in the sixteenth century.[68]

Secondly, settler colonial theory uses a binary framework (colonizer/colonized; settler/Indigenous) which belies the complexity of established settler societies. This stems from its genesis in the study of the anglophone settler world where official, top-down policies attempted to keep Indigenous and settler people separate, socially and sexually. Yet this overlooks a social reality of mixing, both transcultural and sexual, in all culturally mixed societies. Alternatively, Wolfe's idea that assimilation is a form of death can only interpret social or sexual mixing in a destructive way. The shortcoming of binary thinking becomes all the more obvious in settler colonial contexts that are 900+ years in the making, like Wales, and where the colonizing and colonized communities are intimately mixed.

In parallel, Indigenous studies scholarship also charts the violences of assimilation but emphasizes the endurance and ingenuity required to ensure the survival and regeneration of Indigenous societies.[69] The politicization and high profile of Indigenous struggle over the last twenty-five years or so has led many governments to recognize the presence of Original communities as distinct and contemporary societies (not vestiges of the past) who are also here to stay. This 'politics of recognition' accepts that the 'Native' has not been and should not be erased, thus undermining the logic of elimination that underpins the settler quest for utter possession: the land must be shared. However, Glen Coulthard, reflecting on the First Nations/ Canadian example, suggests that this multiculturalism is yet another technique of assimilation through a politics of 'recognition-on-settler-terms' and incorporation with the state, under the guise of 'mutual recognition'.[70] He argues that this strategy activates 'models of liberal pluralism that seek to "reconcile" Indigenous assertions of nationhood with settler state sovereignty', but that this 'reproduces the very configuration of colonialist, racist, patriarchal state power that Indigenous people's demands for recognition have historically sought to transcend'.[71] That is, in order to preserve supremacy, the settler state concedes recognition but only on the terms that it controls. A similar dynamic has been observed by Charles Hale, writing about Guatemala today, and what he calls the *Indio permitido* or 'authorized Indian', a figure who can be an 'Indian citizen' of a multicultural state, so long as they conform to the demands of neo-liberal development and remain subordinated politically and culturally.[72] Indeed, as Coulthard also argues, Indigenous 'difference' can be celebrated so long as it can be set to work for the settler state, for example by boosting tourism or providing national emblems. From a coloniality of power perspective, then, violent assimilation, capitalist development and

multiculturalism are all predicated on the colonization of Indigenous land and imposition of a Euro-centric way of understanding
the world and deciding what is important, and each serves the same
purpose – to consolidate 'civilized' settler power.

Processes of coloniality in Patagonia

Let us now explore the application of these three analytical tools by
using them to shed light on Indigenous Patagonian experience. Their
application to analysing nineteenth-century Wales will be explored in
the following chapter, and subsequent chapters will pick up on these
key themes, though the processes are always intertwined.

Possession
The possession of Patagonia was enacted in two ways: by the purposeful capture of territory (*terra nullius*) and by the laying claim
to Indigenous inhabitants, turning them from people into objects
(*homo nullius*). The *terra nullius* discourse was deployed explicitly
during the Conquest of the Desert, underpinning Patagonia's definition as a deserted space. As Carolyn Larson explains, it was understood as a place of lack, 'empty' of civilization, which must be set to
work for the good of Argentina.[73] This justified the use of military
force to impose the will of the state over 'Indian' savages in order that
both land and people contribute to the prosperity and well-being of
the whole nation. We can witness this macho and possessive narrative in the following quote which cites Nicolás Avellaneda, president
from 1874–80:

> Argentines could only satisfy their own sense of 'propriety, as
> a virile people' through 'the conquest … by reason or by force,
> of a handful of savages that destroy our principal wealth and
> impede us from definitively occupying, in the name of the
> law, of progress and of our own security, the richest and most
> fertile territories of the Republic.[74]

While this was undertaken by a nation state (not a colonizing force),
the desire to make so-called waste land that supposedly belongs to no

one into productive property was at work. Asserting state sovereignty thus entailed the identification of (populated) territories as *terra nullius*, the subordination of those territories (and people) to the state, and the legitimation of such acts (stealing land, oppressing people) by interpreting them as now productive. This process demonstrates the 'coloniality of power' in action – genocidal violence as the shadowy partner of modernity which enabled the imposition of settler sovereignty, legitimated by the logic of economic productivity.

Another means of enacting the possession of land is to mark the state's sovereignty via exploring, mapping and naming – all of which require an intellectual laying claim to landscapes, rivers and significant places. This entailed erasing the Indigenous names that gave meaning to the land that they knew so well: for Indigenous people this was not discovery but epistemological theft.[75] Famous Argentine explorers such as Francisco Moreno and Estanislao Zeballos travelled with and around the military, 'discovering' mountains, rivers and coastlines.[76] They measured the distances, noted the pathways and crossing places, drew the flora, fauna and mountains, and met the people, noting their habits and locations. These travellers provided valuable knowledge and information to the state which supported its state-building initiatives, but as celebrities they also interpreted these 'new territories' for the public, giving them character and names. All these techniques of possession entail pinning down 'wild', barbaric places and promoting a sense of proprietorship, akin to sovereignty. The Welsh too engaged in exploration and map-making, especially Llwyd ap Iwan who went in search of gold and minerals, and whose diaries and journals offer such a vivid account of the Welsh enterprise in Patagonia.[77]

Importantly, the Argentine state also enacted possessive policy over Indigenous people themselves, configuring them as *homo nullius*. Katrülaf, for example, was 'possessed' by the state: he was corralled, tied up, made to march across the desert and forced to enter the army. Many others were confined in internment camps and sent to Diego Garcia Island, where they were sorted and allocated new roles as servants for the growing middle class in Buenos Aires or as workers in the sugar plantations and refineries in the north.[78]

Equally disturbing is the collection of Indigenous people as anthropological items. Katrülaf's story is with us today because it was deemed to be valuable by Robert Lehmann-Nitsche who took time to record his tale, not because he valued Katrülaf as a person, but because he meant to learn something about the 'primitive' inhabitants. Some Indigenous persons were even sent to the Museo de la Plata as living relics which visitors could observe as exhibits. The Museo was founded by Francisco Moreno who brought Caciques Inakayal and Foyel (with whom Katrülaf travelled) to live there until they died. The completeness (and casual violence) of the possessive sensibility that underpins this act is laid bare in Moreno's comment of 1888:

> The death of four adult Indians in the establishment has provided the Museum with four brains that have great scientific value, because they are the only ones of this race preserved in collections ... and their importance increases if we take into account that they belong to individuals from a race that is rapidly extinguishing.[79]

Possessive anthropology also took the form of grave-robbing, as Carolyn Larson charts, whereby wealthy intellectuals uncovered burials and took the skulls and bones back to museums to house, collect, catalogue and study these human remains, often of people actually killed during the Conquest of the Desert.[80] They corresponded with museums in Europe and copied their techniques as well as trading in remains and artefacts. Indigenous people as dead-objects-to-be-collected were prized and valued, while living Indigenous people were displaced from their land, discarded or sent to labour. Both modes objectified and dehumanized Indigenous people, setting them to work for the aggrandisement and Europeanization of the settler state which felt itself to be now in full possession of Patagonia: land and people.

Racialization/barbarization
The racialization/barbarization of Indigenous Patagonians reflected prejudice which tagged both phenotypical and cultural traits.[81] While discrimination was already built into the general colonial mindset of Latin American elites, it took on specific motifs during the nineteenth century, pegged to Argentine nation-building. Not only did elites want land and labour, they aimed to create a 'white' and civ-

ilized Argentina. This was to be an explicitly settler country whose superiority was confirmed by its European character and lack of Indigenous people (in contrast to neighbouring Peru and Bolivia) and the supposed absence of Black people (in contrast to Brazil).[82] This taps into the famous saying (reiterated as recently as 2020 by President Fernández) that 'the Argentines descend from the boats'.[83] Of course, this is a fiction on all counts, but Argentina's claim to power and global status was predicated on creating an image of its racial whiteness – the badge of civilization.[84]

A towering figure in this effort was Domingo Sarmiento whose exile in Europe and the United States, and study of liberal political philosophy, engendered an idealized vision of an orderly, law-based, capitalist, European and well-educated country modelled on the European ideal.[85] He framed this vision in his famous book *Facundo, or Civilization and Barbarism*, and used this trope (civilization/barbarism) to mount a compelling argument enacted through policies when he became president of the republic (1868–74).[86] To enable this future, he proposed the need to erase all those 'undesirable elements' that worked against it: the lazy *gauchos* (cowboys), the crude, populist landowners of vast estates (*caudillos*), the degenerate *negros* and the wild, barbaric *indios*. This 'rabble' were tainted by the 'darkness' of rural life and contrasted with the light, modern and future-facing 'city on the hill': Buenos Aires, citadel of citizens. Thus the desired status of 'citizen' was brought to life through its contrast with the ample and flexible category of 'barbarian', deploying a racial code.[87]

In Patagonia, this effort to implant civilization required that those who embodied barbarism be displaced or killed, imprisoned or assimilated in order to elevate Argentina on the world stage. Racialization/barbarization took three intertwined forms and echo las Casas's classifications of barbarism written 400 years before: they were labelled as savage (immoral behaviour and rebellion) and were relegated to the 'primitive' past (inferior governance and lifeways). First, Indigenous people were condemned for their degenerate and lawless behaviour which enabled their branding as an expendable enemy and justified military action.[88] In particular, the 'Indian' was described as a violent 'internal enemy' who mounted raids (*malones*) against the settlers, sometimes taking their wives and children (the *malón* was an established strategy of inter-Indigenous rivalry). The Mapuche (like

Katrülaf) were marked as the most savage and identified by the state as 'foreign' and 'Chilean' people who quashed the supposedly 'peaceful native Argentine Indians' (though there is little truth to this). This barbarization of 'foreign Indians' allowed the state to claim that 'our Indians' were not fierce, had been decimated by alien Indian forces, and therefore needed state protection. This dimension of barbarization justified war and ennobled the military conquest of Patagonia.

A second form of barbarization emerged from this – labelling the 'Argentine Indigenous' as intellectually and culturally primitive. Positioning the Other as being backwards in time is a key thought-device used in ideas of progress, development and civilization which imagines Western modes of thinking and living to be further along on the evolutionary pathway.[89] Moreover, labelling a person or community as 'backwards' implicitly tags the civilized as being 'advanced' and therefore superior. Here we see modernity/coloniality at work in the nineteenth century, acting to re-assert the hierarchy of culture/races and solidify the power of the settler state by making claims to progressive civilization. In Patagonia, Mónica Quijada identifies contemporary sources which label the *indio* as *inferior* and as 'fossil forms of primitive life'.[90] This, Quijada notes had 'important connotations because it complemented the notion that the "primitive peoples" which came into contact with an element that was "more advanced" were condemned to disappear'.[91] Thus General Julio Roca, ideologue and engineer of the Conquest of the Desert (president 1880–6 and a 'great friend to the Welsh') could state: 'It is in effect a law of nature that the Indian will succumb before the invasion of the civilized man. In the struggle for existence in the same environment, the weaker race must succumb to that better endowed.'[92] This portrayed the 'disappearance' of Indigenous people as being a natural outcome (not purposeful erasure), linked of course to Darwinian principles.[93] European domination is thus configured as natural because of the supposedly innate racial inferiority of the 'native' and corresponding innate racial superiority of the European, as evidenced by the outer trappings of civilization. This form of racialization/barbarization dominates by turning Indigenous people into objects and making the 'pre-Conquest Indian' die. This is expressed succinctly by the common phrase, still heard today, 'there are no Indians – they killed them all', which serves to invisiblize Indigenous people, even in plain sight, and could itself be construed as an act of genocide.[94] Making Indigenous people invisible, even while they stand, is a powerful tool of elimination and one which remains potent today, especially in Wales as we will see in chapter six. The powerfulness of the discourse of Indigenous death (and also, Afro-Argentine death[95]) allowed Argentina to develop its image as 'white' and European. This was a key reason why the Argentine state welcomed the Welsh as settlers, people who embodied their desire to inculcate Anglo-Saxon genes and Protestant values, wealth and civilized behaviour. This does not make the Welsh direct oppressors of the Indigenous Patagonians, but it does make them an integral part of the story.

Assimilation in Patagonia
The experience of Indigenous Patagonians chimes with the highly oppressive approach to assimilation that Wolfe proposes: the logic of elimination-by-inclusion is explicitly at work. This entailed assimilation of Indigenous land within 'Argentina' and assimilation of Indigenous people within Eurocentric modes of development. A key first step, then, is the bodily importation of white settlers (like the Welsh) who would aid Argentina's assimilation within the European model of statehood. Spurred by this ideological project, Argentina underwent a rapid immigration policy in the latter nineteenth century: around three million migrants arrived between 1880 and 1910.[96]

A key ideologue who drove this policy was Juán Alberdi who argued that: 'to govern is to populate in the sense that to populate is to educate, improve, civilize, enrich and enlarge spontaneously and quickly'.[97] In order to create a civilized nation Alberdi argued that: 'to civilize via population it is necessary to do so with civilized peoples; to educate our America [the Americas] in liberty and industry, it is necessary to populate it with the Europeans most advanced in liberty and industry, as occurs in the United States'.[98] Domingo Sarmiento illustrates that archetype by describing the 'German or Scotch colonies' in south Buenos Aires whose 'cottages are painted; the furniture is simple but complete; copper or tin utensils always bright and clean; nicely curtained beds; and the occupants of the dwelling are always industriously at work'.[99] (We might note the virtues of cleanliness and sexual modesty which are inferred.) Y Wladfa, then, is intended to play a key role in assimilating the land formerly belonging to Inakay-al, Foyel and many others within the nation state, capitalist economy and European ideal. The Welsh settlers were at the vanguard of this trend, bringing 'civilization', painted cottages and petty capitalism to the Chubut Valley. While they did not quite realize it, then, they were pivotal players in this assimilation drama, especially because their location is so far to the south in 'Indian land'.

Assimilation policies also, of course, focused on attempts to civilize the 'Indian' and draw them into the national development programme. At first, this entailed an explicit policy of fast-track indoctrination, especially via the military. Claudia Briones quotes Estanislao Zeballos, adventurer and deputy, who claimed in 1882 that:

> the most humanitarian, the most civilized, the most honourable thing that the nation can do with them is to assign them to the Army, where they will be taught to read and write and the first principles of the nation that they have never known. It will put them into contact with civilization and as a result fit them to be useful to their country.[100]

By 1900, the drive to assimilate was deemed to require urgent state action, at least by Deputy Manuel Cabral who would state:

> I don't want to keep the few Indians that speak, for example, a few Toba or a few Chulupí; I want the Argentine schools, the national schools, to go to the Indians in such a way that the little Indians [*indiecitos*] can be converted into Argentine citizens.[101]

In another comment he proposed the virtues of miscegenation: 'I want immediate mixing, with the assurance that, from one generation to the next savagery will disappear, because it is an undeniable fact that the superior civilization will destroy the inferior, it imposes and dominates.'[102] Here we see how racialization works hand in glove with barbarization to disparage, and to engineer the elimination of Indigenous people, proposing their transformation into 'civilized' citizens. We can also identify Wolfe's portrayal of forced assimilation at work as 'a kind of death'.

What to do with 'the Indian Problem' was a concern for a wide range of different governments throughout the twentieth century, ranging from right-wing military regimes of the 1930s to Juan Perón's leftist populism of the 1950s, to the liberal democracy of Alfonsín in the 1980s.[103] While some were more authoritarian or sympathetic than others, each regarded the poverty of Indigenous populations as a blight on the nation, and sought ways to teach, cajole and force their participation in development initiatives. That is, each aimed to promote different versions of assimilation on terms dictated by the state. Policies effectively instructed the *Indios* on how to adopt and utilise the Eurocentric worldview which promoted individual initiative in the capitalist economy. Each government consulted experts (economists, agronomists, etc.) on policy matters, and devised a fresh policy agenda, sometimes following global trends in development economics.[104] Seldom were Indigenous views on such policies sought, nor did experts draw on their knowledge of the environment or skills, practices or preferences. While some of these initiatives were well-meaning, each continued to regard the 'Indian' as an outlier to the nation and therefore an aberration or source of shame for a government that continued to believe that Argentina had a special claim to 'civilization'.[105]

Ultimately, this barrage of policies meant that assimilation has been highly successful. Indigenous people have been forced to adapt to the Eurocentric order to survive and immense damage has been done by the sustained violence of forced acculturation, as Wolfe suggested. Yet this should not necessarily be construed as 'death'. A major change occurred when Indigenous movements mobilized at the Constituent Assembly to gain recognition of the 'ethnic and cultural pre-existence of the Argentine Indigenous Peoples' in the 1994 constitution.[106] This opened the way for Indigenous people to claim rights over territories and places of cultural importance, which itself has served to mobilize and strengthen Indigenous communities. In Patagonia, nineteenth-century ways of life are gone, yet the Mapuche language and social networks are becoming stronger and communities are increasingly politically engaged.[107] Spiritual practices, languages and cultural activities, as well as histories and philosophies that were cherished and passed on in families, have now re-emerged as cultural capital for the community.[108] However, while this 'politics of recognition' has enabled the visibility of Indigenous people, for example by including Indigeneity (and Afro-descendance) in the census,[109] it is the state that controls the terms by which they are made present in the Argentine imaginary and recognized as the rightful recipients of land and rights.[110] The multicultural agenda introduced by the Kirchner governments in the early 2000s did legislate for Indigenous rights in an attempt to solidify, rather than unsettle, the legitimacy of the settler colonial regime, with a good degree of success.[111] Nevertheless, decolonization, reterritorialization and the building of new *Originario* identities continues to challenge the capitalist settler order and its logic of elimination in Patagonia.

Conclusion

I have set out here the conceptual tools that I will be using to understand power relations in Wales and Patagonia, adopting the coloniality of power approach to analysing the settler setting, focusing on three processes – possession, racialization/barbarization and assimilation. Within 'possession' I discussed land, *terra nullius* and the feeling of sovereignty. Within 'racialization/barbarization' I examined theorizations and explored the potential utility of civilization/barbarization as an analytical device. Within 'assimilation' I highlighted the logic of elimination and analysed the politics of multicultural 'recognition'. I then used these theoretical tools to organize and interpret nineteenth-century Argentine policy and Indigenous experiences in Patagonia. Of course, these processes change focus and practice over time, and they developed very differently in Patagonia than in Wales, as we will see in the next chapter. However, the use of a common set of tools in both locales helps us to identify commonalities in the operation of settler states and in the exercise of prejudice based on 'race' or 'barbarity'. We should also note that the processes do not operate in isolation but are intertwined. For example, acts of possession entail the Othering and demeaning of the people already there, and its 'success' in military and political terms obliges the Indigenous to assimilate or face a very difficult future. Processes of racialization and barbarization of the 'Indian' in turn enable the Argentine state's claim to rightful possession of Patagonia and justify the forced assim-

ilation of Indigenous people – including Katrülaf. Assimilation measures, therefore, seem to endorse the project of conquest, possession
and incorporation of Others who are deemed subject to the state by
virtue of their racial colonizability as barbarian Others.

Thinking about both Patagonia and Wales while writing this
chapter has enriched my ideas and challenged my assumptions
about where theories can be applied and to what sort of actors. Taking the origin country, Wales, seriously has opened space to view
marginalized communities in Europe through the lens of colonialism. This helps to unpack what is often viewed as a monolithic and
exploitative actor and to identify earlier or different manifestations
of the key processes identified here: possession, racialization/bar-
barization and assimilation. As we will see in the following chapter,
Wales has a complex relationship to settler colonialism that stretches back over 900 years, and recognizing both the common and distinctive elements in comparison to nineteenth-century Patagonia is
thought-provoking.

Here I have focused on processes that oppress, but there is plenty
of evidence in the following chapters of cultural and political resistance to settler colonial states and the logic of elimination. The capacity to endure oppression and survive as a people should be construed
as tenacious resistance in the face of grasping and acculturating actors. The upsurge in cultural activism, pride, organization and demands for land and greater political power over the last thirty to fifty
years is testament to the agency and political creativity of subordinated actors in both Patagonia and Wales. Yet these two cases are not
alike: the Welsh have not faced massacres, the forced disintegration
of families and societies, and purposeful cultural annihilation to the
same horrifying extent as in late nineteenth-century Patagonia. That
Y Wladfa was part of that genocidal process, however unwitting, is in
my view something that Welsh society must begin to recognize. This
too is a crucial aim of this book.

Notes

1   Ranajit Guha, *Elementary Aspects of Peasant Insurgency in Colonial India*
    (Delhi: Oxford University Press, 1983).

2   Ashis Nandy, *The Loss and Recovery of the Self under Colonialism*, 2nd edn (Delhi: Oxford University Press, 2009).

3   Edward Said, *Orientalism* (London: Routledge and Kegan Paul, 1978).

4   Dipesh Chakrabarty, *Provincializing Europe: Postcolonial Thought and Historical Difference* (Princeton: Princeton University Press, 2000).

5   Gayatri Chakravorty Spivak, *Toward a History of the Vanishing Present* (Cambridge, MA: Harvard University Press, 1999).

6   The first influential book being: Bill Ashcroft, Gareth Griffiths and Helen Tiffin, *The Empire Writes Back* (Abingdon: Routledge, 1989).

7   Jane Aaron and Chris Williams (eds), *Postcolonial Wales* (Cardiff: University of Wales Press, 2005); Kirsti Bohata, *Postcolonialism Revisited: Writing Wales in English* (Cardiff: University of Wales Press, 2004).

8   Walter Mignolo, *The Darker Side of Western Modernity* (Durham: Duke University Press, 2011), p. xxiv.

9   Aníbal Quijano, 'Coloniality of Power and Eurocentrism in Latin America', *International Sociology*, 15/2 (2000), 215–32. Other major figures in the field are collected in this edited volume: Mabel Moraña, Enrique Dussel and Carlos Jáuregui (eds), *Coloniality at Large* (Durham: Duke University Press, 2008).

10 Quijano, 'Coloniality of Power', 216.

11 Quijano, 'Coloniality of Power', 216.

12 Quijano, 'Coloniality of Power', 217.

13 David Weber, *Bárbaros: Spaniards and their Savages in the Age of Enlightenment* (New Haven: Yale University Press, 2005).

14 Quijano, 'Coloniality of Power', 222–9.

15 David Rock, *Argentina 1516–1987: From Spanish Colonization to the Falklands War and Alfonsín* (London: IB Taurus, 1985), pp. 118–61.

16 Geraldine Lublin, 'Adjusting the Focus: Looking at Patagonia and the Wider Argentine State through the Lens of Settler Colonial Theory', *Settler Colonial Studies*, 11/3 (2021), 386–409.

17 Walter Mignolo, *Coloniality, Subaltern Knowledges and Border Thinking: Local Histories/Global Designs* (Princeton: Princeton University Press, 2000); for a flawed yet thought-provoking analysis, see Michael Hechter, *Internal Colonialism: The Celtic Fringe in British National Development* (London: Routledge, 1999).

18 Chris Williams, 'Problematizing Wales: An Exploration in Historiography and Postcoloniality', in Jane Aaron and Chris Williams (eds), *Postcolonial Wales* (Cardiff: University of Wales Press, 2005), p. 5.

19 One exception is Simon Brooks, *Why Wales Never Was: The Failure of Welsh Nationalism* (Cardiff: University of Wales Press, 2017).

20 See Alissa Malcoun and Elizabeth Strakosh, 'The Ethical Demands of Settler Colonial Theory', *Settler Colonial Studies*, 3/3–4 (2013), 426–43. For a nuanced analysis of early work and intellectual connections, see J. Kēhaulani Kauanui, 'False Dilemmas and Settler Colonial Studies: Response to Loren-

zo Veracini "Is Settler Colonial Studies Even Useful?"', *Postcolonial Studies*, 24/2 (2020), 290–6.

21 Patrick Wolfe, 'Settler Colonialism and the Elimination of the Native', *Journal of Genocide Research*, 8/4 (2006), 403.

22 Breny Mendoza, 'Decolonial Theories in Comparison', *Journal of World Philosophies*, 5 (2020), 43–60; Gustavo Verdesio, 'Colonialismo Acá y Allá: Reflexiones sobre la Teoría y la Práctica de los Estudios Coloniales a través de Fronteras Culturales', *Cuadernos del CILHA*, 13/2 (2012).

23 Lorenzo Veracini, *The Settler Colonial Present* (Houndsmills: Palgrave, 2015), pp. 49–94.

24 Wolfe, 'Elimination of the Native', 388.

25 Aileen Moreton-Robinson, *White Possessive: Property, Power and Indigenous Sovereignty* (Minneapolis: University of Minnesota Press, 2020), p. xi.

26 Moreton-Robinson, *White Possessive*, p. xii.

27 Moreton-Robinson, *White Possessive*, pp. xiii.

28 Moreton-Robinson, *White Possessive*, p. 20.

29 Mark Rifkin, 'Settler Common Sense', *Settler Colonial Studies*, 3/3–4 (2013), 322–40.

30 Moreton-Robinson, *White Possessive*, p. xi.

31 Moreton-Robinson, *White Possessive*, pp. 15–18.

32 Jodi Byrd, *Transit of Empire: Indigenous Critiques of Colonialism* (Minneapolis: University of Minnesota Press, 2011), p. xxi.

33 Carole Pateman, 'The Settler Contract', in Carole Pateman and Charles Mills, *Contract and Domination* (Cambridge: Polity Press, 2007), pp. 35–78.

34 Pateman, 'Settler Contract', pp. 51–3.

35 Naeem Inayatullah and David Blaney, *International Relations and the Problem of Difference* (London: Routledge, 2004), pp. 42–83.

36 Pateman, 'Settler Contract', pp. 61–73.

37 Moreton-Robinson, *White Possessive*, pp. 33–46.

38 Moreton-Robinson, *White Possessive*, p. xiii.

39 Just two among a vast scholarship are Kimberlé Crenshaw, 'Mapping the Margins: Intersectionality, Identity Politics, and Violence against Women of Color', *Stanford Law Review*, 43/6 (1991), 1241–99; Patricia Hill Collins and Sirma Bilge, *Intersectionality* (Cambridge: Polity Press, 2016).

40 For example, through the one-drop rule and Reservations system.

41 Michael Omi and Howard Winant, *Racial Formation in the United States* (New York: Routledge, 1986), p. 84.

42 See the discussion by Moreton-Robinson, *White Possessive*, pp. 93–108.

43 Laura Gotkowitz (ed.), *Histories of Race and Racism: The Andes and Mesoamerica from Colonial Times to the Present* (Durham: Duke University Press, 2011).

44 Peter Wade, *Race and Ethnicity in Latin America* (London: Pluto Press, 1997).

45 See the excellent introduction by Bianca Gonzalez-Sobrino and Devon Goss, 'Exploring the Mechanisms of Racialization beyond the Black-White

Binary', *Ethnic and Racial Studies*, 42/4 (2019), 505–10; Steve Garner and Saher Selod, 'The Racialization of Muslims: Empirical Studies of Islamophobia', *Critical Sociology*, 4/1 (2015), 9–19.

46   Garner and Selod, 'Racialization of Muslims', 11.

47   Tzvetan Todorov, *The Fear of Barbarians* (Cambridge: Polity Press, 2011).

48   Yongjin Zhang, 'Barbarism and Civilization', in Mlada Bukovanski, Edward Keene, Christian Reus-Schmidt and Maja Spanu (eds), *Oxford Handbook of the History and International Relations* (Oxford: Oxford University Press, 2023), pp. 218–32, 219.

49   Mark Salter, *Barbarians and Civilization in International Relations* (London: Pluto Press, 2002).

50   Walter Mignolo, *Idea of Latin America* (Oxford: Blackwell, 2005), p. 16.

51   Mignolo, *Darker Side of Western Modernity*, p. 86.

52   Mignolo, *Darker Side of Western Modernity*, p. 105.

53   Mignolo, *Idea of Latin America*, p. 18; my italics in this section.

54   Mignolo, *Idea of Latin America*, p. 18.

55   Mignolo, *Idea of Latin America*, p. 18.

56   Mignolo, *Idea of Latin America*, p. 19.

57   Mignolo, *Idea of Latin America*, p. 19.

58   Mignolo, *Idea of Latin America*, p. 20.

59   Mignolo, *Idea of Latin America*, pp. 15–22.

60   Wolfe, 'Elimination of the Native', 388.

61   Walter Delrio and Pilar Pérez, 'Beyond the "Desert": Indigenous Genocide as a Structuring Event in Northern Patagonia', in Carolyn Larson (ed.), *The Conquest of the Desert* (Albuquerque: University of New Mexico Press, 2020), pp. 122–45, 129–31.

62   For example, Nina Lakhani, *Who Killed Berta Cáceres? Dams, Death Squads and an Indigenous Defenders' Battle for the Planet* (London: Verso, 2020).

63   Wolfe, 'Elimination of the Native', 402.

64   Audra Simpson, *Mohawk Interruptus: Political Life across the Borders of Settler States* (Durham: Duke University Press, 2014), pp. 1–36.

65   Wolfe, 'Elimination of the Native', 397.

66   Claudia Briones, 'Construcciones de Aboriginalidad en Argentina', *Société Suisses des Américanistes Bulletin*, 68 (2004), 73–90.

67   Stephanie Gilbert, 'Living with the Past: The Creation of the Stolen Generation Positionality', *AlterNative* (2019), *https://journals.sagepub.com/doi/full/10.1177/1177180119869373* (accessed 20 February 2024).

68   Diego Escolar, *Los Dones Etnicos de la Nación* (Buenos Aires: Prometeo, 2007).

69   Taiaiake Alfred and Jeff Corntassel, 'Being Indigenous: Resurgences against Contemporary Colonialism', *Government and Opposition*, 40/4 (2005), 597–614.

70   Glen Coulthard, *Red Skin, White Masks: Rejecting the Colonial Politics of Recognition* (Minneapolis: University of Minnesota Press, 2014), p. 3.

71   Coulthard, *Red Skin*, p. 3.

72   Charles Hale, 'Rethinking Indigenous Politics in the Era of the *"Indio Permitido"*', *NACLA Report on the Americas*, 38/2 (2004), 16–21.

73   Carolyn Larson, 'The Conquest of the Desert: The Official Story', in Carolyn Larson (ed.), *The Conquest of the Desert: Argentina's Indigenous Peoples and the Battle for History* (Albuquerque: University of New Mexico Press, 2020), pp. 17–42.

74   Larson, 'The Conquest of the Desert', p. 21.

75   Analía Castro, 'Estrategías de Apropriación Territorial en la Cartografía Histórica de la Provincia de Chubut, Patagonia, Argentina a Finales del Siglo XIX', *Anales del Museo de América*, 19 (2011), 101–21.

76   Susana López, *Representaciones de la Patagonia: Colonos, Científicos y Políticos, 1870–1914* (La Plata: Ediciones al Margen, 2003).

77   For example, Llwyd ap Iwan, 'Dyddiaduron' NLW MS7258. Edited and published as *Diarios del Explorador Llwyd ap Iwan* (Buenos Aires: Patagonia Sur, 2008).

78   Alexis Papazian and Mariano Nagy, 'Prácticas de Disciplinamiento Indígena en la Isla Martín García hacia fines del Siglo XIX', *Revista TEFROS* 8 (December 2010), 1–22.

79   Ricardo Salvatore, 'Live Indians in the Museum: Connecting Evolutionary Anthropology with the Conquest of the Desert', in Carolyn Larson (ed.), *The Conquest of the Desert: Argentina's Indigenous Peoples and the Battle for History* (Albuquerque: University of New Mexico Press, 2020), pp. 97–121, 97.

80   Carolyne Larson, *Our Indigenous Ancestors: A Cultural History of Museums, Science and Identity in Argentina, 1877–1943* (Pennsylvania: Pennsylvania University Press, 2015).

81   Racial dynamics in Argentina are also shaped by the presence of significant numbers of Afro-descendants who arrived as slaves to work in the docks, workshops and private homes. See Lyman Johnson, *Workshop of Revolution: Plebeian Buenos Aires and the Atlantic World, 1776–1819* (Durham: Duke University Press, 2011). Afro-Argentines were most visible in the cities – especially Buenos Aires: in 1800 around one-third of the population was Black, and the story of their 'disappearance' from sight is complex. A still excellent text is George Reid Andrews, *The Afro-Argentines of Buenos Aires, 1800–1900* (Madison: University of Wisconsin Press, 1980). There is no actual evidence of Afro-Argentine presence in or around the Welsh colony, so my discussion is focused on anti-Indigenous prejudice. However, many of the ordinary soldiers were of mixed-heritage which could have included Afro-descendance. See Alejandro Solomianski, *Identidades Secretas: La Negritud Argentina* (Buenos Aires: Beatriz Viterbo Editora, 2003).

82   Emanuela Guano, 'A Color for the Modern Nation: the Discourse on Class, Race and Education in the Porteño Middle Classes', *Journal of Latin American Anthropology*, 8/1 (2002), 148–171; Galen Joseph, 'Taking Race Seriously: Whiteness in Argentina's National and Transnational Imaginary', *Identities*, 7/3 (2000), 333–71.

83 Enrique Garguin, '*Los Argentinos Descendemos de los Barcos*: The Racial Articulation of Middle Class Identity in Argentina (1920–1960)', *Latin American and Caribbean Ethnic Studies*, 2/2 (2002), 161–84; 'Uproar after Argentina President says "Brazilians came from the Jungle"', *The Guardian*, 9 June 2021, *https://www.theguardian.com/world/2021/jun/09/argentina-president-comments-uproar* (accessed 20 February 2024).

84 Paulina Alberto and Eduardo Elena (eds), *Rethinking Race in Modern Argentina* (Cambridge: Cambridge University Press, 2016), pp. 1–24.

85 Juliet Hooker, *Theorizing Race in the Americas: Douglass, Sarmiento, Du Bois and Vasconcelos* (Oxford: Oxford University Press, 2017), p. 66.

86 Domingo Sarmiento, *Facundo, or Civilization and Barbarism* (1845; London: Penguin, 1998).

87 Lucy Taylor, 'Four Foundations of Settler Colonial Theory: Four Insights from Argentina', *Settler Colonial Studies*, 3 (2021), 344–65.

88 Walter Delrio and Pilar Pérez, 'Beyond the "Desert": Indigenous Genocide as a Structuring Event in Northern Patagonia', in Carolyn Larson (ed.), *The Conquest of the Desert: Argentina's Indigenous Peoples and the Battle for History* (Albuquerque: University of New Mexico Press, 2020), pp. 122–45.

89 Johannes Fabian, *Time and the Other: how Anthropology makes its Other* (1983; New York: Columbia University Press, 2002).

90 Mónica Quijada, '"Hijos de los Barcos" o Diversidad Invisibilizada? La Articulación de la Población Indígena en la Construcción Nacional Argentina', *Historia Mexicana*, 53/2 (2003), 489–90.

91 Mónica Quijada, 'La Ciudadanización del "Indio Bárbaro": Políticas Oficiales y Oficiosos hacia la Población Indígena de la Pampa y la Patagonia, 1870–1920', *Revista de Indias*, 59/217 (1999), 675–704, 686.

92 Quijada, 'La Ciudadanización', 687. See chapter 6, n. 8.

93 Darwin himself visited southern Patagonia and his racist response to meeting the people of Tierra del Fuego informed *The Descent of Man*. Nick Hazlewood, *Savage: Survival, Revenge and the Theory of Evolution* (Chatham: Sceptre Books, 2000), pp. 329–46.

94 Quijada, 'La Ciudadanización', 688.

95 See Andrews, *Afro-Argentines of Buenos Aires*; Alejandro Frigerio, 'De la "Desaparición" de los Negros a la "Reaparición" de los Afrodescendientes: Comprendiendo al Política de las Identidades Negras, las Clasificaciones Raciales y de su Estudio en la Argentina', in Gladys Lechini (ed.), *Los Estudios Afroamericanos y Africanos en América Latina* (Buenos Aires: CLACSO, 2008), pp. 117–44.

96 Walter Nugent, *Crossings: The Great Transatlantic Migrations, 1870–1914* (Bloomington: Indiana University Press, 1995), pp. 112–21.

97 Juán Alberdi, *Argentina: Bases y Puntos de Partida para la Organización Política de la República Argentina* (1852; Barcelona: Linkgua Editores, 2006), p. 22.

98 Alberdi, *Argentina*, p. 22.

99 Sarmiento, *Facundo*, p. 17.

100 Briones, 'Construcciones de Aboriginalidad', 79.
101 Briones, 'Construcciones de Aboriginalidad', 79.
102 Briones, 'Construcciones de Aboriginalidad', 79.
103 Morita Carrasco, *Los Derechos de los Pueblos Indígenas en Argentina* (Buenos Aires: IWGIA As. Comm. Aborígenes de Argentina, 2000), pp. 26–32.
104 Carrasco, *Derechos de los Pueblos*.
105 Lucy Taylor, 'Decolonizing Citizenship: Reflections on the Coloniality of Power in Argentina', *Citizenship Studies*, 17/5 (2012), 596–610.
106 Morita Carrasco, 'El Movimiento Indígena Anterior a la Reforma Constitucional y su Organización en el Programa de Partícipación de Pueblos Indígenas' (Visiting Resource Professor Papers: LLIILAS, University of Texas at Austin, 2002), *http://www.utexas.edu/cola/insts/llilas* (accessed 8 September 2021).
107 Sabine Kradolfer Morales, 'Ser Mapuche en Argentina en el Umbral del Tercer Milenio', *Revista del CESLA*, 10 (2007), 37–51.
108 Sarah Warren, 'Mapping Mapuche Territory: Reimagining the Conquest of the Desert', in Carolyn Larson (ed.), *The Conquest of the Desert: Argentina's Indigenous Peoples and the Battle for History* (Albuquerque: New Mexico Press, 2020), pp. 219–38.
109 Barbara Sutton, 'Contesting Racism: Democratic Citizenship, Human Rights and Antiracist Politics in Argentina', *Latin American Perspectives*, 163/35 (2009), 106–21.
110 For example: Axel Lazzari, 'Aboriginal Recognition, Freedom and Phantoms: The Vanishing Ranquel and the Return of the Rankülche in La Pampa', *Journal of Latin American Anthropology*, 8/3 (2003), 59–83.
111 Lucas Savino, *Decolonizing Patagonia: Mapuche Peoples and State Formation in Argentina* (Boulder: Lexington Books, 2022).

CHAPTER 3

Y Wladfa in Historical and Global Perspective

This chapter locates the tiny Welsh colony in the Chubut Valley within global politics, framing the enterprise in the sweep of colonial history.[1] Rather than looking east to England, as is the usual habit, I adopt an Atlantic position and face westwards to Ireland and the Americas. This shifts the way that we conceptualize Wales, but also opens a different view of its relationship to colonialism. Indeed, a key argument of this chapter is that Wales occupies an in-between position both geographically and conceptually being both colonized (from the east) and colonizing (in the west). This strategy is inspired by the 'coloniality of power' approach which takes a long view of colonialism and focuses not on powerful global agents but rather on marginal actors in peripheral locations. It is in these liminal cases with their messy social relations that we can identify the complexities of colonial power.

However, as I argued in chapter two, applying the approach to Wales requires pushing the theory into new directions because, as it was originally conceived, settler colonial theory (and postcolonial thinking more generally) assumes that all Europeans share the same subject position, and that Europe, and Europeans, are a homogenous whole driven only by the desire to exploit. This is precisely not the case with Wales, as the settlers in Patagonia saw themselves as colonized at home and established the colony in order to escape prejudice and assimilation. As such, this case exposes the need to unpack the crude category of 'the colonizer', not only because the colonizing Welsh are themselves subordinated, but also because they simultaneously benefitted from their entanglements with the 'English' drive for conquest. In this chapter I demonstrate that the Welsh have used 'English' colonial enterprises as an opportunity to improve their personal position and their country's political status, cultural life and economic well-being, often by claiming to be the original Britons and thus asserting privilege. Yet they are constantly reduced and demeaned by an 'English' state which asserts its hegemony and brands the Welsh as an inconsequential, over-emotional or untrustworthy barbarian. The ambivalence of the Welsh relationship to England is a constant theme that we will see play out in Y Wladfa as well.

The chapter is divided into two parts. Part one explores key events in Wales's long history of participation in colonialism, whilst part two focuses on the making of Y Wladfa, thinking through the themes explored in the theory chapter: possession; racialization/barbarization; and assimilation. These dynamics help us to analyse the conditions and ideas that propelled the Patagonia project.

Part one: a long-view history of Wales and colonialism

Wales was first conquered in the eleventh century by the Normans, starting with William FitzOsbern's invasion west of the Wye river in 1067. Before then, lands on the border with England had changed hands in local skirmishes but the Norman conquest was the first coherent strategy.[2] Wales might have been England's first colony, but soon the Normans were looking to Ireland, and Welsh people were actively involved in taking this, England's second colony: the colonized took advantage of the colonization of others to the west.

Wales has a long and complex history with Ireland stretching from the seventh century (at least). People living to the west of Wales's mountain spine developed family and trading links with Ireland while political interactions between kings and princes on either side of the Irish Sea entailed cooperation, marriage, intrigue, war and conquest.[3] Following the establishment of Norman power in Wales, both Norman and Norman-Welsh lords (the offspring of strategic marriage alliances with noble Welsh families) invaded Ireland in 1169.[4] They took Welsh peasant soldiers to fight and settled Welsh tenants on their new Irish estates. For elite Welsh-Norman dynasties this was an exceptional opportunity to gain territory, wealth and power, while for ordinary settler families it was a chance to forge a prosperous future. The position of the Welsh in Ireland, then, established the terms of Welsh colonial engagement: their own lands had been colonized, but the colonizing force offered the opportunity to shift position and become actors, not objects, of colonization. Indeed, both processes took place simultaneously.

The settlers who arrived and were planted in the twelfth century, including the Welsh, gradually merged with the indigenous Irish communities and the increasingly amalgamated society earned significant autonomy from the English Crown.[5] However, interest in Ireland was renewed in the Tudor period, driven by both the desire for land and wealth, and concerns about a possible Spanish/Irish Catholic invasion of what was now Protestant England-and-Wales. Once more, Welsh nobles played an important role in this enterprise, providing military captains and low-ranking soldiers. In his fascinating thesis, Rhys Morgan details how many ordinary Welsh soldiers became settlers in Ireland, bringing others to settle in their own right.[6] Indeed, in Munster the Welsh constituted 17 per cent of the settler population and developed important support networks based on their common linguistic and familial bonds, which also echoed back to the 'old country'.[7] In this scenario, the Welsh were enthusiastic colonizers who embraced the English venture in Ireland and understood themselves to be a full constituent part of the so-called 'New English' contingent.

Yet, this is not how the English saw them. They regarded the Welsh as 'Other' people whose position on the scale of civilization and barbarism might have been improved but could still not trusted.[8] They began to doubt Welsh 'civilitie' when rebellions in Ireland in the 1570s and 1580s led to instability and rekindled fears of a Spanish Catholic invasion, supported by the Irish – and the Welsh. Both the Welsh and the Irish were thus identified as having an ethnically and spiritually barbaric 'racial' essence.[9] Moreover, these concerns were political: it was feared that successful rebellion in Ireland could prompt a rejection of English rule in Wales too and that 'the Welsh might join with the Irish, not for religious reasons, but to win back their independence'.[10]

In this scenario, the Irish and the English embody the two binary positions of barbarian and civilized but the Welsh, as colonized subjects yet also fellow colonizers, occupy a middle ground as suspect allies. Their acceptance and trustworthiness are always conditional on conformity with the English ideal, and always doubted due to their inherent barbarism. We will see that this ambiguous middle-ground position finds echoes in the nineteenth (and indeed twentieth and twenty-first) century, in both the British and Argentine context.

The Welsh themselves tried to tackle this situation by sidestepping the binaries at play (Welsh/English and barbarian/civilized) as Morgan reveals in his analysis of a polemic history book written by Revd Meredith Hanmer which promotes the Welsh case called *The Chronicle*.[11] Hanmer made two claims: that the Welsh language and culture is equal to English, so difference-within-civilization is possible; and that their loyalty to the Crown is based on an authentic claim to Britishness. Hanmer counters the cold and suspicious attitude of the English by arguing that the Welsh were not only faithful to the Crown but actually were the original Britons, thus elevating Welsh status by identifying with the Tudor dynasty's Cambro-British roots.[12] He thus rejects the vision of a supine Wales and replaces it with an image of muscular, masculinized conquering agency, asserting a rightful place for Wales at the political table with England, as equals. As we will see, this argument survived to be deployed by Michael D. Jones, the pivotal ideologue of Y Wladfa, as an empowering way to generate Welsh pride.

This spirit of energetic global engagement, including colonization, is captured by the story of Welshman Captain Peter Wynn who, along with several other younger sons of the minor gentry in north Wales, was entangled within turbulent European and colonial politics. Colonized and colonizing, Captain Wynn was a Welsh speaker who honed his fighting skills suppressing Irish rebellions in the 1570s before becoming inveigled as a soldier and spy in pivotal moments of European politics.[13] According to Paul Hammer's engaging biography, these included:

> the Earl of Leicester's expedition to the Low Countries; Sir William Stanley's notorious defection to Catholic Spain; plotting by English Catholic exiles abroad; intrigues with

Sir Francis Walsingham; expeditions under the Earl of Essex to Normandy, Cadiz, the Azores and Ireland; gathering intelligence on the progress of Spain's new Armadas of the mid-1590s; service with Imperial forces against the Ottoman Turks in Hungary; Essex's abortive coup d'etat of 1601; Lord Mountjoy's final conquest of Ireland in 1603; soldiering in Dutch service; and, finally, the desperate struggle to establish and maintain an English colony at Jamestown.[14]

Wynn was the first Welsh person that we know of to set foot in the Americas when he arrived in Jamestown in 1608 with the 'second supply' to support the failing colony, led by Captain John Smith. Actually, Wynn died soon after arriving, but his life indicates that Wales and the Welsh were integrated within this newly globalizing world, driven by Spanish silver, and ready to take advantage of colonial adventure.[15] Yet Captain Wynn was also explicitly Welsh: in Jamestown, Wynn was asked to interpret with the 'Indians', 'because the language of the native people of Monachan sounded "very like Welch"'.[16] This signals that his Welshness was 'visible' as an Othering device, and associated with all forms of 'barbarous' communication that were encountered. Of course, few Welsh people were engaged in such exploits but his story is valuable because it disrupts our image of the Welsh as oppressed victims and invites us to see them in a context of early colonialism, and as its agents, well before the British Empire.

These early colonial examples confirm that Wales has occupied a liminal position, being both colonized and colonizing, long before the Patagonian colony. Indeed, we might argue that it is a constitutive component of the Welsh condition, to be marked by subordination but also enjoy opportunities and strategic alliances which find advantage from the ambiguity afforded by this middle ground. By making arguments about the fundamental Welshness of Britain they stake a claim to equality with the dominant state precisely because of, not despite, that difference. Of course, such arguments do not convince the powerful English elite, but they do provide a source of pride and strength for the Welsh, albeit one based on celebrating a process of domination under which they themselves are caught.

Precursors of Y Wladfa

As we will see in part two, the leaders of the Welsh Patagonian initiative agreed that preserving Welsh culture, promoting Welsh political autonomy and sustaining Welsh community was best served by creating a new homeland – a *Heimat* – in order to physically displace Welshness from under the shadow of English political and cultural domination.[17] However, this was not the first time that these problems were identified and solutions were pursued – solutions which entailed the colonization of Indigenous lands. The two most important settlements were in Pennsylvania: the Welsh Tract and Beulah Land, both of which directly inspired the search for a third Wladfa site – Patagonia. All three, spanning three centuries, are characterized by core traits: they were driven by radicalism and defiance of the 'English' order; they asserted cultural and political autonomy; and they eventually succumbed to the forces of assimilation. We explore the human cost of this domineering anglophone order in the case of David Evans.

The Welsh Tract
The first precursor to Y Wladfa was established in the shadow of William Penn's colony, of which Welsh Quakers constituted the majority for a brief yet pivotal period between 1682 and 1700.[18] Wales had been a hotbed of Quakerism led by prominent families in Radnorshire, Montgomeryshire and Meirionydd, who suffered fines and penalties as well as social ostracism and intimidation. So, when the king granted the province of Pennsylvania to William Penn by Royal Charter, twelve prominent Welsh Quakers jumped at the chance to flee religious persecution. They visited Penn in London to discuss creating a specifically Welsh colony and verbally agreed to take 40,000 acres of land in order to establish a Welsh Tract. The idea was to create a 'distinct settlement composed exclusively of Welsh [which] would give them the opportunity they desired of maintaining undisturbed their own language and institutions'.[19] Richard Allen reports that they succeeded in this aim: 'the Welsh language was used in daily business and evidence suggests that these settlers retained their Welsh customs'.[20] This cultural autonomy was to be matched, according to a quotation cited by Waylan Dunaway, by community

decision-making: 'within which all causes, quarrels, crimes and disputes might be tried and wholly determined by officers, magistrates and juries of our own language'.[21] Thus, the desire for religious freedom was matched by a desire for political freedom, linked to the radical egalitarianism of Quaker religious practice, and enunciated through the language and customs of Wales.

However, the authorities, in the form of its rich, influential and often absentee English leader William Penn, clashed with the well-organized yet ordinary settlers, led by charismatic Welshman, Thomas Lloyd who was president of the provincial council and deputy governor.[22] Penn aimed to shape the new colony in his vision but this conflicted with the desire for Welsh autonomy, so he promoted assimilation to undermine Lloyd's powerbase. Penn denied agreeing to allow the Welsh Tract to be a Welsh ethnic enclave, he imposed a municipal division which split the Welsh Tract in two, planted non-Welsh migrants within the Welsh Tract, and abolished the civil authority of the Quaker meetings which had effectively governed the Welsh Tract, imposing provincial rule.[23] Added to this, assimilation was occurring 'naturally' anyway as more and more English-speaking migrants arrived. Penn's frequent absence in England empowered Lloyd, a 'champion of civil liberties and judicial reform', able administrator and forthright politician who strengthened the power of the assembly and fought for enhanced autonomy.[24] Lloyd challenged Penn's authority in part because the Welsh were disillusioned with Penn's leadership and angry at his broken promise over the Welsh Tract.[25] Moreover, Lloyd advocated the politics of Quakerism, citing the equality of men in the eyes of God and the capacity of Quakers (who were touched by the 'inner light') to discern God's will and reject ungodly laws. In a burst of independence, Lloyd even denied support to King William in his war with France, a defiant move which led the Crown to take back Pennsylvania in 1692 under its own rule, returning it to Penn in 1694.

Yet, while the principles and ideals might possibly be 'Welsh', the language of political activism was mostly English and the council was multiethnic: the drive for the colony's freedom came at the price of Welsh assimilation within what had become an anglophone colonial project. The idea of a Welsh enclave enabling Welsh autonomy and cultural practice had crumbled in the face of larger processes of migration and state-building, eventually creating the United States of America. This tension between the desire to preserve Welsh culture (which required an enclave) and the desire to shape a new colony (which required working in an anglicized atmosphere) also conditioned nineteenth-century Ohio and Pennsylvania. Indeed, as we will see, it was the problem of language and culture loss in the USA that led American-Welshman Edwyn Roberts to suggest that an explicitly separate Welsh colony was required in Patagonia. Assimilation in the colony, as well as at home, is thus a core motif of the Welsh colonial condition, not only because of population size, but also because the modes of domination are repeated in the Anglo-colony. This domination/assimilation is not only political but also affects people's way of life and identity, as the case of David Evans, an ordinary migrant, reveals.

David Evans was twenty-three when he set sail in 1702. Brought up on a farm in Carmarthenshire, he had been a shepherd and weaver but had big dreams as this extract from his diary, cited by Boyd Schlenther, reveals: 'I voyaged over the great seas to Pennsylvania to earn money so that I could buy plenty of books.'[26] Following a period of indentured labour clearing land and learning carpentry, he moved to the Welsh-speaking town of Radnor in 1704 and began teaching and preaching. However, the (English-speaking) American Presbytery heard of this and decreed: 'Evans had done very ill and acted irregularly in thus Invading ye work of the Ministry; And was thereupon censured.'[27] He was thus obliged to study theology (in English) at the fledgling Yale University in 1712 and, after graduating in 1713, went to preach in the town of Pencader (Delaware). There followed several years of conflict in which Evans led his congregation in objecting to the 'Westminster creed' imposed by the American Presbytery authority, and he wrote books providing an alternative interpretation rooted in Welsh culture. However, he also clashed with his parishioners when he refused to preach to them in Welsh.[28] He eventually left his flock for English-speaking New Jersey, parting from them with this astonishing and insulting final sermon (quoted here in full): 'Goats I found you, and goats I leave you.'[29]

What are we to make of this man? For Schlenther, he 'failed to live up to Welsh expectations', adding: 'surely, if any man in colonial America … could have been expected to take the leadership in nurturing a continuing sense of Welsh identity, it was Evans'.[30] Indeed, it is easy to see Evans as a traitor to his Welshness, happier to preach to the English than the Welsh 'goats'. Except that, at the end of a life fraught with personal and professional troubles he wrote a memoir poem, in Welsh. Schlenther proposes that he did so to keep his thoughts safe from prying eyes: this may be true, but perhaps it also reveals a more conflicted inner life than the archive states. David Evans came from a humble Welsh-speaking background but had a passion to learn and think. However, it was not possible for him to do so in Welsh: indeed, he was chastised, stopped and sent to Yale to learn (in English) the correct way to preach. His lay-preaching was disciplined and corrected by a knowledge regime which spoke in English, promoted the Westminster creed, and reflected dominant English understandings of civilization and modern life. If David Evans accepted that success in America depended on performing Englishness, then it is little wonder that he chose to preach and write in English. It might also explain why he insulted Welsh speakers by calling them goats. Perhaps his parishioners were not willing to embrace Englishness as the mark of success; perhaps they made him ashamed of his humble and vilified roots; perhaps they confused his sense of self, and self-worth. For Evans, caught between the binaries of English 'civilization' and Welsh 'backwardness' it was perhaps easier to perform an Anglo-colonial role in a new English-speaking parish – working with the grain of community, church and emerging state – than to preach awkwardly in a Welsh-speaking parish where the people and their language scraped against the grain, creating discord in his soul. Clearly, though, Evans had not forgotten his mother-tongue and reached for it to express his deep emotions. Schlnether describes the poem as 'pitiful in every sense', using 'anachronistic Welsh' and revealing 'the decided gap between his feelings and his abilities'.[31] But his Welsh was that of the farm at home – humble and of the heart – while his English was of Yale – erudite and of the intellect.

This tragic tale reflects the opportunities and agonies of assimilation. David Evans achieved success by becoming a Yale-educated preacher in the New World – stepping up from his impoverished origins by dint of his own ambition and bright intellect. Yet, to echo Wolfe's phrase, this required of him a 'kind of death' – an alienation from the person who crossed the ocean and the adoption of a new persona which never quite fit him.[32] This ambivalence did not generate an exciting new 'Third Space', but rather a permanent displacement, discomfort and despair because his inalienable Welshness was always judged as barbaric in a world that celebrated English civilization. It is David Evans's position between the Welsh/English binary which reveals the everyday and human-scale antagonisms and agonies of assimilation. It was precisely against this personal agony, as well as the ethnic erasure of Welshness, that the Welsh enterprise in Patagonia was founded.

Beulah Land

The second precursor to Y Wladfa developed at the end of the eighteenth century, impelled by a short but fervent period of radical political activism. Jacobin dissent in Wales from the 1770s to 1790s was galvanized by revolutionary events in France and America. Gwyn A. Williams charts, with typical passion and flair, the rise of an intellectual civil society which grasped radical thinking, spread ideas about the 'rights of man' and inspired political protest in a flurry of thinking, writing and printing.[33] Many saw the United States as a land of political freedom where civic equality was being enacted – moreover, the American Revolution proved that the heavy hand of British rule could be challenged. Importantly, the Welsh on both sides of the Atlantic became intellectually connected by the exchange of letters, books and pamphlets in dialogue: for example, political philosophers Richard Price (Neath) and David Williams (Caerphilly) were correspondence friends with Benjamin Franklin.[34] The resulting emigration fever was thus political and nationalist, as well as economic, in character.

One example of these fervent, home-spun intellectuals was William Jones, Llangadfan – a polymath maverick and political radical who, in the words of Geraint Jenkins, had 'a passionate desire to undermine conventional thinking, to expose social and political grievances'.[35] He saw the Welsh as culturally colonized, railing against the 'planting' of English-speaking clergy in Welsh-speaking villages, and the carelessness with which the gentry allowed Welsh manuscripts to 'moulder away in the hands of strangers to the language'.[36] For him, cultural celebration was political work: he proposed a national library; collected Welsh dances and songs; and composed a nation-

al anthem. He thus stood in defence of Welsh culture in the face
of elimination and assimilation. Moreover, Jones burned with anger that tenant farmers like him were overtaxed, overworked and
undervalued. This exploitation led him to distribute a pamphlet at
the 1791 eisteddfod in Llanrwst addressed 'To all Indigenous Cam-
bro-Britons' in which he argued that 'oppressed tenant farmers and
impoverished craftsmen were duty-bound to pack their bags, quit
Wales and sail for the Promised Land'.[37] That is, he proposed emigration to America as the solution to economic exploitation and
cultural suppression, a precursor to nineteenth-century concerns.
Like Michael D. Jones and Edwyn Roberts sixty years later, though,
he worried that those migrating now 'were setting off at random,
ill-prepared and ill-informed and at great expense'; like them, he
aimed to 'establish a separate state whose affairs would be adminis-
tered through the medium of the Welsh language'.[38] This emigration,
then, should be anti-colonial and nationalist – both culturally and
politically empowering.

His vision was realized, briefly, by emigration firebrand Morgan
John Rhys. Born in Glamorganshire, he was a passionate advocate
of the French Revolutionary ideals, promoting political reform and
education, anti-slavery and the abolition of class privilege, an end
to bribery and oppressive taxes for the poor. Rhys believed that he
could best promote this ideal society in the New World and landed in New York in 1794 to form an emigration society. In 1798 he
purchased a large tract of land between Philadelphia and Pittsburgh
called Cambria, with the town of Beulah at its core.[39] However, the
settlement quickly collapsed. It failed to live up to expectations, was
short of money and poorly organized, and was soon torn asunder
by rivalries and factionalism.[40] These events demonstrated that having the Welsh language in common did not prevent lies, antagonism
and bitter recriminations. Ethnic unity is hard to sustain in the face
of adversity and dashed hopes. Thus, many who arrived to settle in
this Welsh-speaking colony quickly moved on in search of better
land and golden opportunities in the plethora of English-speaking
towns and cities springing up to service the accelerating numbers
of European migrants. They became assimilated within the flood of
humanity arriving in the USA. The dream of a Welsh Wladfa slid
from view as its institutions dissolved and its people and lands were

assimilated within the multi-ethnic, English-speaking melting pot of the United States.

* * *

Part two: the making of Y Wladfa Patagonia

As already explained, the Welsh went to Patagonia to build a new homeland where they would rule themselves according to Welsh customs and in the Welsh language. This colonial enterprise was driven by experiences of economic exploitation and cultural oppression linked to English domination at home, but also in the anglophone destinations for Welsh migrants: Australia, Canada, New Zealand (Aotearoa), South Africa and especially the United States of America. Migrants to these destinations left to escape poverty and abusive working conditions imposed by landowners, ironmasters or mining barons.[41] For example, migrants from the iron district around Tredegar and Merthyr Tydfil fled economic depression, labour unrest, collapsing wages and foundry closures in the 1840s, lured by job prospects in Ohio's expanding coal and iron works. Others went to find better prospects, excitement and participation in the imperial project, helped by family, friends and village networks of those already settled.[42]

There is no doubt that poverty also motivated the Welsh Patagonian enterprise. As Glyn Williams shows, many *gwladychwyr* [colonists] had already migrated to English towns and cities in search of work and 'were willing to relocate in the hope of obtaining free agricultural land'.[43] Questions of poverty were a key theme of the handbook, *Llawlyfyr y Wladychfa Gymreig* [Handbook of the Welsh Colony] which aimed to 'sell' the enterprise, authored by firebrand organizer Hugh Hughes (Cadfan). As well as practical advice, the handbook spelled out a class-based political message. Hughes declared the Welsh to be 'the most servile class in Great Britain' because of their economic situation and exploitation wages, saying 'the nation of Wales is entangled in nets which have been thrown across Wales'.[44]

What set Y Wladfa Patagonia apart, though, was its aim to counter the political and cultural domination of England and Englishness, underpinned by the realities of rule from London, anti-Welsh prejudice and the drive to assimilate. Let us now turn to chart the role of the core logics – possession, barbarization and assimilation – within Wales's complex, double-edged position. That is, while Wales was subject to these dynamics at home, it enacted those same processes in Patagonia.

Welshness and dispossession/possession

The Norman colonization of the territory that became Wales predated the *terra nullius* discourse and Lockean concepts of 'waste and 'productive' land. Land was taken – 'possessed' – by the Planter lords, but such colonization was patchy and reflected local dynamics rather than a coherent ideology.[45] The nation itself was 'possessed' by the English Crown as the nascent state began to grow and its structures solidify, and its position was institutionalized by the Acts of Union in 1536 and 1542, drawing Wales formally within London's ambit.[46] By 1865 (the year when the *Mimosa* left Liverpool for Patagonia) most of the land was drawn into capitalist development and its ownership was endorsed by the laws of property and market. Moreover, the 'fact' of Wales's incorporation into Britain was largely unquestioned, though many Welsh thinkers (like Meredith Hanmer) contested its subordination and asserted the Welsh origins of Britishness. Indeed, it is this spirit of Britishness and the global environment of colonial endeavour which shaped Welsh ideas about 'possession' of Patagonia.

The right of the Welsh to take stake a claim to a piece of Patagonia was never questioned by the founding leadership – indeed, quite the opposite. Michael D. Jones revealed the possessive sensibility which endorsed colonization when he suggested that: 'other lands are available and they are in complete possession of savage people, such as Patagonia, and it is undoubtedly possible to make a colony in a land like this, as William Penn did in Pennsylvania'.[47] This sense of a 'right to possess' amongst the wider public, especially when they felt oppressed at home, is reflected in the report that 'hundreds' sang 'Let's take possession of the land! [*'Awn a meddianwn y tir!*']' at a migration meeting in Mountain Ash.[48] This 'right' to take possession of land was not merely acquisitive but entangled in a sense of thwarted pride and resistance based, in part, on prowess. In the very first paragraph of his pamphlet promoting Y Wladfa, Jones declared, in a reiteration of the 'original Britons' argument, that British civilization was founded on Welsh foundations:

> Since the earliest times, the Welsh have distinguished them-selves as migrants [*ymfudwyr*]. Even before the time of the Romans, they came from the east to the extreme west of Eu-rope, not as unskilled barbarians, but bringing high levels of civilization in their wake.[49]

The Welsh excelled in many areas, including the practice of war: 'They could fight according to the best methods of the heroic age'; agriculture: 'they worked the land, grew wheat, reared animals and lived in open cleared ground'; and industry: 'The Welsh knew how to work metals; and they were the first miners that we can identify in history.'[50] The Welsh had thus 'civilized' Britain – a place imagined as *terra nullius*, and as such a land that they could justifiably take. In addition, he portrayed British civilization (measured in buildings, money, written language and law) as being fundamentally Welsh:

> Only the Welsh established the cities of Britain which be-came the most important in the world. They used curren-cy to trade. They had learned men and used Greek letters to write like other Celtic peoples. The Welsh language is a founding element of the English language. Their laws are the foundation for laws in Britain, the United States and all the British settlements.[51]

In addition, Jones (a preacher himself) drew on the increasingly strong dynamics of religious nonconformism which dominated moral discourse in Wales. He framed migration as righteous, claim-ing it was blessed by God's law:

> Indeed, migration is a right that comes down from the Heav-ens … through migration Noah's descendants will populate the world, and according to the same law the world will be-come filled with men. The Welsh will take up their part, and

it will be pleasant for them to do this in the most wise, orderly and effective way.[52]

This religious justification fills Y Wladfa with moral purpose because
it would enable the Welsh to live according to their own norms which
are imbued with nonconformist ideals. As we will see, this moral element is essential to Welsh Patagonian identity, especially linked to
'friendship' with Indigenous Patagonians, and enables the continued
pride in Y Wladfa and its feat of survival.

Perhaps the most explicit claim to the rightful possession of Patagonia, though, came from Edwyn Roberts, an American Welshman
and driving force behind Y Wladfa. He claimed the 'right' to settle
land in the Americas because it was the Welsh who first 'discovered'
the continent (note how he sees Indigenous presence as irrelevant).
He devoted the first three and a half pages of his book to the story of
Madog and Welsh Indians.

> The first discovery of America is hidden in great darkness,
> but there is no doubt that Europeans were there a good while
> before Columbus ... It is alleged by some Welsh and English
> historians that Madog ab Owen Gwynedd sailed from Wales
> with a number of ships towards the end of the eleventh cen-
> tury or the beginning of the twelfth. It is said that he discov-
> ered America and *the fact that there are Welsh Indians on the
> American Continent even today*, that a lot of Welsh words are
> in the Indian languages, and that the tribe called Mandan
> came from Wales.[53]

This tale may have roots in a real voyage, but there is certainly no evidence that the fabled 'Welsh Indians' existed. These were supposed to
be the offspring of Welsh sailors and Native Americans and captured
the popular imagination in both Wales and the USA throughout the
nineteenth century. Newspapers reported their discovery, Jefferson
charged the Lewis and Clark expedition to find them, and tales of
Welshmen saved from the clutches of 'savages' by speaking Welsh to
their long-lost brethren thrilled people in both America and Wales.[54]
Edwyn Roberts drew on this fable, which he perhaps believed, to
embed Y Wladfa within a heroic narrative of Welsh pride and destiny.

In particular, he used ideas about ideal manhood to substantiate the Welsh-Indian story, saying that Columbus identified some Indians as: 'strong and energetic people, who were brave in battle; and that their habits and rituals were similar to those of old residents of Europe ... who were these people if they weren't of the old Welsh race?'[55] The wider purpose of this claim is made clear by the next sentence:

> We, the Welsh, have as much right as anyone else to declare publicly to the whole world that we, the Welsh people discovered America first. It is our possession, America, south and north. As it belongs to us, fair and by rights, is it not right for us as a nation to possess a small portion of country which previously belonged to our forefathers?[56]

This argument is a powerful rallying cry, designed to stir the blood and promote the Welsh Patagonian project, and also reveals Roberts's attitude to colonization. He understood it to be justified because the Welsh were there first and the Welsh Indigenous were a superior 'race' to the Other 'Indians', given that even after hundreds of years, their (highly masculinized) qualities of energy and courage were what made them stand out. At the same time as claiming rightful possession, then, he refuted Welsh subjugation and asserted rightful pride.

Welshness and barbarization/pride

Anti-Welsh prejudice has been called the 'last permitted bigotry' and is as old as Wales itself.[57] As yet, Cymrophobia has been described but not yet theorized, so my observations here are merely an opening to a far wider analytical project. However, anti-Welsh bigotry seems to have two key characteristics. First, it is promulgated almost exclusively by the English and reflects English colonial attitudes, even up to today. Pritchard and Morgan, for example, found that Welsh culture and language was a positive draw for overseas tourists, but was off-putting for English audiences who preferred to imagine Wales as a landscape with tourist activities (a *terra nullius* playground).[58] Secondly, anti-Welsh prejudice over the centuries has linked Welshness to 'backwards' and rebellious behaviour, inadequacy (including sexual) and its supposedly incomprehensible language. All this makes culture a central arena of both oppression and resistance.

Although anti-Welsh prejudice has rarely been researched, it clearly has early and colonial roots. Geraldine Heng has identified Cymrophobia with medieval 'Celtic' identity, albeit very briefly, while Coral Lumbley explores the racialized 'dark Welsh' characterization in key medieval texts.[59] Matthew Stevens and Teresa Phipps have charted in greater detail the application of discriminatory rules and their impact in medieval Wales.[60] For example, only the English could take up important political and trading positions by law while the Welsh were systematically excluded and labelled as hyper-emotional, argumentative, deceptive, malingering, criminal and English-hating.[61] Perhaps these 'traits' are evidence for imaginative strategic responses to the colonial situation Welsh people found themselves in: talking-back to authority might be construed as 'being argumentative and hating the English', for example, and exploiting loopholes or avoiding legal channels might appear as 'deception' and 'criminality' – compounded, perhaps, by use of Welsh to forge deals.

We also have evidence of prejudicial views from the mid-sixteenth century onwards, linked to everyday behaviour, sexuality and language, often tagged together. For example, Lloyd Bowen analysed anti-Royalist pamphlets during the Civil War period and cites the politician William Ebery describing Wales as a place 'where gross ignorance, idolatry, superstition and all manner of sins abound everywhere'.[62] Bowen also identified several pamphlets and plays where Wenglish was used to deride Welsh syntax or the language itself. While Welsh support for the Crown motivates much of this vitriol, ideas about (English) civilization and (Welsh) barbarism actively frame anti-Welsh bias.[63] Welsh sexuality was a key theme identified by Pritchard and Morgan in illustrations from the same period, especially the trope of the 'randy' big-horned Welsh goat.[64] This barbaric virility has become skewed today by the commonplace 'jokes' about Welshmen having sex with sheep, jibes which hint at lonely failure as well as bestial barbarity.[65] Alongside sex, a caricatured Welsh diet (of the poor) of cheese, leeks and herring, the 'preposterous' Welsh pride in their ancestry and of course the 'incomprehensible' Welsh language were targets for ridicule.

Nineteenth-century portrayals of Welshness are framed by the experiences of empire which taught both English and Welsh that

(white) Englishness was superior. The Welsh were depicted, as Kirsti
Bohata shows, as Black or simian in English-language Welsh literature, as these 'in-between' authors grappled with their own identity
and urged the whitening/anglicization of the Welsh.[66] Indeed, many
Welsh speakers wanted their children to be educated in English so
that they could enjoy the opportunities that the British Empire offered. The pivotal documents in this regard were the infamous Blue
Books – the 1847 report on education in Wales written by three English commissioners, who toured Wales collecting data and (prejudiced) social impressions.[67] Gwyneth Tyson Roberts's excellent, detailed and nuanced analysis of the reports reveals the elite English
mindset to function around a series of desirable/despise-able traits.[68]
Instead of identifying and denouncing poverty, the commissioners
linked poor living conditions with moral degeneracy. For example,
Commissioner Symons reports: 'the cottages are formed of a few
loose fragments of rock and shale, piled together without mortar
or whitewash. The floors are earth … [and] comprise one room,
in which all the family sleeps', and adds, blaming the Welsh, 'these
squalid huts appear to be the deliberate choice of the people'.[69] For
Symons, squalor is linked to sexual depravity: 'the cottages and beds
are frequently filthy … [and] the people also are very dirty', while his
link to bestial behaviour ('the pigs and poultry have free run of the
joint dwelling and sleeping room') serves to debase and dehumanize
the poor.[70]

The commissioners also blamed religious Nonconformity. Religion often served as a proxy for political dissent (as we saw with the
Quakers and William Jones, Llangadfan) and the fierce, independent-minded and community-oriented Methodism which dominated
Wales at the time provided a political outlet and focus for community
action. Commissioner Symons (again) observed: 'Welsh methodism
sprung from this immediate neighbourhood (Tregaron) … the extreme filthiness of the habits of the poor … are … striking in this
place'.[71] It is from this filth, he implies, that Methodism arose, and in
this moral (dis)order that Methodism thrives.

The final target for their repudiation was, of course, the Welsh
language – a key marker for a kind of racial essence. Around
three-quarters of the Welsh population were Welsh speakers in the mid-nineteenth century and the commissioners used

'Welsh-speaking' and 'Welsh' interchangeably.[72] For Commissioner Johnson, Tyson Roberts explains, the Welsh were backwards because their language was inadequate to express and enable modernity, saying: 'the language had "limited resources", which ... "remain obsolete and meagre"'.[73] Commissioner Lingen, linked Welsh to 'an obsessive interest in religious sectarianism, and "utter want of method in thinking and acting" leading to "wild fanaticism" and "a widespread disregard of temperance, chastity, veracity and fair-dealing"'.[74] These statements justify the Commissioners' advocacy of teaching in English and the eradication of the Welsh language: if the language is the root cause of barbarism, civilization requires the English tongue.

While Welsh public leaders responded with anger and dismay in press and pamphlets, the negative impression 'remained the abiding image for many English people, especially those with power and influence'.[75] This sparked a desire to assimilate, as the next section shows, but it also galvanized pride. Many countered the accusations of degeneracy by performing their virtue to the world, for example by forging temperance societies or presenting symbolic white gloves to circuit judges to demonstrate that no crimes had been committed.[76] Others, though, took 'pride' in a different, anti-colonial direction and dreamed of Y Wladfa, where they would not have to try to win the approval of the English in order to walk with dignity.

Wales and assimilation/autonomy

The desire to build a new Welsh homeland entailed a political rejection of English 'racial' disparagement (barbarization), but also a rejection of social processes designed to erase Welsh culture and language (assimilation) which entailed grappling with Britishness. We have seen how Britishness was claimed by some Welsh thinkers as originating in Wales, but in reality the Wales-Britain relationship is complex.

Welsh philosopher J. R. Jones's work *Prydeindod* gives us a view of Britishness from its margins. He understood it as an ideology of belonging aimed at everyone – including the English working class.[77] However, while Britishness proffers the dream of equal rights and a common membership of the union, its strong identification with

Englishness as the model of desirable ethnicity (and a certain vision of Englishness, at that) sustains the civilizational hierarchy-as-usual amongst the component elements of Great Britain. This illusion of equal membership, in Dewi Z. Phillips's words, 'tempts the Welsh to believe they can participate on equal terms within the framework of Britishness, and yet they are also aware of the unreality of this hope' because they butt up against prejudice every day.[78] As such, Britishness consolidates the hierarchy of 'races' in Britain (and also the class system), even whilst denying their relevance and obfuscating the colonial aspect of the relationship.

The promotion of Britishness developed in tandem with burgeoning industrialization and imperial expansion as a source of pride and belonging to a bigger, successful project.[79] In Wales, this paved the way for linguistic assimilation, spurred by the opportunities and adventures offered by industrialization in English cities (Liverpool, Manchester, Birmingham, London), or by the empire whose expansion in Asia and Africa was beginning to quicken. Where languages reflect social and economic hierarchies, it is inevitable that elevation requires anglicization, especially when Englishness is a stand-in for 'civilization'. Assimilation was not just imposed from above, then, but actively pursued from below. Indeed, as Tyson Roberts suggests, 'many … Welsh working-class parents wanted their children to learn sufficient English to improve their chances of well-paid and higher-status employment'.[80]

Michael D. Jones identified the hard-to-resist logic of assimilation within everyday Victorian capitalism in *Y Ddraig Goch*, a fortnightly journal closely linked to the Wladfa enterprise:

> Our children are taught in English schools; the English language is on all our railway stations; English managers curse the Welsh in almost all of our factories – and soon enough, foreigners will have eaten all the Welsh meat, and once the Welshman has completed his work, they use the bones to beat him. Should it be like this? Can it be like this? I hear the answer, 'No – a free Welshman in a free country'.[81]

In the Handbook promoting Y Wladfa, Hugh Hughes Cadfan argues that assimilation leads (in Wolfe's terms) to a kind of existential death:

> If they consent to melt themselves into the English mould,
> [the Welsh] have to leave behind their own feelings at the
> first step, and all steps thereafter they must sell their inde-
> pendence and their honour, until at last [they are] wretched
> and worthless.[82]

Thus he links poverty with assimilation and cultural collapse, and
argues that autonomy is the answer to these problems. Although he
does not speak in anti-colonial terms, the handbook rings with the
desire for self-determination as a people, as in this example: 'So now,
beloved Wales, be courageous! [*Ymwrolwch!*] Stand up straight, and
pull yourself up to your full height, or if you like, the height of your
ancestors.'[83] He directly links personal and national autonomy and
honour to the Welsh language: 'Our wonderful language is like a
weakling [*musgrellyn*] without arms, but when we regain the precious feelings of independence and honour, how can we not – then
we will be a lively and capable "national body".'[84] It is this mixture of
economic with political power and cultural dignity which makes Y
Wladfa distinctive within the vast array of other colonizing initiatives at the time, and it is on this foundation that the celebration, yet
also romanticization, of Y Wladfa is built.

However, assimilation was not just a problem in Wales. Indeed, it
was after Michael D. Jones travelled to the USA in 1848 to study settler
prospects that the idea to create Y Wladfa Patagonia emerged. Once
there, and especially after meeting Edwyn Roberts, he realized that dynamics of barbarization and assimilation were as powerful in the colonies as they were back home. In *Gwladychfa Gymreig*, he explained:

> It is a wrench for both the English and the Welsh to leave
> the places where they were born but when the Englishman
> lands in any British settlement he will be greeted in his own
> language ... The feeling of the Welsh settler is very different
> ... he is greeted in a foreign language and ... he must spend a
> good deal of time catching up with the Englishman.[85]

That is, piecemeal, individualized migration meant that Welsh people
were disadvantaged and needed to assimilate to prosper. He also recognized that an ethnically ordered system empowered and enriched

English Americans, observing: 'Welshmen pay tax just like the English, and every British colony has been won, planted and kept by the Welsh, just like the English. But to the Englishman only goes the praise, the profit and the enjoyment.'[86] The replication of ethnic inequalities in America had a depressing effect on the Welsh, he argued, who felt excluded – if not vilified – unless they adopted an (Anglo) American stance and melted into the new society, in an echo of assimilation experiences back home. The solution thus became clear – the need for a Welsh-only colony which gathered together Welsh women and men from Wales but also from anglophone states like the USA to create a community with enough critical mass to sustain a Welsh way of life.

Some 'American Welshmen' were drawing the same conclusion. In 1848, Morris Roberts of Remsen, New York State observed that the Welsh were being swallowed up by 'Saxon waves' and argued for:

> somewhere that the Welsh may settle together, where their language would be safeguarded and where they could enjoy political and religious advantages through the medium of their own language, without being in poverty or under the kind of oppression that they face in Wales, or lost among the English as they are on the Welsh borders, in English towns and in small settlements in the United States.[87]

Moreover, a Welsh Settlement Society was founded in Camptonville, California in 1856 to 'seek land … to establish a Welsh settlement so that the nation is elevated to its previous status among the nations of the world'.[88] Thus, concern to raise Wales's stature globally was important in America, just as in Wales.

Y Wladfa's fortunes were particularly shaped by Edwyn Roberts who would eventually not only campaign in Wales but found the first settlement in New Bay (now Puerto Madryn), Patagonia. The charismatic American from Oshkosh, Wisconsin was also worried about culture loss in the USA and argued that Welsh migration should be concentrated for maximum effect, like many before him. Interestingly, he was well aware of the precursors to Y Wladfa and was inspired by John Morgan Rhys's Beulah Land colony of 1793. He agrees with Rhys's analysis and cites his speech which demands 'a stretch of land in this country for the nation [Welsh] to settle on together, instead of dispersing all over this extensive land.[89] He was inspired too by Rhys's letter to the US government which demanded that land should be 'the property of the Welsh and no one else ... that the laws be in the Welsh language' and that it should 'be like a State'.[90] Michael D. Jones agreed – cultural strength against the tide of assimilation required political autonomy:

> if there was a Welsh colony, the Welsh migrants would feel more at home; and if they felt that the foundations of a Welsh nation were being laid down, where there would be a Welsh Government, and the laws would be administered in Welsh, they would be more courageous and more public-spirited to carry out nationalist schemes.[91]

The whole purpose of the colony, then, was to resist assimilation and this is what differentiates Welsh Patagonian colonization from British imperialism. In contrast to most settler colonial initiatives, the Welsh had no desire (nor capacity) to 'eliminate the native' but neither did they aim to exert power over them through assimilation. This led them to a model of coexistence in which the two societies, Indigenous and Welsh, existed in parallel. It is this model of interaction that has been labelled 'friendship'. However, the Welsh were harbingers of Argentine settler colonialism, accelerators of capitalist development and pioneers in the possession of Patagonian land, and in that sense they were colonizers.

Conclusion

The political and nationalist character of Y Wladfa is clear from the crest that adorns Lewis Jones's book, and heads some of the letters in the archive. On it, a proud dragon is encircled by the slogan '*Fy Iaith, Fy Ngwlad, Fy Nghenedl*' (My Language, My Country, My Nation), set into an attractive wreath of leeks.[92] Thus, a close link is made between national pride and the Welsh language, just as the Blue Books made the opposite connection. The history of Wales's relationship to colonialism is far from binary, though, if (inspired by coloniality thinking) we take a long view of colonialism, foreground race-class structures and think from an Atlantic position. Indeed, if we examine Wales's role in Ireland and the Americas, a key conclusion is that being *both* colonized *and* colonizing simultaneously is a central pillar of the Welsh subject position. Wales occupies a kind of middle ground (akin, but also different, to the term proposed by Richard White)[93] where, while it cannot escape subordination, it can certainly seize opportunities that arise from enforced association with the colonizing English/British state, as we saw in the case of Captain Peter Wynn. Importantly, the subordinate position of the Welsh travels with them, as political subjugation, relative poverty and linguistic status are quickly reasserted in anglophone settler colonies like Anglo-Ireland, Pennsylvania and Beulah Land. The same processes of barbarization (anchored in prejudices forged and nurtured in Britain) and assimilation (required to succeed in the dominant society) operate in the colony. As the case of David Evans and his pitiable poem attest, they serve to reassert the 'natural order of things' which entails Welsh subordination to the English.

A second key theme is the importance of radical dissent in driving Welsh colonial enterprises: from the Quakers' Welsh Tract to William Jones Llangadfan's vision and John Morgan Rhys's Beulah Land, religious dissent and political radicalism run together. This finds echoes in Y Wladfa itself, whereby political radicals such as Hugh Hughes Cadfan and Michael D. Jones assert the need for an autonomous homeland, driven by experiences of poverty, centuries of cultural disdain and the Blue Books assault. Once again, this dissent led to a colonizing movement paradoxically driven by anti-colonial impulses. Indeed, one of the reasons why Y Wladfa is such a powerful trope is because, finally, this anti-colonial strategy worked (at least for a time) and endured (in one form or another) to today.

A third theme to emerge as important is the ambiguous relationship of the Welsh to Britishness. On the one hand the Welsh are portrayed as key protagonists in the story of Britain (Welsh as agents of colonization), but on the other Welshness is disparaged and assimilated within an idea of Britain that is essentially English (Welsh as colonized). Interestingly, both Meredith Hanmer and Michael D. Jones square this circle by asserting the distinctive Welshness of their contribution and their equal status on the basis of that difference, rather than measuring Welshness against an English gold standard.

However, this claim could not erase the reality of English political and economic domination within Britishness and the irresistible lure of participation within the colonizing projects in Ireland and the wider empire.

Using key processes identified by settler colonial theory has helped to identify how power inequalities operate in colonial settings in Europe and the Americas. However, the ambiguity of the Welsh example also mounts two key challenges to the theory. First, it complicates the assumption that colonialism occurs in the global south, and is exercised by 'developed' nation states. The Welsh case shows that colonial relationships can and do exist in Europe and that they are very complex – we might think here of the inter-relationships between Norman and later Tudor England, Wales and Ireland discussed in part one. This is important because, while Indigenous people are viewed as complex actors negotiating a complex world (quite rightly), settlers are often portrayed as cardboard cut-outs in decolonial depictions, mere pawns in the grand games of colonial power politics. Yet settlers arrive with their own complex subject positions and motivations which might not toe the imperial line. Understanding both Indigenous and settler to be complex actors is essential if we wish to develop decolonizing strategies which will have resonance and long-term impact.

Allied to this insistence on complexity is the second insight: that the binary distinction between the colonized and the colonizer, which forms the mainstay of settler colonial theory, cannot make any sense at all of a colonizing community like the Welsh. While the Indigenous/settler distinction might be of strategic use when discussing government policy or advocating Indigenous rights, the example of the Welsh casts doubt on the validity of this dichotomy. The Welsh subject position places them – as a nation and as individuals – in both positions simultaneously, muddying the easy arguments about whose land is occupied, whose sovereignty is usurped, who is barbarized and whose culture is at risk of elimination. This is not to argue that both are in the *same situation* (the Welsh were not killed for their lands; Indigenous Patagonians were) but rather that similar processes were at work for both groups of people. It is by looking at non-typical cases such as the Welsh in Patagonia that we can identify and interrogate the fuzzy, tricky margins of ideas like Indigenous and settler. And it is only by taking conditions in the origin country seriously that we can see settlers as whole and complex humans who are themselves also caught up in global dynamics such as capitalism, modernity and racial hierarchies. Things become even more complex when the Welsh arrive in Y Wladfa, and it is to Patagonia that our analysis now turns.

Notes

1   Neil Evans also notes the paucity of historical work on imperialism in his review of the historiography: 'Writing Wales into Empire: Rhetoric, Fragments – and Beyond?', in H. V. Bowen (ed.), *Wales and the British Overseas Empire: Interactions and Influences 1650–1830* (Manchester: Manchester University Press, 2011), pp. 15–39.

2   R. R. Davies, *The Age of Conquest, Wales 1063–1415* (Oxford: Oxford University Press, 1987), pp. 3–23.

3   Davies, *The Age of Conquest*, pp. 11–12.

4   Seán Duffy, 'The 1169 Invasion as a Turning-point in Irish–Welsh Relations', in Brendan Smith (ed.), *Britain and Ireland 900–1300: Insular Responses to Medieval European Change* (Cambridge: Cambridge University Press, 1999), pp. 98–113.

5   S. J. Connolly, 'Settler Colonialism in Ireland from the English Conquest to the Nineteenth Century', in Edward Cavanagh and Lorenzo Veracini (eds), *Routledge Handbook of Settler Colonialism* (London: Routledge, 2017), pp. 49–64.

6   Rhys Morgan, 'From Soldier to Settler: the Welsh in Ireland 1558–1641' (unpublished PhD thesis, Cardiff University, 2011).

7   Morgan, 'From Soldier to Settler', 152–82.

8   Morgan, 'From Soldier to Settler', 189.

9   John Patrick Montaño, '"Dychenyg and Hegeying": The Material Culture of the Tudor Plantations in Ireland', in Fiona Bateman and Lionel Pilkington (eds), *Studies in Settler Colonialism: Politics, Identity and Culture* (Houndsmills: Palgrave, 2011), pp. 47–62.

10   Morgan, 'From Soldier to Settler', 191.

11   Morgan, 'From Soldier to Settler', 200.

12   Morgan, 'From Soldier to Settler', 209.

13   Paul Hammer, 'A Welshman Abroad: Captain Peter Wynn of Jamestown', *Parergon*, 16/1 (1998), 59–92, 62, 65.

14   Hammer, 'Welshman Abroad', 61.

15   Hammer, 'Welshman Abroad', 70.

16   Hammer, 'Welshman Abroad', 62.

17   I discuss *Heimat* – the concept of a home that we can sense as a potential ideal but have never achieved – in Lucy Taylor, 'Welsh–Indigenous Rela-

tionships in Nineteenth Century Patagonia: "Friendship" and the Coloniality of Power', *Journal of Latin American Studies*, 49 (2017), 143–68.

18   Wayland Dunaway, 'Early Welsh Settlers of Pennsylvania', *Pennsylvania History*, 12/4 (1945), 251–69, 254.

19   Dunaway, 'Early Welsh Settlers', 252.

20   Richard Allen, 'In Search of New Jerusalem: A Preliminary Investigation into the Causes and Impact of Welsh Quaker Emigration to Pennsylvania, *c*.1600–1750', *Quaker Studies*, 9/1 (2004), 31–51, 37.

21   Dunaway, 'Early Welsh Settlers', 252.

22   Allen, 'In Search of New Jerusalem', 39.

23   Dunaway, 'Early Welsh Settlers', 259–60.

24   Allen, 'In Search of New Jerusalem', 39–40.

25   Vivienne Sanders, *Wales, the Welsh and the Making of America* (Cardiff: University of Wales Press, 2021), p. 21.

26   Boyd Stanley Schlenther, '"The English is Swallowing up their Language": Welsh Ethnic Ambivalence in Colonial Pennsylvania and the Experience of David Evans', *Pennsylvania Magazine of History and Biography*, 114/2 (1990), 201–28, 204.

27   Schlenther, 'The English is Swallowing', 206.

28   Schlenther, 'The English is Swallowing', 215.

29   Schlenther, 'The English is Swallowing', 215.

30   Schlenther, 'The English is Swallowing', 216.

31   Schlenther, 'The English is Swallowing', 222.

32   Patrick Wolfe, 'Settler Colonialism and the Elimination of the Native', *Journal of Genocide Research*, 8/4 (2006), 397; see chapter two.

33   Gwyn A. Williams, *The Search for Beulah Land* (London: Croom Helm, 1980), p. 7.

34   Williams, *Search for Beulah*, pp. 11–25.

35   Geraint Jenkins, '"A Rank Republican [and] a Leveller": William Jones, Llangadfan', *Welsh History Review*, 17/3 (1995), 365–86, 372.

36   Jenkins 'A Rank Republican', 378.

37   Jenkins, 'A Rank Republican', 383.

38   Jenkins, 'A Rank Republican', 384.

39   'Rhys Morgan John', *Dictionary of Welsh Biography*, https://biography.wales/article/s-RHYS-JOH-1760 (accessed 29 October 2021).

40   Williams, *Search for Beulah*, pp. 142–73.

41   Aled Jones and Bill Jones, 'The Welsh World and the British Empire, *c*.1851–1939: An Exploration', *Journal of Imperial and Commonwealth History*, 31/2 (2010), 57–81; Anne Kelly Knowles, *Calvinists Incorporated: Welsh Immigrants on Ohio's Industrial Frontier* (Chicago: University of Chicago Press, 1997), pp. 13–25.

42   Bill Jones, '"Raising the Wind": Emigrating from Wales to the USA in the late Nineteenth and early Twentieth Centuries', Annual Public Lecture, Ysgol y Gymraeg, Prifysgol Caerdydd (2004).

43 Glyn Williams, *The Desert and the Dream: A Study of Welsh Colonization in Chubut, 1865–1915* (Cardiff: University of Wales Press, 1975), p. 35.

44 Hugh Hughes, *Llawlyfyr y Wladychfa Gymreig* (Liverpool: L. Jones, 1862), pp. 5, 4.

45 Davies, *The Age of Conquest*.

46 Gwyn A. Williams, *When was Wales?* (London: Penguin, 1985), pp. 114–67.

47 Michael D. Jones, *Gwladychfa Gymreig* (Liverpool: J. Lloyd, 1860), p. 14.

48 Edwyn Roberts, *Hanes Dechreuad Y Wladfa Gymreig yn Mhatagonia* (Bethesda: J. F. Williams, 1893), p. 33.

49 Jones, *Gwladychfa Gymreig*, p. 3.

50 Jones, *Gwladychfa Gymreig*, p. 3.

51 Jones, *Gwladychfa Gymreig*, p. 3.

52 Jones, *Gwladychfa Gymreig*, p. 5.

53 Roberts, *Hanes Dechreuad y Wladfa*, p. 8; my italics.

54 Gwyn A. Williams, *Madog: The Making of a Myth* (London: Eyre Methuen, 1979); Meriwether Lewis and William Clark were charged by President Jefferson in 1804 to explore and claim lands to the west acquired though the Louisiana Purchase, pushing the boundaries of the USA and laying claim to Indigenous land.

55 Roberts, *Hanes Dechreuad y Wladfa*, pp. 10–11.

56 Roberts, *Hanes Dechreuad y Wladfa*, p. 11.

57 Jan Morris, 'Mocking the Welsh is the last Permitted Bigotry', *The Spectator* (25 July 2009), https://www.spectator.co.uk/article/mocking-the-welsh-is-the-last-permitted-bigotry (accessed 19 July 2024).

58 Annette Pritchard and Nigel Morgan, 'Culture, Identity and Tourism Representation: Marketing Cymru or Wales?', *Tourism Management*, 22 (2001), 167–79.

59 Geraldine Heng, *The Invention of Race in the European Middle Ages* (Cambridge: Cambridge University Press, 2018), p. 37; Coral Lumbley, 'The "Dark Welsh": Color, Race and Alterity in the Matter of Medieval Wales', *Literature Compass*, 16 (2019), 1–19.

60 Matthew Stevens and Teresa Phipps, 'Towards a Characterization of "Race Law" in Medieval Wales', *Journal of Legal History*, 41/3 (2020), 290–331.

61 Stevens and Phipps, 'Towards a Characterization', 310–13.

62 Lloyd Bowen, 'Representations of Wales and the Welsh during the Civil Wars and Interregnum', *Historical Research*, 77/197 (2004), 362.

63 Bowen, 'Representations of Wales', 360.

64 Annette Pritchard and Nigel Morgan, 'Representations of "Ethnographic Knowledge": Early Comic Postcards of Wales', in Annette Pritchard and Adam Jaworski (eds), *Discourse Communications and Tourism: Multilingual Matters* (Bristol: Channel View Publications, 2016), pp. 53–75, 62–3.

65 Mike Parker, *Neighbours from Hell? English Attitudes to the Welsh* (Talybont: Y Lolfa, 2007).

66 Kirsti Bohata, 'Apes and Cannibals in Cambria: Literary Representations of the Racial and Gendered Other', in Charlotte Williams, Neil Evans and Paul

O'Leary (eds), *A Tolerant Nation? Revisiting Ethnic Diversity in a Devolved Wales*, 2nd edn (Cardiff: University of Wales Press, 2015), pp. 85–105.

67   Gwyneth Tyson Roberts, *Language of the Blue Books: Wales and Colonial Prejudice* (Cardiff: University of Wales Press, 1998).

68   Tyson Roberts, *Language of the Blue Books*, p. 186.

69   Tyson Roberts, *Language of the Blue Books*, pp. 137–8.

70   Tyson Roberts, *Language of the Blue Books*, p. 132.

71   Tyson Roberts, *Language of the Blue Books*, p. 172.

72   Tyson Roberts, *Language of the Blue Books*, p. 193.

73   Tyson Roberts, *Language of the Blue Books*, p. 196.

74   Tyson Roberts, *Language of the Blue Books*, p. 199.

75   Prys Morgan, *Brad y Llyfrau Gleision* (Llandysul: Gwasg Gomer, 1991); Tyson Roberts, *Language of the Blue Books*, p. 199.

76   Russell Davies, '"Hen Wlad y Menig Gwynion": Profiad Sir Gaerfyrddin', in Geraint H. Jenkins (ed.), *Cof Cenedl VI: Ysgrifau ar Hanes Cymru* (Llandysul: Gwasg Gomer, 1991), pp. 135–59.

77   J. R. Jones, *Prydeindod* (Llandybïe: Christopher Davies, 1966).

78   Cited in Kirsti Bohata, *Postcolonialism Revisited: Writing Wales in English* (Cardiff: University of Wales Press, 2004), p. 6.

79   Paul O'Leary, 'Languages of Patriotism in Wales 1840–1880', in Geraint H. Jenkins (ed.), *The Welsh Language and its Social Domains, 1801–1911* (Cardiff: University of Wales Press, 2000), pp. 533–60.

80   Tyson Roberts, *Language of the Blue Books*, p. 195.

81   Dafydd Tudur, 'The Life, Work and Thoughts of Michael D. Jones (1822–1898)' (unpublished PhD thesis, University of Wales Bangor, 2006), 184–239, 223–4.

82   Hughes, *Llawlyfyr y Wladychfa Gymreig*, p. 6.

83   Hughes, *Llawlyfyr y Wladychfa Gymreig*, p. 7.

84   Hughes, *Llawlyfyr y Wladychfa Gymreig*, p. 7.

85   Jones, *Gwladychfa Gymreig*, pp. 6–7.

86   Jones, *Gwladychfa Gymreig*, p. 7.

87   Cited in Tudur, 'Life, Work and Thoughts', 181. For more examples see Jones, *Gwladychfa Gymreig*, pp. 20–4.

88   Tudur, 'Life, Work and Thoughts', 195; for a spirited account of the meeting, see Roberts, *Hanes Dechreuad y Wladfa*, p. 15.

89   Roberts, *Hanes Dechreuad y Wladfa*, p. 11.

90   Roberts, *Hanes Dechreuad y Wladfa*, pp. 11–13.

91   Jones, *Gwladychfa Gymreig*, p. 7.

92   Lewis Jones, *Y Wladva Gymreig yn Ne Amerig* (Caernarfon: W. Gwenlyn Evans, 1898).

93   Richard White, *The Middle Ground: Indians, Empires and Republics in the Great Lakes Region, 1650–1815* (Cambridge: Cambridge University Press, 1991).

CHAPTER FOUR

Possession in Y Wladfa

This chapter is the first of three which follow the historical trajectory of the Welsh settlement in its formative years. Following on, chapter five explores the theme of racialization/barbarism and charts Welsh-Indigenous relations, focusing on the period up to 1875, while chapter six narrates the arrival of the state into the Chubut Valley and assimilation into the Argentine national project. First, though, this chapter charts the settlement's founding events, people and principles, examining the process of acquisition, journey from Liverpool and the adversities the settlers faced in navigating and establishing their new homeland. It focuses on processes of possession – legal, material and psychological – and explores how Welsh experience of subjugation at home, coupled with religious fervour, created a unique possessive sensibility which combined God's endorsement of the enterprise with nationalist feeling. The belief that they were fulfilling God's will imbued the project with spiritual strength and moral action, and signalled their superiority within the ranks of colonizers, a move which, even today, endorses the enterprise and empowers its people. Appreciating these core dynamics is only possible by integrating the origin country within analysis of the settlement.

The Welsh Patagonian settlement

The book's first chapter introduced the reader to the living, breathing people of Indigenous Patagonia by sharing the testimony of Katrülaf. In turn, this section introduces the Welsh settlers as people, and we have far more material to work from. A good number of diaries survive which offer close and direct accounts of events, and published memoirs (by middle-class men) of those first eventful years. The story of Y Wladfa is often related as something of a heroic saga, becoming an ideal of adversity, ingenuity and triumph. The purpose of this section is not to refute that legend but rather to people and contextualize it, thus drawing out the complexities and ambiguities that are obscured by the gloss of hindsight and the deceptive clarity of a story often told.

One hundred and fifty-three people boarded the ship *Mimosa* on 24 May 1865 in Liverpool and set sail for New Bay (which was to become Puerto Madryn), Patagonia. Abraham Matthews (a good-hearted preacher and father of five from Llanidloes) tells us that they sang a patriotic song as the anchor was raised to the tune of 'God save the Queen'.[1]

Ni Gawson wlad sydd well	We've found a better land
Yn y Deheudir pell	In the far-off South
A Phatagonia yw	That's Patagonia
Cawn yno fynd mewn hedd	There we can live in peace
Heb ofni brad na chledd	Not fearing treachery
A Chymro ar y sedd	And Welshmen there will reign
Boed mawl i Dduw	Praise be to God

The conditions were fair on board according to Joseph Seth Jones (an excitable young man from Abergele, trained as a printer) who kept a diary during the trip.[2] He reported on regular religious services, as well as accusations of thievery and some arguments, and on the four children who died. There were moments of high jinx too, such as when everyone went through the drenching ceremony as they crossed the equator, or when (in calm seas) they were lowered down on a rope from the bowsprit to be dipped in the water, like sheep, as the ship gently pitched and tossed. He says they saw whales and 'porpoises or tortoises or something, which went really fast in the same direction as the ship, but even faster than us. As if they were jumping.'[3] They arrived on 28 July 1865 and Lewis Jones met them. He and Edwyn Roberts had arrived earlier to organize the animals, foodstuffs and materials that they would need, plus building basic housing and a store. Joseph Seth Jones reports that he told them he had:

> 16 houses and a good storehouse, 2 carts, 90 horses, 30 cattle, 500 sheep, 30 white men, one Patagonian and a black man, a tame one (Indian from Calcutta), 3 or 4 cannons (that had been found in old wrecks in the bay) ... In the stores there were 300 sacks of wheat, 3 tons of bread ... and oats ... and potatoes ... and lots of other dry goods such as rice, sugar, coffee ... picks, iron ... wood ... and that he had 500 cattle and 200 horses coming across country ... and later 3000 cattle and 500,000 sheep on the way.[4]

Looking towards land from the anchored ship, it seemed that this truly would be a land of milk and honey peopled only by 'white men' and 'tame' racial others. However, as Abraham Matthews tells us, life was not to be easy. The wooden 'houses' in New Bay were very rough; there was a serious lack of fresh barrelled water with the nearest spring 3 miles away;[5] the soil was dry, the scrubland difficult, there were no roads and their carts were too cumbersome for the terrain; plus the wind was relentless and whipped across the wide-open expanses and vast skies. What a contrast to the rain-soaked mountains, villages and steep-sided industrial valleys of Wales this must have been.

The foundation of the settlement was to be commercial farming yet they had great difficulty even feeding themselves during the early years. The Argentine government had been very generous (and would continue to be so) in supplying the means to establish farms and significant numbers of animals were provided.[6] However, there was a big gap of misunderstanding between the two cultures when it came to husbandry. The animals were wild and used to being herded on horseback, not a sedentary life in fields (besides, there were no fences or fields), so herds simply wandered off in search of food and water. This was deeply troubling for the Welsh, not only because their stock was disappearing but also because the animals they thought they knew were alien and hostile. Abraham Matthews, for example, tells us about Mrs Eleanor Davies's shock:

[she] was used to cattle all her life. One day she went out with
a milk ewer in her hand intending to milk a couple of cows
with young calves. She walked after them, trying to catch
their attention by saying 'Come here, my girl [*dere di, 'mor-
wyn i*], come here, my big girl' but the cows looked at her as if
she was a slavering monster ... Mrs Davies walked up to one,
unsuspectingly, but the cow rushed her, so Mrs Davies threw
the ewer at her and did her best to escape, saying ... 'these are
cursed cattle, God save us, these are cattle with an evil spirit'.[7]

The 'tame' man 'from Calcutta', who had brought the cattle from Patagones, told them the Argentine method:

if they wanted to grab a cow or a horse, that a man on horseback would throw a leather rope around the creature's head,
lead her to a post sound in the ground and bind her to the
post before attempting to milk her, and if she was really wild,
you would also tie her back feet together.[8]

This was a far cry from taking a stool and jug to the field. Moreover,
they were supplied with oxen trained to work in the yoke, but these
animals did not obey the Welsh commands (probably because they
were accustomed to a different technique) and 'it took great effort to
teach the oxen, who were called Brian and Spidwal, to work'.[9] Their
knowledge was all wrong and they could not complete even basic
farming tasks, so their food and future prospects were in jeopardy.
Still, the leadership organized the small community to solve short-
term problems: fetch and ration water, distribute the government
food and improve the housing.

Before long the community decided to transfer from the sandy,
barren soils of New Bay to the alluvial earth of the Chubut river valley,
always their final destination. The men set off in groups of 10–12 to
make the 40 km hike, but again their ideas were confounded and had
to be remade. They lacked basic maps or orientation skills and took
two, sometimes four days, wandering in the 'desert' (a few years later
they would be able to make the journey in a day on horseback). The
Welsh expected to find water along the way and to shoot food, but
they suffered thirst and hunger – even eating foxes and birds of prey

'creatures that were not sanctioned by the law of Moses' to keep body and soul together.[10] The women and children travelled by ship, the *Mary Ellen*, but this ran aground in the mouth of the river Chubut. They were stuck there for seventeen days in bad and worsening conditions: the food became spoiled, they suffered badly from a lack of water for cooking and drinking, and one baby died.[11] Meanwhile, the men watched for the ship that, each day, failed to breech the turn of the river – worried that their loved ones had perished at sea.

These ordeals of arduous travel and intense anxiety became a founding experience of pioneer life. Settler colonial studies suggests that experiences such as these bind settlers to the new land which they feel they have won through the blood and tears, births and deaths of their communities. Anna Johnston and Alan Lawson, for example, discuss the way that 'hardship' seemed to justify 'ownership' for the Afrikaners undertaking the so-called Great Trek into non-settled parts of south-east Africa (1836–40).[12] Living through this emotional conquest of the land is a founding moment which generates the sensibility of possession.

Eventually the women and children arrived, disembarked and the settlement began. The memories of Thomas Jones 'Glan Camwy' are vivid of that time (even though he was a youngster of sixteen) and he published his recollections in the Welsh Patagonian newspaper, *Y Drafod*, sixty-one years later. He recalls that they used an old 'fort' as the starting point, as it had a well, and built rough houses within its enclosure: this was to become Rawson.[13] Each had their tasks and 'everyone took up their work with enthusiasm' Thomas Jones tells us, including the builders and joiners, the preachers and farmers. Jones explains: 'as we lived within a 100-metre radius, we were one large family. The goods store was in the middle of the circle and there they held the religious services.'[14] They made a make-shift open-air chapel using planks, boxes and sacks with a big box on which to place the Bible. Chapel life was at the centre of their community, giving a familiar rhythm to the week. The two preachers (Abraham Matthews and Lewis Humphreys) took turns to lead the Sunday service, and to run the Ysgol Sul (adult Sunday school) and Friday social gathering.[15]

In terms of political decision-making, the community was run by the council of twelve people who had been elected in Liverpool: 'the council was the authority which governed matters within the Welsh

Colony and legislated as was necessary'.[16] Because of the low numbers
and the common problems faced by everyone (food, shelter, security), they practised a kind of town hall democracy which meant that,
although decision-making was male-dominated, the adult women
could also speak freely and may have been able to vote. Lewis Jones
clearly acted as leader, though, closely followed by Richard Jones
Berwyn and Edwyn Roberts, aided by the two preachers. They also
elected a Justice of the Peace who would oversee any disputes, calling
a jury of twelve.[17] In terms of money, the council issued bank notes in
order to monetize funds arriving from the government. These were
signed by the colony's first secretary of the council, Thomas Ellis (a
druggist by trade who had migrated to cure his rheumatic illness,
along with his brothers David and John).[18] However, as the state only
provided stock, not finance, the exchange of goods and labour rather
than money dominated this early economy. This fact, and dire want,
promoted an egalitarian impulse and the fair distribution of the government's largesse, rather than the laws of supply and demand.

The question of security loomed large for many settlers who
feared the arrival of violent 'Indians', as we will see. To counter this,
Edwyn Roberts set up a militia, perhaps thinking of himself as an expert in 'vicious savages', being from the United States. Thomas Jones
recalls that they had military training every Wednesday night with
revolver and sword, and kept guard whenever there was a full moon.
They had found an old metal tank which they would bang on as an
alarm should danger arise, and petitioned the government for old
rifles with fixed bayonet to help defend themselves.[19] Such, then, was
the Welsh state-in-miniature perched on the banks of the Chubut river, complete with government, legal and economic system, spiritual
and cultural institutions, and defence.

Yet all was not happy in the new idyll. Many felt that they had
been deceived by the stories of bounty and verdure.[20] Scouts went to
look for better pastures but found just more of the same flat, windswept scrubland. Following two failed harvests 'everyone was very
disheartened', so 'a general meeting was called to gather the opinion
of all the colonists, and the unanimous decision was made to leave
for New Bay [Puerto Madryn] as soon as possible to another, better
place'.[21] After a lot of heartache and discussion there was a split and
forty-four people went, some to the town of Patagones, and some to

Santa Fe (Argentina). One (Robert Meirion Williams) composed a song that conveys the sense of dashed hopes and bitter experience that led some to abandon Y Wladfa Patagonia:

> The Children of Gomer seriously thought
> To establish a Colony for the skilful Welsh
> In Patagonia, to improve the lot of the weak
> And to raise him from poverty.
> Though they scattered seeds and plants on the earth
> So that they might bring forth fruit, this did not happen
> The devastating and poisonous dryness, and the wind,
> Withered them, they did not grow as had been promised
> (chorus)
> Country! [*País!*] Country, it is an unproductive country
> Sterile, the whole surface is arid
> From the north, to the east and the south.[22]

The sixty who returned to the Chubut Valley had an arduous task to start again and gather hope for the new season.[23] They fixed the houses, planted and nurtured, but also suffered hunger, sometimes reduced to eating wild plants.

Now committed to the settlement, the Welsh who remained began to adapt and generated an identity not just as Welsh but as Welsh Patagonians. Thomas Jones also tells us about everyday ingenious solutions that the Welsh devised. They made 'glass' for their windows to keep out the incessant wind by stretching finely cleaned 'ostrich' skin over a frame. They also made soap from boiled animal intestines mixed with the ashes from burned river-bank reeds, and used these reeds also as the wick in candles fashioned from animal fats, particularly from seals who were killed precisely to fulfil this purpose.[24] They probably adapted some methods from those practised in rural Wales: I recall my husband's father John Roberts (Taid), born 1921 in Llanerfyl, telling me that he would be sent by his mother to gather rushes to make candles.

Perhaps the most important adaptation was the development of irrigation. This innovation was started by Aaron Jenkins, a former miner from Mountain Ash. As E. F. Hunt tells the story, Aaron Jenkins ('of cheerful disposition [and] kind heart') had planted his crop close to the river.[25] He observed his crop withering and the river nearby, and hatched a plan:

> he ran to his house to fetch a spade and commenced to cut a narrow ditch ... The parched ground was covered with wide cracks and fissures into which the water ran as into open mouths ... as if it was a sentient being quenching a great thirst ... [And] in a few days the wheat revived like magic.[26]

Others attribute this eureka moment to his wife Rachel, whose own good sense may well have been overlooked in the telling of the story, given the habit at that time of ignoring women. Still, irrigation quickly became standard practice and neighbours would work together to develop and maintain the system of canals which are still in use today. This became institutionalized in the Irrigation Society which operated through a shareholder system and remains an important public sphere institution.[27] This was the gateway technology which heralded capitalist modernity in Y Wladfa and endures as a legacy of the Welsh proto-state.[28]

The colony's prosperity attracted settlers and led to migration waves in 1868–75 and 1881–91. Migrants originated in Wales and also the United States, with 500 arriving in 1875–6, drawn by the foundation of Gaiman in 1874.[29] Most arrivals were families and the gender split was roughly even, though some arrived as single men. They came from rural areas (where agriculture was suffering depression) and also the industrial valleys. By 1876, then, the population was 690 and the lingua franca was Welsh: Captain Bedingfield of the Cracker observes in his report to the government in 1871 that all but one man and three women spoke Welsh, and they were 'rapidly acquiring that language'.[30] Most spoke English more or less perfectly while some were acquiring Spanish, 'that being the trading language of the Indians ... one or two have a slight acquaintance with the Indian language'.[31]

For ten years, the Welsh fulfilled their dream of political autonomy and created a (virtually) monolingual Welsh-speaking community. This brief period – a kind of utopia, or the Heimat fulfilled – continues to beguile the image of Y Wladfa in the popular imaginary or is seen as a fleeting golden age. While distinctively European, it is still somehow outside the ravages of capitalist modernity (they do not use money) and avaricious colonialism (they live peaceably with the 'Indians'). It seems a place of moral action, collective decision-making and cooperation, a simple life built on sharing fears, adversity, triumphs and the goods provided by the state. As we will see later, though, this image masks a more complex reality, just as we would expect.

Already we have a sense of the character of a few settlers. This is important because while they reflected prevailing ideas about colonialism, capitalism and race they built the colony and its social relations in a certain way. So, let us get to know a few of them. Richard Jones Berwyn (already briefly mentioned) was a leading protagonist in Y Wladfa, who arrived on the *Mimosa*. Born near Llangollen, he became a pupil teacher at fifteen and then went to London for teacher training. There, he worked as an accountant, taught Welsh in evening classes, wrote for the Welsh press and organized Welsh music concerts. He is described as able, versatile, genial and obliging, and in Patagonia undertook a wide range of roles from registrar to weather-officer, editor to miller and, as the main teacher, he wrote the first Welsh-language textbook.[32]

Most settlers did not conform to that archetype, though, and arrived at all ages, from all backgrounds and contributed in a range of ways. David Bowen, for example, was a skilled miner in the Rhondda Valley who arrived in 1879. He used his geological skills to help canal construction and was 'a patriot, an especially obliging and willing neighbour, and a steadfast, quiet, affectionate and likeable character'.[33] Twin brothers Maurice and Lewis Humphreys both sailed on the *Mimosa*. Lewis was an ordained minister and began the school in 1865, teaching in the open-air chapel, but was forced by ill-health to return to Wales in 1867.[34] Another first arrival was David Williams of Aberystwyth who was keen as mustard for Y Wladfa Gymreig and read out sections of the settler's handbook on the deck of the *Mimosa* to inspire the travellers. It was perhaps he who composed the alternative words to God Save the Queen, as we know that he composed a similar treatment of the Lord's Prayer, beginning 'Great Englishman who lives in London'.[35] Sadly, David was so eager to see the Chubut Valley that he set off alone in that direction – and was never heard of after: they found his body 1868.[36] John Murray

Thomas also arrived on the first sailing but quickly settled in Buenos Aires and became an important trader linking Y Wladfa and the capital. He was also a keen explorer, gold prospector and early photographer.[37] Thomas Benbow Phillips from Tregaron was also well travelled: he had already tried – and failed – to establish a Welsh colony in Brazil (1851–4) when he arrived in 1872, later running the Chubut Mercantile Company. At the age of seventy-five he married Florence Elizabeth Elbourne, who was nineteen, and had two children, Gilbert and Marjorie.[38] Benjamin Brunt also came later (1881) at the age of forty-four with his second wife Ann and eight children. He described his farm as a 'howling wilderness' but there he grew wheat which won first prize at the International Exhibition in Paris, 1889, and in Chicago.[39]

We know very little of the women who also set sail on the *Mimosa*. We do have the writings of Eluned Morgan, daughter of the colony's pre-eminent leader Lewis Jones, which shed some light on women's conditions, tasks and concerns.[40] However, her family background and high level of education set her apart from the ordinary settler women, and her highly romanticized work paints a rosy picture of what must have been a hard-graft life. In the archive, women appear as mothers, wives, daughters, sisters and aunts, but there is almost no information on their own experiences, hopes and fears, or daily lives. We can only imagine how they worried about the health of their children: were they eating enough? Was there enough water? Were they warm enough at night? Would they get lost in the desert? This reflects women's invisibility in the archive, rather than omission, though a few scraps of information do emerge. Gwen Williams is noted as 'a skilful seamstress and a faithful member of her chapel', and we know that Elizabeth Evans was sent into service at an early age.[41] She came to Patagonia in 1874, though her family was originally intending to go to the USA. She died 'nine days short of her hundredth birthday' in 1931.[42]

Similarly, we know little about what life was like for children. The litany of tragedies which befell the children of Thomas Dalar Evans and his wife Esther (born in Trelew, Patagonia) gives a sense of the dangers. Their son Buallt was drowned in the Chubut river aged eight and another son Madryn (also at eight years old) disappeared on 6 June 1904, his body found near the house the next day, killed and hidden, as if by a puma.[43] John Coslett Thomas, on the other hand, gives us a rare insight into children's games. In his autobiography he recalls that:

> 'Indians' we played most of all, that is riding each other without being thrown off, injuring each other as if we were wild animals, bowling at poles as if they were the legs of horses or the necks of guanacos or ostriches, and hunting each other in the bushes as if we were partridges.[44]

Children learned to ride at a young age (like the Indigenous children) and enjoyed the freedom of 'the camp' but also attended school which, as we have seen, was a priority for all settlers from the very first weeks.

These stories (and people) are real and to be cherished. Yet this does not obviate the logics and practices of possession which their colonization of the Chubut Valley entails, nor does it somehow justify their racialized and barbarizing attitude towards Indigenous people. Yet we must never lose sight of the humanity of the Welsh and always recall that they too were caught up in processes of possession, barbarization and assimilation back home and in a wider world which perpetually portrayed them as inferior to the English.

Possession: acquisition and belonging

The Welsh understood that they had a rightful claim over the lands of Y Wladfa, according to both the law and the social norms of the period. They were not doing anything illegal or even unusual at that time – indeed, they acted peaceably, choosing trade and mutual coexistence over physical violence and domination. Given the naked force and brutality of many settler colonies at the time, this is certainly something to be proud of. My purpose here is not to condemn, then, but rather to reveal the complexities of their human response, drawing on archival evidence. Doing so helps us to tease out the logics of possession, both Welsh and Argentine, which enabled the dispossession of Indigenous lands, and the state's policy of 'Indian elimination' which consolidated Argentina as a settler colonial society.

Legal possession and tenuous sovereignty

First, and most obviously, possession of the land allocated to the Welsh by the Argentine government was facilitated by a legal regime, grounded in the logic which underpins all nation states: national sovereignty. The Argentine state aimed to use settlers in order to stake a claim to lands currently in the hands of Indigenous people and thus to extend the weight of the state across the whole territory on the map. Argentina was far from 'fixed', so granting legal status (and land) for Y Wladfa not only established a legal footing for the Welsh but strengthened Argentine sovereignty claims and reinforced the existence of the 'imagined community' of the nation and the machinery of state. There was much at stake for both parties.

The legal process was appropriately bureaucratized. The Welsh Emigration Society in Liverpool opened correspondence with the Argentine consul, Samuel Phibbs, who was very encouraging, though he doubted that Argentina would allow the Welsh to have 'everlasting possession of the country' as Hugh Hughes Cadfan desired.[45] Lewis Jones and Captain T. Love Jones-Parry then went to Argentina in 1863 as agents to see the proposed settlement zone and negotiate with the government. Dr Guillermo Rawson (minister for the interior) was very enthusiastic about their scheme and together, they drew up a proposal which contained the following: Point 7: 'The urban or local government will belong completely to the settlers, and according to their own organization'; point 8: The settlers are to be free from any military taxes for the first ten years ... but they must defend themselves from the Indians'; and point 9 suggested that when they reach 20,000 in number they could become a province.[46] This proposal attempted to enshrine Welsh self-government, and the aim to become a province opened the possibility for real autonomy for a substantial Welsh community, thus fulfilling the desires for a Welsh Heimat. However, this proposal was rejected by congress which viewed it as a British colonial enterprise. The confusion might be the result of linguistic elision – in Spanish 'the British' is translated as *los Ingleses* ('the English') – but their caution was well grounded, given that Britain had already claimed the Falkland Islands.[47] Their reluctance is therefore understandable given the tenuous hold Argentina had over this vast landscape – and the avaricious activity of the British Empire elsewhere in the world.

As we can see, legal possession was 'made real' by regulations and nominated actors who proceeded according to a legal logic which seems natural when seen from today: the rule of law (male, elite), representative democracy and lots of paperwork. But Aileen Moreton-Robinson suggests that we should see these structures and legitimated habits-of-thought as techniques of power, designed to dispossess Indigenous people of their land. The Argentine state, its consul and its ministers made a claim to ownership of Patagonia – to rightfully possess it – based on assertion, rather than fact. Indeed, the 'fact' was that Indigenous leaders and their people 'owned' Patagonia. While they did not have the kind of bureaucratic structures that Europeans recognized as 'the state', they exercised governance over the region, engaged in political alliances and conflicts, and had a complex normative code which regulated social action and punished transgressors. Because these institutions did not look like a European-type state (no neo-classical architecture here), they were interpreted as absent or at best 'savage'. Thus, Patagonia could be imagined as *terra nullius* and its people as *homo nullius* because its society appeared to have no structures – *socio nullius*. This disavowal of Indigenous territory, government and society enabled the Argentine state to perform its claim to sovereignty over Patagonia, and it was this which enabled the consul to offer land to the Welsh.

This legal performance proclaimed Argentina's right to possess Patagonia, but actually the state knew full well that 'Indians' were owners of the 'empty' lands. During the 1830s and under President Rosas, the government made war in order to 'extinguish' the Rankülche (Ranquel People) between Rio Negro and the Neuquen river, but made a political pact with Cacique (leader) Calfucurá who ruled below the Rio Negro line.[48] Making both wars and pacts implies recognition of Indigenous sovereignty and land-ownership. (Later, they signed a military alliance with Cacique Cipriano Catriel and Ignácio Coliqueo, and made war against Calfucurá.) Far from ignoring Indigenous leaders and the governance regimes that they represented, the reality behind the rhetorical 'claims to sovereignty' was the presence of leaders such as Calfucurá who was a political rival, described as 'charismatic and diplomatic; an accomplished strategist with a gift for words'.[49] The legal claims, then, meant little unless backed up by military force and genocidal violence, a fact that the Welsh seem to be blissfully unaware of until the arrival of the Conquest of the Desert to the Chubut Valley in the early 1880s.

Property as possession
As well as legal recognition, a second foundational trope of capitalist modernity helped to justify the settlement: the market in property. Of course, in both Wales and Argentina the concept of land as property, was foundational to understanding the relationship between people and land. The practices associated with property were similarly naturalized: buying, selling, renting and eviction. The rule of law was used to ensure that people could trust the market, and therefore be confident of speculating in land.

Settler colonialism requires a few preliminary moves before land can be constituted as property, including mapping, naming, demarcating and allocating: thereafter these parcels of land could become property.[50] This latter process is precisely what happened in the Chubut Valley. A few months after the Welsh arrived, a surveyor from the Argentine government landed to measure and delimit the plots that were to be allocated. Lewis Jones tells us that the government sent Captain Murga from Patagones to give formal possession of the country to the settlers, and a surveyor called Díaz, along with an (alcoholic) Englishman to translate.[51] These functionaries brought the colony officially to life: Abraham Matthews tells us that 'On 15th September, the Argentine flag was raised over the Chubut Valley on a clearing by the river.'[52] This ceremony performed the moment when a claim was staked by the Argentine government, and it was Welsh presence that provided tangible proof that Patagonia was the property of Argentina that could be gifted, marked out and transferred from state possession to settler possession. The surveyor laid out the farm plots in a grid pattern, and they were distributed by drawing names from a hat. Thus the Indigenous homeland was parcelled and reallocated to the Welsh.[53]

The sight of a surveyor parcelling land to make properties and a settlement ceremony to confirm possession must have seemed natural to the Welsh – this process had been enacted countless times in settler colonies, but also the enclosure of common land in Wales. However, the Welsh were well aware that this land had belonged to someone else first. Quite often in the archive the 'Indians' are referred

to as 'the rightful owners of this land'. For example, the Revd W. Casnodyn Rhys observed that the Indigenous were 'the rightful owner of
the soil on which the settlers had located themselves'.[54] This presented
a moral problem (were they stealing this land?) that was resolved by
invoking the 'moral market' and the principle of fair exchange. For
example, Hugh Hughes Cadfan reported that 'there are four [Indig-
enous] tribes who consider eastern Patagonia to be their common
possession between them'.[55] He then added: 'We cannot disregard the
rights of the Indians of the land but, rather following the example of
our famous countryman William Penn, we should attempt to make
friends of them, giving them whatever is honest, whatever is just'.[56]
The liberal regime of property-owning rights which regulated the
operation of the market, enabled the exchange to be 'fair', where fair-
ness is judged in terms of price. Michael D. Jones agreed, stating in
an 1856 article in *Yr Anybynwr*: 'I am completely opposed to taking
land, unless the principles of fair trade allow it'. As Dafydd Tudur (his
biographer) explains, he believed 'that the Indigenous people should
be recognized as "the land's owners" … and [he] claimed that they
should receive full compensation for the area to be populated by the
Welsh'.[57] These two aspects (liberal property and the market) are, as
we saw in chapter two, thus fundamental to the rules, moral order
and sensations of possession which condition the Welsh colony.

Indeed, 'purchase' was adopted as a key strategy by the Argentine
government, a concept which in itself recognized the prior ownership
of Patagonia by Indigenous peoples. Interior Minister Rawson noted:

> the treaty that we have just celebrated with the Indigenous
> owners of these lands [*dueños de aquellas tierras*], [which]
> gives us the undisputed proprietorship of them, through
> significant compensation which they have agreed to, being
> obliged at the same time not only to respect the properties
> of the colony but also to defend it, should that be necessary,
> from possible aggression from other tribes.[58]

The Welsh were thus reassured that the land had been bought, fair
and square, from the Indigenous communities who owned it, and
they too proposed market-based norms of ownership. For example, in their proposal to congress they suggested 'a price [of] £10 a

year per square league ... [with] an option to purchase at a price of 500 silver dollars for each square league on expiration of the lease.[59] However, norms of capitalist interaction justified the possession of Indigenous land.

Importantly, trade was also fully embraced by Indigenous communities who not only subsisted via hunting and gathering, but were enmeshed in global capital relations, fully comprehending both economic worlds, as we saw in Katrülaf's testimony. We can gain a clearer understanding of their economy and society by reading a letter from Cacique Antonio which deserves to be quoted at length. It was dictated by him to Georges Claraz, a Swiss adventurer and botanist. He recalls that they all gathered to write the letter together:

> Chilapata and all the others added their ideas in the middle of this meeting, some lying on their stomachs, others on their side, others on their backs and some reclining in the gay guy's tent [*toldo del maricón*], I wrote. Then I read what I had written. They all told me 'lovely, lovely, very lovely: you speak very well'. Then I said that the letter should be sealed. This we did with the wax.[60]

One assumes that the letter was written in Spanish but it only survives in the following English transcription.

To Mr Jones, Superintendent of the Colony of Chupat.
                            Tschetschgoo, December 8, 1865.

Very distinguished Sir,
Without having the pleasure of knowing you personally, I know as a fact that you are peopleing the Chupat with a people from the other side of the sea. You, doubtless, do not know that in the country south of Buenos Aires there exist three distinct sets of Indians. To the north of the Rio Negro ... lives a nation of Indians denominated 'Chilenos' ... Between the Rio Negro and the Rio Chupat ... lives the nation called 'Pampa' and speaking Pampa. I and my people belong to it. To the south of the Chupat lives ... the 'Tchuelcha'. Now

I say that the plains between the Chupat and the Rio Negro are ours and that we never sold them. I am the Cacique of the tribe of Pampa Indians ... I have a Treaty of Peace with Patagones but that does not touch on selling lands. I know very well that you have negotiated with the Government to colonize the Chupat but you ought also to negotiate with us who are the owners of these lands. But never mind my friend ... Our plains have plenty of guanacos and plenty of ostriches. We are never in want of food [...]

I was desirous of going to Buenos Aires to present the government my claims ... but I know that they are fighting with the people of Paraguay and ... also that bad diseases are raging in Buenos Aires ... This is the reason why I did not go.

I remained and had arranged with the Comandante [Murga, of Patagones] who is my very good friend to ... visit you and your people ... Ere I come I hope to receive a letter from you making me know what your answer shall be. Afterwards I shall go and put up my tents ('*toldos*') in front of your village in order that I may become acquainted with you and you with me and with my people; you see that I have a good heart and a good will.

Be not afraid of us my friend, I and my people are contented to see you colonize on the Chupat, for we shall have a nearer place to go to in order to trade, without the necessity of going to Patagones, where they steal our horses and where the '*pulperos*' (tavern keepers) rob and cheat us. If you treat us well ... we shall always negotiate with you.

We sell ostrich feathers of those ostriches called '*petisos*' ... We also sell guanaco skins and ... guanaco mantles ('*quillangos*') [which] rich persons ... put ... as carpets. Enquire as to the prices of those articles in order that you may pay us properly when we come in the winter.

Tell me in your letter what kind of money you are using at the Chupat, whether paper or silver money. Try to get an interpreter. We all know a little Spanish but English we do not understand. Also do not forget to have liquor, yerba for mate (tea), sugar, flour, bread, biscuits, tobacco, ponchos (cloaks), handkerchiefs, cloth or blanket, fine ones for our women for they have no other dresses except blankets. See to it that those things which we buy and want are good but, moreover, the yerba (Paraguayan tea) ought to be good. ... You ought, for my portion of the land, to negotiate with the Government. See you what they can pay me for it. Everywhere they sell and buy but they do not colonize without buying ...

Mr Aguirre has read a letter of the Government to me in which I am told to leave you to increase in numbers.... I promised to do all in my power for you... and if you should want labourers and heads to show and lead the way, in order to bring cattle you can engage my people who will faithfully serve you.

I send this letter by my grandson, who is Francisco Hernandez... if you take an interest in us and mean to enter into friendly intercourse with us make us some presents ... I shall tell you frankly what we like best is some good liquor, a little flour, yerba, sugar and tobacco, and if you can get it, a saddle which is called the English saddle ...

I wish you much happiness and salute you with my best estimation. All my people who are collected here to see this letter written send you many salutations. From the Cacique Antonio.[61]

This rich text is a jewel-box of insights but the following key points stand out. First, Cacique Antonio speaks with a voice of authority, confidence and power, freely invoking his role as representative and leader. Secondly, he has a clear grasp of Argentine politics, being well aware of events in Buenos Aires and the dispute with Paraguay, and is well connected to the regional military leader, Captain Murga, and the prominent businessman Mr Aguirre, both in Patagones. Through them, he is informed of government action, but he also has a clear grasp of politics within the Indigenous world in both the past and present, negotiating both arenas of power with ease. In terms of colonization, he comprehends this, as does the government, as a market transaction which sees land as property, and insists that while he has been asked to support the colony, the lands have not been purchased. Such matters need to be resolved by the settlers, he adds, and not by him – a mark of his sense of ownership and natural pride. An air of beneficent authority infuses his proposed relations with the settlers. He patiently explains the social world of different 'tribes' that they have entered, extends the hand of peace and offers them labourers and guides to facilitate their settlement. Finally, this letter explicitly invites a business deal. Cacique Antonio is well aware of the quality and value of his goods and their market destination and would like to trade with the Welsh, in the hope of a fairer treatment and a better price, added to the greater convenience of the Welsh settlement.[62] He proposes to utilise both money (paper or silver) and barter (for goods) as modes of trade, understanding both to be useful and neither to be superior – a mark of his fluency in both economic mechanisms.

Overall, this is not the letter of a 'primitive savage' but of a capable politician and astute businessman who did not shun colonization and capitalist modernity, but sought to make his own way, on his own terms, through this world. For example, he suggested Indigenous social conventions such as 'put[ting] up my tents ("toldos") in front of your village in order that I may become acquainted with you and you with me and with my people', and proposed that 'if you take an interest in us and mean to enter into friendly intercourse with us make us some presents'. We know from a range of sources, including the travelogue written by George Musters, that siting tents close to another group and then going to visit, with presents, was an important diplomatic convention.[63] Importantly, Cacique Antonio also mediated between European and Indigenous understandings of possession. He utilized ideas and practices embedded in Europeanized conventions of market-driven property but also evoked a claim to sovereignty based on belonging, ancestry and the connection between people and their lands when he referred to 'the animals which are our property that were given to us by our God, the God of the Indians, so that we might chase them for food'.

We can see that parallel ideas about what it means to own, the relationship between trade and possession, making pacts and sovereignty are at work here. However, Cacique Antonio's letter gives us a glimpse of a time when they were held equally in the balance, but soon the logics of capitalist property and state sovereignty would be imposed, both by the geo-political powerfulness of their logics and by military domination.

The possessive sensibility Cymreig
As well as the material and structural dimensions of possession (linked to the legal and market realms), possession also entails an emotional connection to what is possessed: in the context of settler colonialism, this means land. Like most European settlers in the nineteenth century, this sensibility was channelled through liberal capitalist logics embedded in the Lockean thinking. That is, land is understood as a commodity whose value to society emerges from the utilization of resources to extract the greatest benefit for humankind from the earth, in the form of food, fuel or raw materials with which to make useful objects. It entailed an attitude to nature which saw the natural world as simultaneously a wasteland and a potential asset (social and financial), and also a sensibility which legitimated Man's mastery over nature as well as 'unused' territories owned by Indigenous people. This (highly gendered) sensibility is what justified settler colonialism.

Naturally, for them, the Welsh intended to take land that was currently unproductive in Lockean terms and transform this space using their agricultural techniques to establish productive farms. This was also the intended wish of the Argentine government – to import settlers who knew how to transform the 'desert' into a fertile resource to enrich the state.

On top of this, though, the Welsh desire for political autonomy and their anti-colonial mission led them to see this not just as agricultural land, but *the promised land*. In his perceptive book, *Entre el Desierto y el Jardín* (Between the Desert and the Garden), Fernando Williams argues that for the Welsh 'the Bible story is what links them to the territory'.[64] The foundational moment between people and land is written in the arduous journey from New Bay to the Chubut Valley, which he suggests was interpreted as 'the desert of the Old Testament, where God's People are tested in their march to the promised land, a march where, despite all the difficulties, God communicates with his people, guiding and helping them'.[65] For example, the arrival of a hunting dog on the trek which caught a hare was understood as the intervention of divine providence. The experience also inspired the first sermon preached after the journey 'the Children of Israel in the Desert' where they sang the hymn '*Diwedd y Daith*' (End of the Journey), which includes the stanza 'O! the hills of Jerusalem can be seen / all through the desert journey'.[66] This experience, Williams argues, defines the land, the colonizing project and the people, and justifies the presence of *this* colony on *this* land (possession) in terms of God's will. It reinforced what was already a strong, Calvinist sense that the Welsh were God's chosen people (predestination) which, when melded with their sense of persecution at home, strengthened the certainty that this God-blessed colony was their nationalist political destiny.[67] The possession of the Chubut Valley was justified by a complex intersection of emotions and teachings which created a powerful sensibility that they rightfully belonged there. Interestingly, it is the supposed emptiness of Patagonia (the desertedness of the desert) that enabled the fulfilment of that destiny, thus a sensibility of possession, justified by *terra nullius*, was central to the colonial effort.

The counterpart to this vision of the 'desert' is its envisioned transformation into a garden (*el jardín*). The protestant work ethic is pivotal to this transformation in which labour and improvement of the soil is matched by the effort and improvement of man. This approach to nature (both land and man's natural inclinations) dovetails with Locke's utilitarian approach. Fernando Williams points out that the two strong dynamics at work in the idea of the garden are in tension. On the one hand 'the garden is an expression of order in construction' (a garden concerns the human effort to control nature), linking self-improvement of moral, God-fearing Man and improvement of the 'desert': on the other hand, gardening entails Man meddling with God's work which began with a perfect Eden, prompting nostalgia (*hiraeth*) for the loss of 'a virgin world whose desecration is linked to fear for its probable extinction'.[68] This is resolved by making the link between culture and cultivation.[69] Thus the Welsh can create a manufactured garden that may not be an Eden but can be an oasis of both productive farms and a moral, God-loving society: thus 'the garden becomes the proof of the community's faith'.[70]

Central to this was irrigation. We have already discussed its practical impact, but irrigation also generated a sensibility of rightful possession. Water is what makes the desert productive, enabling both Lockean utility and God's blessing, as this Patagonian eisteddfod poem infers:

Here we have land for good agriculture
now we can sow clover.

Where there were wild plants
one can see grasses and daisies.
Under the plough and harrow
there will be moist soil.
By making banks and ditches
we guide the water to meadows and fields
Giving drink to the poor, dry earth
like in beautiful Italy or ancient Eden
It will be like the lands of the Nile.[71]

The idea of making a garden from an empty place echoes with the parable of the sower who casts his seed upon the ground:

Listen! Behold, a sower went out to sow. And as he sowed, some seed fell along the path, and the birds came and devoured it. Other seed fell on rocky ground, where it did not have much soil, and ... withered away. Other seed fell among thorns, and the thorns grew up and choked it ... And other seeds fell into good soil and produced grain, growing up and increasing and yielding thirtyfold and sixtyfold and a hundredfold. (Mark 4: 3–9)

Thus, while all around the desert remained dry and spiny, the seed of the gospel flourished in the Welsh settlement, as did the prize-winning wheat, because the water that they channel and the cultivation that they practice is matched by their purity of heart and diligence in fulfilling God's will. Crucially, as Fernando Williams argues, creating a garden depends on imagining Patagonia to be a wasteland, without Indigenous people, alternative sovereignties – or the physical violence that, sooner or later, makes their settlement possible. In this mode, the possessive sensibility must close its eyes to the reality of settler colonialism in Patagonia. This disavowal of Indigenous presence did become possible once the Conquest of the Desert had, rhetorically, eliminated Indigenous people from Patagonia, yet during the first twenty years of the colony, the story – and discourse – was very different. This is the topic of the next chapter.

Conclusion

Using a coloniality of power approach allows us to see that while Y Wladfa was being created, something else was being destroyed – Indigenous sovereignty. In the early years, the settlement was not strong enough to impinge significantly on the de facto power of Cacique Antonio and his fellow Indigenous leaders in their homelands but it established the Argentine claim to ownership over the land through reciprocal recognition with the Welsh. The drive to Indigenous 'elimination' would then (almost) inevitably follow. The case illustrates how liberal law and capitalist ideas of property operate together to generate possession. Yet it also shows how experiences back in the origin country shape the possessive sensibility enacted in the colony, melding a sense of colonial oppression back home and of predestination, anchored in spiritual belief and religious teachings. Thus possession is conditioned by both general principles and embedded in specific cultural traits which are only intelligible if we both humanize and contextualize the settler.

However, ideas about possession during this early, colonizing period were complex and still ambiguous. The Welsh themselves were uneasy about whose land this *really* was, and therefore the legitimacy of their colony, but they solved the problem by adopting a 'fair dealing' strategy. Indeed, this became the basis for a successful economic relationship with the Indigenous people for at least the first twenty years of Y Wladfa. The Indigenous too mediate between modes and concepts of possession in the Chubut Valley, acknowledging the force of property as a principle. Yet they also assert the principle of being the 'rightful owners of the land' due to their prior occupancy, ancestral/spiritual connection and exercise of a governance regime which might not look like a state to Western eyes, but which functions to regulate all aspects of life in Patagonia. The tone of self-assured powerfulness in Cacique Antonio's letter, a man at home in the Chubut Valley, contrasts to the superficial claim to possession that was forged in the ceremony by the riverbank when Argentina asserted its ownership of the land by granting it to the Welsh, and the Welsh staked their faith in that ownership by accepting the concession and drawing their lots from a hat. Yet this performance was backed by a modern legal regime endorsed by the new Argentine state, the concepts and mechanisms of capitalist property-ownership and the sense of spiritual destiny which drove the Welsh to feats of endurance. What clinched Argentine supremacy, though, was the arrival of the army twenty years hence, and what made military conquest possible was not only money and guns, but the belief that Indigenous people were primitive, barbarous and obsolete savages. It is to the topic of racialization/barbarization that we now turn.

Notes

1   Abraham Matthews, *Hanes y Wladfa Gymreig yn Patagonia* (Aberdâr: Mills ac Evans, 1894), p. 13.

2   Joseph Seth Jones, 'Dyddiadur a Gadwyd gan Joseph Seth Jones yn Adrodd Hanes ei Daith ar y Mimosa i Batagonia ym 1865, ac ar gyfer 14–21 Mawrth 1866', NLW MS 18176B (1865).

3   Jones, 'Dyddiadur', p. 24.

4   Jones, 'Dyddiadur', pp. 31–2.

5   Thomas Jones, *Historia de los Comienzos de la Colonia en la Patagonia*, trans. Fernando Coronato (1926; Trelew: La Bibioteca Popular 'Agustín Alvarez', 1998), p. 31; see also Glyn Williams, *The Desert and the Dream: A Study of Welsh Colonization in Chubut, 1865–1915* (Cardiff: University of Wales Press, 1975), pp. 39–43.

6   Williams, *Desert and the Dream*, pp. 54–6.

7   Matthews, *Hanes y Wladfa*, p. 17.

8   Matthews, *Hanes y Wladfa*, p. 17.

9   Jones, *Historia de los Comienzos*, p. 33.

10 Matthews, *Hanes y Wladfa*, p. 18.

11 Matthews, *Hanes y Wladfa*, p. 19.

12 Anna Johnston and Alan Lawson, 'Settler Colonies', in Henry Schwartz and Sangeeta Ray (eds), *A Companion to Postcolonial Studies* (Oxford: Blackwell, 2005), pp. 360–76, 361. See also Travis Wysote and Erin Morton, '"The Depth of the Plough": White Settler Tautologies and Pioneer Lies', *Settler Colonial Studies*, 9/4 (2019), 479–504.

13 Williams, *Desert and the Dream*, pp. 44–51.

14 Jones, *Historia de los Comienzos*, p. 50.

15 Jones, *Historia de los Comienzos*, pp. 49–50.

16 Jones, *Historia de los Comienzos*, p. 50.

17 Jones, *Historia de los Comienzos*, p. 84.

18 See R. Bryn Williams, *Y Wladfa* (Caerdydd: Gwasg Prifysgol Cymru, 1962), images 1 and 2, opposite p. 96; Eirionedd Baskerville, *Companion to the Welsh Settlement in Patagonia* (Cymdeithas Cymru-Ariannin, 2014),

http://www.cymru-ariannin.com/uploads/companion_to_the_welsh_settlement_in_patagonia.pdf (accessed 15 November 2022), p. 29.

19 Jones, *Historia de los Comienzos*, p. 85.

20 Matthews, *Hanes y Wladfa*, pp. 33–41.

21 Jones, *Historia de los Comienzos*, p. 75.

22 Jones, *Historia de los Comienzos*, p. 82. Original in Welsh, translated by the author from Spanish.

23 Matthews, *Hanes y Wladfa*, pp. 46–50.

24 Jones, *Historia de los Comienzos*, p. 99.

25 E. F. Hunt, 'Aaron Jenkins: the Man who Saved the Welsh Colony, Patagonia', *The Welsh Outlook*, 16/12 (1929), 371–3, 372.

26 Hunt, 'Aaron Jenkins', 373. Aaron Jenkins was killed in 1878 by prisoners who had escaped from a Chilean penitentiary in the south.

27 Williams, *Desert and the Dream*, pp. 64–5. See also Glyn Williams, *The Welsh in Patagonia: The State and Ethnic Community* (Cardiff: University of Wales Press, 1991).

28 See the excellent presentation by Fernando Williams, 'Agua y Poder en el Valle de Chubut', Symposiwm Ymchwil 2021: Ailddehongli'r Wladfa Gymreig/Reinterpreting Y Wladfa/Reinterpretando Y Wladfa (2021), *https://www.youtube.com/playlist?list=PLcohw1amF9-JRKRVeNDADCO5M9iHjrutM* (accessed 25 July 2024).

29 Williams, *Desert and the Dream*, pp. 69–77. For a detailed breakdown, see Marcelo Gavirati, 'El Contacto entre Galeses, Pampas y Tehuelches: la Conformación de un Modelo de Convivencia Pacífica en la Patagonia Central (1865–1885)' (Doctorado Interuniversitario en Historia, Universidad del Centro de la Provincia de Buenos Aires, 2012), 425–6 and 429–30.

30 'Correspondence respecting the Welsh colony on the River Chupat, Patagonia, address dated July 3 1871', in *Papurau'r Llywodraeth 1867–1898*, NLW MS 20903 D, p. 18.

31 'Correspondence respecting', p. 18.

32 Baskerville, *Companion*, pp. 10–13.

33 Baskerville, *Companion*, pp. 14–15.

34 Baskerville, *Companion*, p. 65.

35 Williams *Y Wladfa*, pp. 85–6.

36 Jones, *Historia de los Comienzos*, p. 29.

37 Baskerville, *Companion*, pp. 104–7.

38 Baskerville, *Companion*, pp. 83–6.

39 Baskerville, *Companion*, pp. 16–18.

40 Eluned Morgan, *Dringo'r Andes a Gwymon y Môr* (1904, 1909; Talybont: Honno/Y Lolfa, 2001).

41 Baskerville, *Companion*, p. 106.

42 Baskerville, *Companion*, p. 39.

43 Baskerville, *Companion*, p. 46.

44 *Autobiography of John Coslett Thomas*, NLW Facs 919 (n.d., c.1925), p. 88. See also Baskerville, *Companion*, p. 102.

45   Dafydd Tudur, 'The Life, Work and Thought of Michael D. Jones' (unpublished PhD thesis, University of Wales Bangor, 2006), 217. See also Williams, *Desert and the Dream*, pp. 29–33.

46   A full copy of the original proposal is printed in Hugh Hughes Cadfan, *Y Wladychfa Gymreig: Atodiad i'r Llawlyfyr* (Liverpool: Lee and Nightingale, 1863), pp. 13–16.

47   Williams, *Y Wladfa*, pp. 67–73.

48   Carlos Martínez Sarasola, 'The Conquest of the Desert and the Free Indigenous Communities of the Argentine Plains', in Nicola Foote and René Harder Horst (eds), *Military Struggle and Identity Formation in Latin America* (Gainesville: University Press of Florida, 2010), pp. 204–23, 209–11.

49   Martínez Sarasola, 'Conquest of the Desert', p. 205.

50   Analía Castro, 'Estrategias de Apropiación Territorial en al Cartografía Histórica de la Provincia de Chubut, Patagonia, Argentina a Finales del Siglo XIC', *Anales del Museo de América*, 19 (2011), 101–21.

51   Lewis Jones, *Y Wladva Gymreig yn Ne Amerig* (Caernarfon: W. Gwenlyn Evans, 1898), pp. 48–9. He adds that Díaz was 'an example of the smooth and polite Argentinian, and through his position as surveyor, the settlement came into contact with the government and became accustomed to all the twists, turns and arts of that office'. Jones did not get along with Díaz and, following arguments, took his family to Buenos Aires.

52   Matthews, *Hanes y Wladfa*, p. 20.

53   Williams, *Desert and the Dream*, p. 48.

54   William Phillips, 'Fifteen Years in Patagonia' (NLW MS1653B, n.d.), p. 23, handwritten notes.

55   Hugh Hughes 'Cadfan', *Llawlyfr y Wladychfa Gymreig* (Llynlleifiad: Lewis Jones, 1862), p. 20.

56   Hughes, *Llawlyfyr*, p. 19.

57   Tudur, *Life, Work and Thoughts*, p. 208.

58   Williams, *Desert and the Dream*, p. 29, n. 37.

59   Williams, *Desert and the Dream*, pp. 30–1.

60   Georges Claraz, *Viaje al Rio Chubut: Aspectos Naturalisticos y Etnologicos (1865–1866)*, ed. Rodolfo Casamiquela (Buenos Aires: Ediciones Continente, 2008), pp. 101–3. I have translated *maricón* as 'gay guy' because this captures the relaxed and uncontroversial way in which his sexuality is dealt with in the text. Indeed, choosing to write the letter in his tent is a mark of high status, as is its presumably capacious size. In North America Two-Spirit people often undertook roles as diplomats or negotiators, so perhaps he played a similar ministerial role in Antonio's camp.

61   'Correspondence respecting the Establishment of a Welsh Colony on the River Chupat, in Patagonia, presented to both Houses of Parliament by command of her Majesty, 1867' (government papers relating to the Welsh Colony in Patagonia, NLW 20903D), pp. 33–5. Chupat was often used in place of Chubut at this time.

62   See Gavirati, 'El contacto entre Galeses'.

63 George Musters, *At Home with the Patagonians* (1871; Stroud: Nonsuch Publishers, 2005).

64 Fernando Williams, *Entre el Desierto y el Jardín: Viaje Literatura y Paisaje en la Colonia Galesa de la Patagonia* (Buenos Aires: Prometeo, 2010), pp. 25, 89.

65 Williams, *Entre el Desierto y el Jardin*, pp. 88–9.

66 Williams, *Entre el Desierto y el Jardín*, pp. 89–90.

67 Williams, *Entre el Desierto y el Jardín*, p. 105.

68 Williams, *Entre el Desierto y el Jardín*, p. 137.

69 Williams, *Entre el Desierto y el Jardín*, p. 150.

70 Williams, *Entre el Desierto y el Jardín*, p. 182.

71 Dewi Wyn Eifion, extract from *Arwyrain Amaethyddiaeth* (Elegy to Agriculture), cited in Williams, *Entre el Desierto y el Jardín*, p. 188; translated from Spanish by this author.

CHAPTER FIVE

Barbarization and the Myth of Friendship

The myth of friendship between the Welsh settlers and the Indigenous 'original owners of this land' is foundational to the claim to legitimacy of the Welsh colony, Y Wladfa Patagonia. In contrast to other colonial enterprises, this was founded not on physical violence, nor political subjugation nor forced acculturation within the new dominant order, but rather on living side-by-side and respecting one another. This story is largely true, as we will see. However, if we examine events in Welsh Patagonia using a 'coloniality of power' approach and pay heed to the insights of Indigenous and settler colonial theory, we can observe how global processes of capitalist modernity and the logics of possession, racialization/barbarization and assimilation are at work at the same time. These insights lead us to question the story of friendship in the desert by focusing on the hierarchal relationship between the Welsh settlers and Indigenous communities.

These structural inequalities, which heighten as the colony becomes consolidated, are clearly visible in the archive too, and three modes of relationship emerge from the records, memoirs and diaries of the colonists: comradeship between unequals; righteous Christian love; and suspicion of savagery. Examining these relationships shines a light on the myth of friendship and how it is framed by ideas of civilization/barbarism. It helps us to understand that this story of happy neighbours is a political strategy to elevate Welsh status on the basis of conviviality and righteousness. It does not matter that this myth and its image of Welshness stretches no further than Wales, for it is in Wales that it matters most, and where it has been burnished as a beacon of Welsh endurance, success and virtue in the face of anglicization from over the border. In the process, both the Indigenous and the Welsh have been caricatured, stereotyped and homogenized in a glossy discourse which remains of vital importance, as we will see in chapter seven. However, while the Welsh are empowered by this story, the Indigenous are romanticized, infantilized and relegated to the past, and thus made invisible as real people. This is how racialization/barbarization works in the stories of Y Wladfa.

Comradeship between unequals

The myth of friendship promotes an interpretation of the Indigenous-Welsh relationship which tells a story of comradeship, yet one in which the 'natural geopolitical order of things' is sustained. That is, hierarchies of civilization and barbarism operate to maintain Welsh superiority as Europeans in a global order that celebrates European ways of life and promotes its knowledge. These European lifeways justify commerce and colonialism, under the guise of bringing development, modernity, science and higher culture to benighted peoples. However, this idealized 'friendship' took place in a messy context in which Welsh skills and knowledge was inadequate to the task of milking cows, ploughing land or traversing the landscape where they lived. The Welsh thus found themselves in a strange position, whereby people who, to their eyes, looked like primitive ancestors ate well and travelled with ease across a landscape that to them was completely hostile.

The story of the first visit of the 'Indians' is addressed throughout the archive but the fullest account (which I have analysed in detail elsewhere) comes from Richard Jones Berwyn.[1] It occurred eight months after the Welsh landed when Cacique Francisco and his wife arrived to make contact (on a double wedding day), leaving their group camped a few miles hence. The meeting was nervy on both sides, but eventually they shook hands with the Welsh, and shared smiles and bread, communicating as best they could with the help of a Spanish dictionary. The sense of exchange and trust-building that began that day is what enabled peaceful coexistence and trade to be established in the Chubut Valley. The peaceable nature of the

Welsh reaction is easily explained because they were in a vulnerable position – they were few, badly armed and barely subsisting – so diplomacy was their best course of action. Moreover, domination over others was not their objective: rather they wanted land and personal freedom, and desired to live, learn, worship and rule themselves in Welsh and according to Welsh custom. Neither of those aims entailed dominating 'The Natives'.

The Welsh and various Indigenous communities thus built relationships based on mutual autonomy and cautious respect, as is quite common in the earliest years of settler activity.[2] Both kept to their own laws and cultural norms, spiritual practice and communities: the Welsh did not attempt to convert the Indigenous to Christianity in any serious way. Indeed, although Jonathan Ceredig Davies corresponded about missionary activities and declared his desire 'to convert infidels and pagans of South America', there is no record of action.[3] Moreover, while the two communities did interact socially, there is no evidence of sexual encounter or intermarriage. This model of parallel, intermittently intersecting social worlds suited both parties, and while the Welsh looked down on the strange habits of the Indigenous, they in turn might well have puzzled over the foolish inadequacy of the Welsh.

This sense of egalitarian social relations was fostered by the act of trade which relied on Indigenous people bringing goods to sell. Marcello Gavirati's detailed examination of the colony's economy reveals, for example, that in 1876 the value of feathers (£1,750) and *quillangos* ('Indian rugs', made by women; £1800) combined (£3,550) exceeds the value of wheat exported in the same year (£2,500). Despite the growth of the colony's population and economy, they remained vital to its success: in 1881, feathers accounted for 42.7 per cent of the colony's exports; wheat 43.4 per cent; *quillangos* 12.4 per cent; and cattle/dairy only 1.4 per cent.[4] Even after the Conquest of the Desert (and the massive expansion of wheat production), one ship reported in 1893 that feathers (Arg. $32,241) and guanaco rugs (Arg. $14,160) were the second and fourth most valuable exports, after wheat (Arg. $280,952) and wool (Arg. $18,434).[5] Trade mostly took the form of barter – much as we saw in the case of Katrülaf – whereby products such as flour, tea, rice and sugar were exchanged for feathers and *quillangos*, as well as horses, saddles, etc., that the Indigenous could supply. The sale onwards of 'Indian goods' to Buenos Aires enabled the Welsh to invest in stock and machinery, develop the community, attract new migrants, build towns, schools and good houses of stone equipped with parlours, pianos and the best china. Thus, Indigenous trade enabled the Welsh to fulfil, albeit briefly, their dream of a homeland which nurtured their culture and allowed them to live an autonomous, dignified life.

Welsh-Indigenous relations were also framed by gratitude for the knowledge and help offered by Indigenous people, and here the hierarchy of knowledge was momentarily upturned. Cacique Francisco realized soon after contacting them that the Welsh lacked the skills to navigate their new homeland and set about teaching them how to hunt. This activity became an essential source of food, a vital skill for travellers and a source of joy and palpable freedom for those (men) taking part. W. Casnodyn Rhys recalls:

> He taught the colonists how to manage the horses and cows, how to use the bolas and lasso and how to turn rawhide into whips, lassos, fetters, halters and saddles. They learned of him also the mysteries of the preparation of puchero [stew], asado [barbeque] … One day he … suggest[ed] that the young men should come along with him to hunt ostrich and guanacos. 'Come with me' said Francisco and I will lend you horses and dogs and will show you how to surround and entrap these wily and fleet creatures of the pampas. His offer was readily accepted … Francisco was … an expert huntsman and under his able and sympathetic tuition … they looked forward with joy to a day of hunting under the direction of Francisco. Mounted on his well-trained horses they would scour … for quarry … Exhilarated by the chase … the men returned … dispersing clouds and discontent as they rode in bringing their quarry behind them.[6]

These skills were not just useful, though. Learning how to hunt was thrilling and joyful, the comradeship palpable, and the admiration for Francisco heartfelt:

> the huntsman would regale them with tales of the chase, of the prowess of their leader Francisco, his marvellous dexterity with the bolas and lasso and the fleetness of his horses, the

cleverness of his dogs and his kindness and patience with the inexperienced gringos.[7]

Marcello Gavirati argues convincingly that Cacique Francisco's generosity was partly motivated by his desire to ensure that this new trading hub was a success.[8] Doubtless, Francisco (described as naturally shrewd and observant) also enjoyed being fêted too.

These experiences allowed the Welsh to flourish and make an emotional connection with the landscape that could be a life-affirming source of food and excitement – a key component of masculinized possessive sensibility. John Daniel Evans observed that 'for a Tehuelche, to be prevented from riding, with the freedom of the wind, the freedom of life, is fatal', and it seems that the Welsh, especially those forced previously to doff their caps to landowner and ironmaster, learned to feel this freedom too.[9] This is borne out by one rare opinion elicited by Captain Brent who asked settlers in 1895:

> 'Are you better off here or at home?' [one] working man answers 'yes, at home one had to keep working without cessation to earn daily wages … Out here I have to work hard at times, but then there are times when I need not work but can go two or three days hunting in the camp. Each man however poor has a horse and a good one.[10]

Thus, both economic and personal freedoms were enhanced by settler life: the site of freedom is the *camp* (from the Spanish 'campo' meaning 'countryside') or *paith* (Welsh for 'prairie'), and its key activities are hunting and travel.

The context of the 'desert', then, fostered more egalitarian relationships between Indigenous and Welsh, summed up by a phrase occurring often in the archive: 'brothers of the desert'. On journeys, the Welsh and Indigenous used the same tracks and both peoples helped one another, camping together at night and sharing fire and food (following Indigenous practice). We can see this sense of solidarity in the journey diaries of John Murray Thomas:

> Monday July 23rd [1877] – After Indians arrived in camp gave them mate and bread; packed up and started about

9½ am. Met Galatch [Gallech] in the upper Valley, gave him a letter for home. Followed the Indian track and camped behind first red rocks about ½ hour before sunset. Severo [guide] is there – catching hares with dogs.[11]

In this mode, Welsh-Indigenous relations are relatively egalitarian – indeed the Welsh express gratitude to Francisco, in particular, for his help and 'friendship'. They also understand that trade with the Indigenous is a vital economic opportunity and they take care to cultivate good trading relations which are mutually beneficial. This image of happy coexistence is what remains prominent in the story of friendship between the Welsh and Indigenous people, and continues today.

Yet there are also strong undercurrents of patronizing superiority in evidence, even from people who clearly liked 'The Indians'. Jonathan Ceredig Davies, for example, remembers fondly that he knew:

A chief named Gallech who had a son and two daughters almost as white as Europeans ... a homely good-natured old man ... [and] quite a favourite with the Welsh people ... Gallech had a son Kingel who could speak Welsh well ... My old Italian friend Mr Oneto ... sometimes asked Gallech and his family to his house to dine with him and whenever they came they were good humoured and behaved almost like civilized people, using knives, forks and spoons.[12]

For Davies, Indigenous people were always inferior and uncivilized, which in turn configured himself as superior and civilized. This civilization is colour-coded according to the whiteness of skin (it is racialized), and is observed in everyday habits like cutlery use which reflect a way of life (barbarized). He uses the yardstick of European civilization to order those sitting around the dinner table, yet he sees no trouble in making this ontological hierarchy a foundation for friendship. This is unsurprising as Davies is enmeshed within the global hierarchies that stratified human relationships in the nineteenth century, and condition racialization or barbarization today. This is not to condemn him, but rather to illustrate the ease with which racialized thinking infused even quite affectionate relationships for the settler.

What Gallech and Kingel thought is not known, but we should assume that they understood the sting of being patronized. Perhaps they had come to dinner because they were curious, maybe they were accustomed to such invitations from dignitaries in Patagones, or maybe it was a matter of courtesy and diplomacy, as with other encounters between Indigenous leaders.[13] Perhaps they attended the dinner in order to gain intelligence about the Welsh, the Argentines or other Indigenous groups (one suspects that this was Mr Oneto's motive, to hear about 'some wonderful lakes which were then unknown to white people, but have since been discovered'[14]). That is, their motives may well have been political rather than friendly, and it is certainly unclear whether they reciprocated the Welsh view that this sort of meeting was a matter of 'friendship'. It is true that Cacique Antonio and later Cacique Sayhueke refer to the Welsh in letters as 'my friend' but this usage is probably rhetorical or strategic. The phrase 'my friend' was often used when writing to Argentine officials – with whom they certainly were not friends. For example, in a letter from Juan Calfucurá (Kallfükura) to Major Francisco Iturra (12 September 1856) the Cacique addresses the military leader as 'Dear brother [*querido hermano*]' and signs off as 'your friend [*desde tu amigo*], Calfucurá.[15] 'Friend' was also used as a lever of political strategy, as we see here in this letter from Cacique Valentín Sayhueke to the comandante in Patagones, Julián Murga (30 April 1863):

> My dear friend [*mi querido amigo*] would you be so kind as to send me a saddle, complete with silver-plated stirrups, spurs, reins, all of silver. Friend: neither me nor the commanders [caciques] who have been in Patagones have asked anything from you and I hope that you will do me this favour, so that one day I may reciprocate. God keep you for many years, Valentín Saihueque.

This use of *amigo* implies not only obligation and the social economy of reciprocity so important in Indigenous social relations, but also a veiled threat if the account is not reckoned. Similarly, *amigo* can also be used as a term to facilitate diplomacy, and this was perhaps its intended use when directed at the Welsh colony. Thus, Sayhueke addresses Lewis Jones as 'my friend' when he asks the Welsh to intercede with the government on his behalf during the Conquest of the Desert.[16] Often, the use of 'friend' seems to indicate the presence and reassertion of an alliance. Cacique Antonio Modesto Inakayal (whose group Katrülaf joined, with Cacique Foyel's, when he was captured), for example, addressed the president of the republic, Bartolomé Mitre, as 'my most Respected President and friend [*mi respetado señor Presidente y amigo*]' and signs it 'your devoted friend [*su adicto amigo*]'.[17] This indicated an acknowledgement of Mitre's supremacy but also asserted the importance of Inakayal's loyalty, which in turn implies his role in high-level political networks and relationships of obligation and alliance – which work both ways. *Amigo* was thus a highly political term that oiled the wheels of Indigenous society.

Still, it is also clear that friendly relations between the Indigenous and Welsh were possible and not just cynical manoeuvres. As we saw in Katrülaf's testimony, the Welsh were generally regarded positively and favourably. The well-known book by George Musters, an Englishman who spent around a year travelling with several Indigenous groups, includes reports that Cacique Hinchel's people thought 'the honest Welsh colonists were much pleasanter and safer to deal with than "the Christians" [Argentines] of Rio Negro', and adds '[Cacique] Jackechan often expatiated on the liberality of the colonists and the goodness of their bread'.[18] The Welsh strategy of nurturing non-violent relations and adopting fair trading practices was genuinely appreciated, it seems, and (given how often it is mentioned by the Welsh) their bread was indeed relished.[19] For the Welsh, though, it was about more than bread and dinner-time conversations – this relationship went to the heart of their identity as righteous Christian settlers.

Righteous Christian love

As we have seen, nonconformist Christianity was extremely important to Y Wladfa and its people, and the desire to create a morally 'good' society was vital to the entire enterprise. This was for two key reasons: first, it was the heartfelt belief and teaching of Y Wladfa's ideologues and chimed with cultural norms in Wales; secondly, moral capital was a key commodity and essential to Welsh self-identity, as well as its status in the wider world, being used to rebuff those who sought to disparage them. A central moral concern, then, was the nature of the colonial society and the place of Indigenous people within the new settlement.

We recall that Michael D. Jones demanded that dealings be legal and fair, and the principle that: 'we cannot disregard the rights of the Indians ... giving them whatever is honest, whatever is just' was set out in the settlers' handbook.[20] How, though, should this be enacted in personal relationships? Let us return to the first meeting. Once bread was broken and a stilted conversation was had, Richard Jones Berwyn reported that:

> One of the main officers of the colony came forward and said 'Well I think that we have had enough of looking at the wild animals now. I think that it is time to draw an end to the preaching and bring these two along at once and put an end to them. They are just robbers and spies, and they came here just to spy on behalf of a swarm of other savages. Kill them both!'
>
> 'I will not do that', said one ...
>
> 'The face of this man' added another 'is not that of a savage killer. Let us show more courage and more of our Christian nature than rushing to take the life of an old man and his wife.'
>
> Everyone agreed with this ... In this way we laid the foundation of friendship.

This moment, which has a ring of truth to it despite being written twenty years after the event, was pivotal because it founded Y Wladfa on Christian fellowship (not violence) and thus established its moral legitimacy. This choice and the wider policy of peaceful engagement is praised by all the voices of the archive and is credited as the foundation of their security and prosperity. It is also lauded as morally right.[21]

W. Casnodyn Rhys tells us what happened next: 'a resolution was [then] adopted "to treat the Indians exactly as we treat each other and even to extend to them, as we do to children, the leniency due to ignorance"'.[22] This phrase tells us a lot about Welsh attitudes which use the (nuclear, patriarchal) family as a metaphor for virtuous yet hierarchal social institutions. The familial model for human relations makes sense of a seemingly paradoxical 'Indian policy' wherein equal human value is cherished ('treat the Indians exactly as we treat ourselves') at the same time that paternalistic hierarchies are affirmed ('extend to them, as we do to children'). The infantilizing motif is quite common. For example, Rhys referred to Indigenous people as 'children of the pampas', 'shy and simple children of nature' or noted that 'very much like children they would pick up articles such as spoons, knives etc.'[23] This elicited a paternalistic response: 'The colonists treated the natives consistently with ... wonderful patience and indulgence. Yet they deemed it wise to be firm and never to permit wrongdoing or tolerate any undue advantage being taken.'[24] This portrayal of the 'savage' as not 'violent' but childlike is a way of disarming and depoliticizing Indigenous agency, as well as empowering those who bestow generous patience.

We have seen that Caciques Antonio and Francisco are clearly astute diplomats, businessmen and politicians, so such portrayals are not designed to describe the Indigenous but to tell a story which celebrates Welsh moral righteousness. Righteousness entails obeying God's law which is enacted by implementing the principles of Christian love. Christian love should guide all personal relationships, especially those with the weak or inferior and takes the form of forgiveness, pity, mercy and charity.[25] The superiority of the righteous is not a position from which to abuse power, then, but rather a place from which to nurture the less fortunate and bring the ignorant to the knowledge of God's love. This love-infused hierarchy takes the (heteronormative) family as its model (God the Father), and its paternalism makes sense of the equal worth, yet unequal status, of Indigenous 'heathens' as well as children and women.

The parent-child motif, teleological thinking and the power of righteous love, work together to square the circle of equal-but-inferior. People are all equal because they are all God's children so, as Rhys explains: 'Those who believe in the fatherhood of God must, to be consistent, believe also in the brotherhood of man'. Yet he then immediately says: '[the Welsh] will regard the murder of a savage as heinous fratricide'.[26] This statement assumes Indigenous (savage) inferiority in the order-of-things, and claims virtue for the Welsh who love their brothers despite that inferiority. In this way, racial/civilizational hierarchies are made entirely compatible with equal human worth. Naturally, the Welsh are in an advanced position on the teleological trackway from barbarism to civilization, in terms of both (Welsh) spiritual faith and (European) capitalist modernity. Hidden behind the word 'savage', of course, are racialized ideas about a barbaric way of life, so 'savage' also casts an invisible ray of light on the ideal of 'Welsh civilization', a category that combines both geopolitical superiority and godliness.

The Welsh are not just comparing themselves to the Indigenous, though, but also to other 'civilized' countries. Here they pull out a moral yardstick and assert their own advanced position by measuring the British Empire ('England') and Argentina ('the Spanish') according to their treatment of the 'Indians', and find them morally wanting. For example, Rhys reflects that:

> The wrong done to the savage population ... is one of the blackest blots on modern civilization. I would not fasten this blot on any one nation it belongs to the white man whatever his tongue or flag. The Spaniard mal-treats him abominably but so does the north American whose name for Indians is 'varmient'. So also do the British in South Africa. Can we forget the clearing of Rhodesia and the remorseless hunting down of Lobengula?[27]

These other colonizing nations state a claim to civilization, then, but this is shallow because of their immoral actions – their colonies are stained with blood. Only the Welsh colony can claim to enact moral colonization as its relations with the 'native' are righteous. This leads Rhys to demand that Wales be celebrated within the pantheon of great colonizing nations. He declares:

> This decision [friendship, not violence] is worthy of record; let it be written in the history of colonization in letters of gold. Is there anywhere an instance of a nobler levelling up? Even the Quaker settlement of Pennsylvania did not surpass this.[28]

This device elevates the Welsh above the British, Argentine – and American – colonizers, for while they are not the richest or most powerful colonizing nation, they have proof that they are the most righteous: as I say elsewhere 'Wales is the moral giant'.[29]

The specificity of Welsh experience not only makes theirs the most moral colonial enterprise, according to Rhys, the colonial experience of the Welsh back home, is, paradoxically, what makes them the most perceptive of colonizers and ideally suited to the role. He invokes the Celtic/Welsh spirit and a sense of anti-colonial solidarity, explaining:

> In this decision [friendship, not violence] the true Celtic instinct was true to its history for … there is none that exceeds the Celtic people for swift and accurate perception of the true principles of liberty. The sense of common right and brotherhood amounts to a passion in the Celt that is abundantly proved by the modern history of Brittany, Wales and sad and suffering Ireland.[30]

He is calling up the anti-colonial impulse which drove Y Wladfa and marries this Welsh culture to Christian righteousness, linking both to their unique colonial enterprise. Moreover, he argues pragmatically that the policy of friendship leads to the most effective governance, saying: 'Would to God all settlements of white people pursued the same line of conduct towards aborigines! No other is sound, no other is politic, no other is legitimate for Christian People.'[31] This is not only because relations are smoother, but also because Welsh superiority is demonstrable and therefore more readily accepted by the colonized.

The mode of barbarization configured through righteous Christianity uses the hierarchal relationship between Indigenous and Welsh to demonstrate Welsh Christian virtue. Indigenous people are reduced to an infantilized caricature, turned into child-like objects, treated as if they are all the same. The Welsh are more advanced in a teleological sense, being just as modern as other colonizers by virtue of their European-ness. Yet they are different in one crucial and very Welsh way – they exercise power by behaving with righteous Christianity and thus create a morally good (and effective) colony based on friendship, not force. According to this logic, the proof of this excellence is that not only do the Welsh love the 'Indians', but the 'Indians' love them back.

There are several oft-told stories in the archive which aim to demonstrate Indigenous love of the Welsh. There is the story about how they had a special name for the Welsh – 'los Galensos' – which they used because they were not like the 'Spanish', (Argentines) who they called 'Christians' but with contempt because they 'rob and cheat'.[32] The Welsh, by contrast, 'are honoured with a distinctive name which is endearing to every Indian and that name is 'Galensos'.[33] There is also the remarkable interpretation of the killing of three Welshmen by 'Indians' (the Malcara incident) as a terrible accident of misrecognition rather than a massacre.[34] W. Casnodyn Rhys recounts the 'kindly feeling' demonstrated when Cacique Francisco was lying on his deathbed in Buenos Aires. He is reported to have said 'I am going to the heaven of the Galenses ... for the place where these good people go to must be a happy place!'[35] This is taken by several sources to be proof of their love for the Welsh. The Welsh registered this 'love' in small, everyday ways too. For example, like many memoirists, Jonathan Ceredig Davies mentions the Indigenous love for Welsh bread: 'The Welsh word *bara* (bread) ... became an ordinary word amongst the natives for a distance of one thousand miles or perhaps further and it was very seldom that I ever heard Indians making use of the Spanish word "pan"'.[36] All of these anecdotes point to the exceptionality of the Welsh as colonizers who are 'good'.

While they are affectionate and describe Indigenous people in a positive light, these misty-eyed reminiscences portray Indigenous people as merely harmless and child-like. In turn, this creates an image of the Welsh as indulgent parents who also exercise no harm and even draws the sting of violence from the murder of three Welshmen, explaining it away as mistaken identity. This story of the happy Patagonian family, ruled by paternalistic love and gilded with righteousness is enabled by a policy based on the exercise of Christian love. Yet the peace and kindness on display obscures the fundamental assumption that underpins the relationship: that Indigenous people are backward, simple and primitive souls, a kind of noble savage. This portrayal is important because it allows the Welsh to claim first place in the pantheon of civilized nations based on their moral conduct towards the Indigenous. Yet the purpose of this discourse is not to humanize and support the Indigenous in their struggle against dispossession; it does not acknowledge their political agency or appreciate the complexity of their culture – it does not help people like Katrülaf; rather, its role is to portray the Welsh as 'moral giants'.

This performance (and policy) of moral righteousness is deployed as a claim to power and elevated status. As such, it is aimed towards those who would disparage the Welsh, though I doubt that London or Buenos Aires were paying attention. The greater impact, perhaps, was felt among the Welsh public for whom Welsh conduct in Y Wladfa could be a source of pride, invigorating nationalist politics even today. It is telling that I have drawn often from the lectures and newspaper articles of W. Casnodyn Rhys delivered twenty or sometimes forty years later than the events he described, and in London or Swansea. These stories are meant to be consumed by a Welsh nation hungry for exotic stories well told of a phase in Y Wladfa's history that was now over. The tales of fear, faith and ingenuity can now safely be fixed, complete with cut-out 'Indians' and courageous Welshmen – women are very seldom mentioned. This barbarization using Christian righteousness had roots in the teachings and actions of real people, but was glossed and burnished to elicit pride. The memoirs, which so often stand in for an accurate account, must be put to one side and we need to turn to the diaries to discover something closer to the messy truth of the relationship, its tensions and antagonisms, and the colonial condition. For, more than anything, the discourse of Christian righteousness strips away the colonial reality of Welsh settling and the racial and civilizational hierarchies which enabled the 'elimination of the Native' in Patagonia.

Suspicion of savages

The most obvious hook on which the label of 'barbarism' is hung entails behaviours, whereby barbaric actions are understood to reflect a savage essence. Barbarization results when those in powerful positions identify their own civilization by naming the actions of others as 'barbaric'. Welsh accounts of Indigenous behaviour, though, always imply two hidden aspects: the agency of Indigenous people whose actions disrupt well-ordered Welsh society; and a disjuncture between two social worlds whose ways of knowing and being start from fundamentally different assumptions. It is the powerfulness (not passivity) and contemporaneity (not backwardness) of Indigenous agency which results in the sense of threat or unease. While these discomfiting feelings are usually skipped over in the memoirs, they become vivid when we analyse diary entries which chart social relations far more frankly and without the benefit of hindsight. This Welsh unease takes a number of forms which I shall explore in this section: fear, suspicion, miscomprehension and latent violence.

The Welsh began their relationship with the Indigenous as an imagined savage Other to be feared, even before they arrived. This is not surprising given that the rhetoric of imperial Britain portrayed Others as dangerous, rebellious and exotic.[37] More directly, many Welsh people knew settlers in the USA and received letters alluding to 'Indian Trouble', some of which were printed in the Welsh press.[38] The armed resistance offered by Native Americans in the USA led some prospective American settlers, even ordinary, chapel-going folk, to normalize and embrace anti-'Indian' violence. The colonizing society in New York state, for example, established a 'military company [who] were learning to handle arms so they would be ready to keep the Patagonian Indians in check'.[39] More generally, Indigenous people are spoken of in the same breath as wild animals, solidifying their barbarism. Edwyn Roberts, for example writes of the potential settlement as 'possessed by Indians and where wild beasts lie', while his relatives fear for him in 'the land of cruel Indians and fierce beasts'.[40]

Once in Patagonia, they had met 'tame Others' who drove the cattle but feared the unknown 'wild Indian' of the wide-open spaces. W. Casnodyn Rhys recalls camping out that first night on their trek from New Bay to the Chubut Valley. They felt: 'in real peril from savage beast and still more savage man', and were awakened by 'a strange yelping' which they thought was a dog 'betraying the proximity of Indians', though it was a prairie fox.[41] Next morning:

in the distance was something like the smoke of an extensive crescent of fire. The guide, a Missouri Welshman [Edwyn Roberts] was in fear. His interpretation of the phenomenon was that the Indians were setting the prairie on fire in front of them with a view to enveloping them in flames [it turned out to be a dust storm].[42]

One suspects that Edwyn Roberts regarded himself as an expert on 'Indians' and it was also he who led and drilled the militia in Rawson. Following the arrival of Francisco and the commencement of trade such fears were largely allayed. However, 'fear of the Indian' did not simply transform into the 'brothers of the desert' discourse, as the memoirs often suggest, but persisted as suspicion. The diaries suggest that the undercurrent to peaceable relations was a cautious, uneasy co-existence, and suspicion framed by racial/civilizational hierarchies. We have already encountered the diary of John Murray Thomas which charted a friendly encounter whilst on a desert journey. His journal also reveals, though, the tension behind such encounters:

> Tuesday August 7th – began our march about 10am went by SWly some 9 miles, in the distance saw some horses ... we were seen by the Indians... had a *parlamento* [conversation] and went with them to the tents. They turned out to be Galatch's [Gallech] men they were only 9 men and we saw only 5 lances, the others were women and children. They put up another tent for us but we slept in our own. They were all very kind not too forward, we gave them some yerba, biscuit and rice ... Went to bed and slept without being troubled with the natives. They behaved better than they generally do in Chupat [Chubut].[43]

This notation speaks of caution, mistrust (though not distrust) and a veiled sense of irritation. Even though Gallech's people were 'very kind', the Welsh remained aloof and did not sleep in their tent, a decision that speaks not of friendship but toleration (at a distance). While it suggests the exercise of patience, one can almost hear the gritted teeth in this diary entry, rather than Christian love. Whether Gallech's people thought their response rude is not known. A similar sense of tense humouring accompanies Rhys's observation that: 'the Indians' had 'thievish propensities' when they came to visit people's houses. He explains that: 'You would treat the whole thing in the light of a joke and create a little merriment and would guard against the least sign of a vindictive spirit.'[44] These observations show the presence of a gap in behaviours and expectations between the two social worlds but also the certainty that Welsh behaviour was superior. The misunderstanding of lifeways and habits was viewed through the lens of nineteenth-century racial and civilizational hierarchies to interpret difference as barbarity.

We also see miscomprehension at work in accounts of possible robberies. Some were genuine, such as that reported by Abraham Matthews when sixty horses were rounded up and taken by 'a group of spiteful Indians' in 1871.[45] Far more common were 'misunderstandings' concerning horses and cattle. W. Casnodyn Rhys recalls an incident in which Welsh horses were 'mixed up' with others belonging to Cacique Gallech's group and taken along by an advanced party. The Welsh were sure that this was a robbery but Gallech denied it: '"Certainly" said he "my people have no idea of stealing your horses" insisting that the horses had got mixed.'[46] The argument became 'somewhat bitter' and a shot was fired by mistake during the confrontation, and yet a tense goodwill was eventually restored. These cultural dissonances created suspicion and unease. They were read through the logics and experiences of nineteenth-century settler colonialism which barbarized Indigenous people and assumed their natural proclivity for stealing, aggression and duplicity.

It was the suspicion of a 'savage' and potentially aggressive Other that encouraged the purchase of guns and introduction of latent violence. Thus, and despite being a devout young man, T. G. Pritchard brought thirty Snider rifles from Liverpool to sell to settlers when he migrated to Y Wladfa in 1875. His diary gives us a unique insight into the colony as it was beginning to expand and the place of Indigenous people within it. One entry reads:

> [Sunday, 2 January 1876] Lovely day. After a wash and eating bread and butter for breakfast we called at A. Matthews' house, and had a glass of milk from the maidservant. We also called with Aaron Jenkins. We talked to him about his brother who is in Ohio … Mrs Jones didn't speak Welsh but she gave us a frank account of the character of the Old Settlers in English. She also showed us Indian paint in different colours and also strong Indian thread. It was agreeable to hear Edwyn CR [Roberts] recite *Myn Gafr*. They had two guanacos … that would approach white men and kiss them but they did not favour Indians and spat in their faces … Mrs Jones

had an Indian 13 years old called Gawell as a servant, who
was quick in his perceptions and Mrs Jones said he was perfectly honest. She said that the Indians are deceitful and envi-
ous, and that the Welsh get them drunk and swindle them.[47]

This diary extract presents a window onto life in the settlement: the
productivity of farms; the family connections to Welsh Americans;
the integration of Indian goods within households; the enduring presence of Welsh traditional culture. It also demonstrates the presence of
casual racism as an everyday mode of thinking and relating: it stereotypes 'Indians' as deceitful; suggests that Argentine guanacos reject
Indigenous people and prefer the 'civilized' colonists; and although
praising Gawell, she implies that his honesty and intelligence are the
exception to the rule. (True, she also says that some Welsh are manip-
ulative swindlers, and we will return to this feature shortly.) A few
weeks later, though, Pritchard's entries convey not only tension, but
also stereotyping, othering and dehumanization of 'Indians':

[Friday, 18 February] a *gaucho* told me that the Indians intend to come down unexpectedly in the night to destroy all
the souls here ... because so many settlers arrive and possess
[*meddianu*] their hunting lands.[48]

[Tuesday, 28 February] Just come back from talking about
the Indians. Fear what is in their hearts.

[8 March] Sells four guns to Edwyn Roberts.[49]

[Monday, 8 April] Powell and me are writing ... Tonight two
Indians were killed, another Indian called Sam Slick fled having stolen two horses belonging to I. Lloyd Jones and A. Matthews. Terrible row in town, Cognac reigns.[50]

These entries are redolent of suspicious undercurrents, fuelled by a
fear of savagery, the presence of guns and the deep anxiety of being
a settler on land that belongs to others. Indigenous people are caricatured here as vicious and deceptive killers, robbers, drunkards and
dead items. We do not know who the 'Indians' were, nor their names,

why they were killed or by whom, but this diary entry certainly does not reflect relations based on comradeship or Christian love.

As suggested earlier, the 'savagery' mode of barbarization focuses on Indigenous behaviour and the reactions of Welsh settlers in response. We have seen those reactions manifested as fear, suspicion, miscomprehension and violence. The latter took the form of both casual racism and the purchase and ownership of guns whose purpose was to intimidate (at the very least) Indigenous people in their homeland. These relationships took place within a geopolitical hierarchy which celebrated European-ness as civilization and regarded Indigenous people and their behaviour as primitive and barbaric. Yet we cannot simply apply this binary and observe that the hierarchy oppresses – things are more complicated than that. Pritchard's own diary goes on to observe much calmer arrivals and departures of Indigenous traders, and his own notations on the Bible readings in Sunday school. Life, as ever, was complicated, and Indigenous-Welsh relations were not just configured through one mode, but rather each coexisted – comradeship, paternalism and suspicion. While dominant understandings of civilization and barbarism, often configured through racialized as well as barbarized prejudice, provided the meta-script for settler colonialism, lived reality was far more complex.

One additional layer of complexity was, of course, that while the Welsh were indeed acting as colonizers, they remained colonized in their relationship to England. Although the English were barely active at all in the Patagonian milieu, their shadow lingered to question the 'civilization' of the Welsh. We have already seen that this backward glance over the shoulder to relationships back home shaped the Welsh claim to elevated status based on the Christian righteousness of their colony. An important fly in that ointment, though, was the question of alcohol.

We have already noted in T. G. Pritchard's diary that liquor was a contentious issue. While the Welsh were often teetotal (Pritchard tells us that he was reading a classic temperance novel *Three years in a Mantrap* by S. S. Arthur), liquor was in high demand as an item of trade for Indigenous people.[51] Pritchard deplored the sale of it in his diary, calling its trade 'shameful'. He even reported that it was the main preacher Abraham Matthews who began the trade, saying: 'such is the greed of others for profit!'[52] The father figure of Y Wladfa,

Michael D. Jones was very much against its sale too. He wrote to Thomas Benbow Phillips, who opened a highly successful grocery warehouse, saying: 'allow me to pray that you do not take liquor to the Indians. The colonists have done so and it is without doubt profitable. But it will end up damaging the colony. The Indians should be well treated and guided on the virtuous path.'[53] However, Jones was ensconced in Bala and only came to Y Wladfa once in 1882: he could retain his high principles and virtues at a distance. For those caught up in the situation it was more difficult. Abraham Matthews himself explains: 'They had become accustomed by the Spanish to having alcoholic drink and ... one of the first things that they asked for was Cognac or Brandi.'[54] He tells us that there was nothing in the settlement except three bottles of gin that had been given to the secretary (Lewis Jones) by the surveyor, plus a little medicinal brandy. He explains the situation:

> Many blame the settlers for starting to give liquor to them but at the beginning, especially the first time they came down, it was very difficult to refuse them anything they asked for, as we were rather afraid and quite undefended, and very concerned to keep them as friends.[55]

Matthews gave them the gin and, after they had shared it around and enjoyed themselves, the Cacique – Chiquichano – gave him 'a very lovely mare'. That was all the liquor they could give that year as there was no more in the colony, but 'when [the Welsh] saw how desperate they were for liquor, and the great bargains that they offered for it some made a big effort to get a large quantity [swm pur fawr] ready for next season'.[56] This turned out to be, he says, 'a great source of grief' for the Indian trade.

Trading liquor went against the ideal Welsh morality and the virtuous image of righteous living that underpinned their claim to moral supremacy and high standing in the pantheon of nations. It went against the Temperance movement, so powerful in late nineteenth-century Wales, and had an evidently corrupting influence on the 'children of the desert' who the Welsh were supposed to protect and support as their betters, rather than sowing corruption and degradation. Moreover, its trade had a degenerating effect not just on Indigenous people who became excessively drunk but also on the Welsh who, in the words of Mrs Jones 'get them drunk and swindle them'. The diaries are dangerous, in a way, because they unsettle the impression of universal Welsh moral goodness and a purely righteous society. Perhaps this is why Pritchard's diary has gone missing, though a copy had fortuitously been made.

There is a lot at stake for the Welsh reputation – and that of families and descendants who still live there – in exposing these very human decisions, and their unravelling repercussions, made with good intentions. That first exchange of gin for a horse was undertaken in a milieu shaped by all the aspects discussed here: fear, suspicion, miscomprehension and latent violence. Recognizing this requires that we discard the racial and civilizational hierarchies which paint the colonizer as superior and instead recognize both Welsh vulnerability and Indigenous powerfulness and the personhood of both. The assertion of white, European domination and Indigenous subjugation a few years afterwards, especially after the Conquest of the Desert, entailed a turn to the geopolitical 'natural order of things' and had devastating consequences for Indigenous communities. But this assertion of dominant modes masks what were far more complex interactions in which Welsh subordination at home was played out on the plains of Patagonia. The anxieties and opportunities of being both colonizer and colonized continue, thus, to shape Y Wladfa as an emblem of Welshness.

The 'myth of friendship' and the Conquest of the Desert

The myth of friendship was tested during the Conquest of the Desert. It was President Roca who drove the decisive phase of the Conquest of the Desert, a man who would later become a 'great friend' to the Welsh colony. He describes its aims in his presidential address to congress in 1881: 'to ensure the conquest of the Pampas territories, allowing their colonization and to expand the Chubut colony into the fertile Andean valleys', which entailed an 'expedition against the only two remaining great tribes … those of Shaihueque [Sayhueke] and Renquecura [Namuncura]'.[57]

In response to the resulting wave of repression, Sayhueke appealed to the Welsh, in the name of friendship, to intervene on behalf of the Native Government (a coalition of Indigenous people formed to resist the Conquest of the Desert). Sayhueke's letter tells of: 'the terrible attack made upon me … when three armies set upon my bands, killing without warning a large number of my people. They … stole into our living tents, as if I was an enemy and a murderer.'[58] He explains his situation:

> I have serious agreement with the government since many years and therefore I cannot fight … I am not unmanly my friend … I am not a criminal … not a stranger from another land but born and raised on the land and an Argentinian faithful to the Government.

Sayhueke thus affirmed his status as a leader, a man and a citizen of Argentina, emphasizing simultaneously the righteousness of his conduct and illegitimacy of the Argentine offensive. He then asks for help:

> I now find myself ruined and sacrificed – my lands, which my father and God left me, stolen from me, as well as all of my animals … and a numberless mass of women, children and old people. Because of this, friend, I ask you to place my complaints in full … before the Government … I therefore beg you to intercede on my behalf with the authorities to protect the peace and tranquillity of my people, to return to us our animals and all our silver possessions, but mainly my lands.[59]

The Welsh were genuinely concerned about these events. Everywhere in the archive they lament the injustice and violence of this era. For example, W. Casnodyn Rhys calls it: 'a cruel and indiscriminate slaughter in which many old Indian friends of Chubut fell.'[60] Jonathan Ceredig Davies says 'my sympathies were on the side of the poor Indians; and I think most Welshmen in the colony felt as I did.'[61] This view was echoed by Captain Brent of the Amethyst who noted in 1885: 'the Welshmen regret all that has been done towards [Indigenous] extermination and do not forget the kindness the Tehuelchis showed them in their distress.'[62]

The Welsh heeded Sayhueke's request, writing a letter to General Winter (Vinnter) who led the army in the region:

> We, the inhabitants of Chubut, implore … on behalf of the natives known to us in this region. As ones who are long acquainted with the native people, we … hope that you can show them every compassion and assistance that are consistent with your obligations. On our part … we have received much kindness by the hands of these natives and … the Indians have been a source of protection and assistance to us. We believe that small native communities in the region would be a continual assistance to push new settlements into the interior as has been their trade to us here. We hope … you will see possible … to leave our old native neighbours in their homes while they remain as peaceful and harmless as has been their custom (signed by all the colonists 20 July 1883).[63]

They were caught in an in-between situation: sympathetic to the colonized yet promoting colonization. On the one hand they are supportive of the Indigenous cause and have good pragmatic reasons to take this stance: despite a few disputes, their relationship has been peaceable – and profitable. Moreover, they disliked the Argentine authorities and had a very low opinion of the army. On the other hand, the letter does not condemn settlement and the expansion of state sovereignty – indeed it embraces it – and its tone is paternalistic, steeped in the assurance of their own 'civilization' and always portraying Indigenous people as a race apart, and below. However, whatever the reasoning and calculation, their letter was not acknowledged and did not alter the military's course: they would smash onwards regardless.

Conclusion

The centrality of the 'myth of friendship' gets at the heart of Y Wladfa's significance as a heroic endeavour and iconic cultural moment. The aim of this chapter has not been to condemn the Welsh, then, but rather to show how the logics associated with possession (liberal law, capitalism and nonconformism) and barbarization (civilizational norms, Eurocentrism and suspicion of 'Others') shape social relations and actions in the Chubut Valley. In the end they were like everyone else – unpredictable, kind, prejudiced, generous, fearful and caught in situations which offered little option. Indeed, the archive shows that relationships with Indigenous people were far more ambivalent than the myth of friendship suggests, though it is built on some truth. The comradeship of struggle and joy in the desert was real, as was appreciation for Indigenous skills and knowledge, though tempered by the still dominant understandings of civilization and European supremacy. The Christian impulses of mercy, kindness, forgiveness and love were genuinely felt, though these infantilized Indigenous people. The 'righteousness' of the colony, meanwhile, legitimized their presence as settlers, generated cultural pride and announced their superiority to other colonizers. The third relationship mode – suspicion of the savage – reflected the lived realities of life in a precarious settlement where everyday casual racism merged with portrayals of Indigenous barbarism.

Yet, it seems that some friendships were sincere, and it is this spirit of human affection and fellow feeling, despite differences of culture, worldview and status, which we might harness moving forwards when building decolonial relationships today. The best example is John Daniel Evans's sincere distress at finding a friend, wretched and imprisoned, at Valcheta in June 1888. On his way to buy animals in Patagones, Evans passed the internment camp where people were corralled, sorted and distributed as workers or soldiers. Here they were treated as mere items on a list, while two-thirds of the 600 people at Valcheta – the old, children, women – were referred to as an agglomerated rabble: *la chusma*.[64] (We might pause here to remember Katrülaf, his mother and father, brothers and sisters and cousins – were they in this despised 'rabble'?) Evans recalls that, as he was riding past he heard someone calling to him '*bara bara*' (bread, bread):

> At first I didn't recognise him but … I saw him running alongside the barbed-wire fence … it was my childhood friend, my BROTHER OF THE DESERT, with whom I had shared so much bread. This situation filled my heart with an-

guish and pain, I felt helpless, I felt that I could do nothing to alleviate his hunger, his lack of freedom, his exile, his eternal banishment after being the owner and master of the vast lands of Patagonia, to be confined in this little plot.[65]

Evans bribed a guard to help his friend but the guard broke his word. He recalls: 'later, I returned for him with enough money to get him out of there whatever the cost, to bring him home, but he couldn't wait for me, he died of sorrow a little time after I passed by Valcheta'.[66]

This heart-rending story of two friends on either side of a barbed wire fence – one free and one imprisoned – is a graphic portrayal of how settler colonialism depends, ultimately, on enacting an unbreachable binary between colonized and colonizer. In Patagonia, the largely peaceable early period of fluid social relations was smashed and reordered by the state, splitting the population into two categories: desirable, 'civilized' white settler and despisable, 'barbarized' Indian – one to make live, one to let die. A future for the Welsh colonists meant assimilation, which required them to accept their place in this binary and embrace their role as settlers and citizens within the Argentine national project. Yet this was not easy, and their ambivalent response to the drive for assimilation is the topic of the next chapter.

Notes

1   Richard Jones Berwyn, 'Gyda'r Gwladvawrwyr yn Nyfryn y Camwy, Patagonia: Gweled Brodorion Anwar', *Cyfaill yr Aelwyd*, VII/2, Tachwedd (1886), pp. 40–2. See Lucy Taylor, 'Welsh-Indigenous Relationships in Nineteenth Century Patagonia: "Friendship" and the Coloniality of Power', *Journal of Latin American Studies*, 49 (2017), 143–68, 148–50.

2   See, for example, David Preston, *The Texture of Contact: European and Indian Settler Communities on the Frontiers of Iroquoia, 1667–1783* (Indiana: University of Nebraska Press, 2009); Colin Calloway, *White People, Indians and Highlanders: Tribal Peoples and Colonial Encounters in Scotland and America* (Oxford: Oxford University Press, 2008).

3   For example, Jonathan Ceredig Davies, handwritten notes for 'Patagonia: a Description of the Country' (NLW MS 8545-8B, book 2, n.d. *c*.1890), 326.

4   Marcelo Gavirati, 'El Contacto entre Galeses, Pampas y Tehuelches: la Conformación de un Modelo de Convivencia Pacífica en la Patagonia Central (1865–1885)' (Universidad del Centro de la Provincia de Buenos Aires, Doctorado Interuniversitario en Historia, 2012), 428, 434.

5 Report by Captain W. M. Lang of Her Majesty's ship *Sirius*, 11 April 1893', *Papurau'r Llywodraeth 1867–1898*, NLW 20903 D.

6 W. Casnodyn Rhys, 'Book Manuscript', in 'Collection of writings by W Casnodyn Rhys', NLW MS 16654C (n.d.), p. 47.

7 Casnodyn Rhys, 'Book Manuscript', p. 48.

8 Gavirati, 'Contacto entre Galeses', 241–7.

8 Richard Ellis, *Diary 1865–1916*, NLW Facs 1011.

9 Clery A. Evans (ed.), *John Daniel Evans, 'El Molinero: una Historia entre Galeses y la Colonia 16 de Octubre* (Esquel: Grafica Alfa, 1994), p. 24.

10 Papurau'r Llywodraeth 1867–98, 'Extracts from Captain Brent's Report on the Welsh Colony at Chupat 1895', NLW 20903 D, p. 2.

11 John Murray Thomas, 'Dyddiadur Taith John Murray Thomas i'r Andes', Facs 396 in NLW Facs 3960404 (1877); no page numbers.

12 Davies, handwritten notes, 273–5.

13 Examples of this practice abound in George Musters, *At Home with the Patagonians* (1871; Stroud: Nonsuch, 2005).

14 Davies, 'handwritten notes', 277–8.

15 Jorge Pávez Ojeda, *Cartas Mapuches Siglo XIX* (Santiago: CoLibris/Ocho Libros, 2008), pp. 285–6.

16 Lewis Jones, *Y Wladva Gymreig yn Ne Amerig* (Caernarfon: W. Gwenlyn Evans, 1898), p. 116.

17 Pávez Ojeda, *Cartas Mapuches*, pp. 412–13.

18 Musters, *At Home with the Patagonians*, p. 97.

19 For example, Davies, handwritten notes, 268.

20 Hugh Hughes 'Cadfan', *Llawlyfr y Wladychfa Gymreig* (Llynlleifiad: Lewis Jones, 1862), p. 19.

21 See also my analysis of a famous novel where the same theme emerges from the 'first encounter' between two mothers which includes the sharing of bread – and a baby. Lucy Taylor, 'The Welsh Way of Colonization in Patagonia: The International Politics of Moral Superiority', *Journal of Imperial and Commonwealth History*, 47/6 (2019), 1069–99, 1081–2.

22 W. Casnodyn Rhys, 'Fifteen years in Patagonia' (lecture), NLW MS 1653B, p. 24. For a closer analysis, see Taylor 'Welsh-Indigenous Relationships', 153.

23 Rhys, 'Fifteen years in Patagonia', p. 30; W. Casnodyn Rhys, 'Borderland of Civilization: a Lecture given at the Free Library, Swansea', Articles, NLW MS 20549E (1902), p. 4; W. Casnodyn Rhys, Notes for a Book, 'Chapter 6 John Bull Looks In', NLW 16654C (n.d.), p. 56.

24 Rhys, 'Notes for a Book', p. 57.

25 Taylor, 'Welsh Way of Colonization', 1078–9.

26 Rhys, 'Fifteen years in Patagonia', p. 26.

27 Rhys, 'Articles', p. 27.

28 Rhys, 'Fifteen Years in Patagonia', p. 24.

29 Taylor, 'Welsh Way of Colonization', 1087. I develop the comparison to Britain and Argentina here.

30 Rhys, 'Fifteen years in Patagonia', p. 26.
31 Rhys, 'Fifteen years in Patagonia', p. 26.
32 William Phillips, 'Darlith "Fifteen years in Patagonia"', NLW MS1653B (1902), pp. 1–69, 27–8.
33 Rhys, 'Fifteen Years in Patagonia', pp. 27–8, discussed in Taylor, 'Welsh Way of Colonization', 1088.
34 Discussed at length in Taylor, 'Welsh Way of Colonization', 1089–91.
35 Rhys, 'Fifteen Years in Patagonia', pp. 38–9.
36 Davies, handwritten notes, 112–13.
37 Anne McClintock, *Imperial Leather: Race, Gender and Sexuality in the Colonial Contest* (London: Routledge, 1995).
38 William D. Jones, '"Going into Print": Published Immigrant Letters, Webs of Personal Relations, and the Emergence of the Welsh Public Sphere', in Bruce Elliott, David Gerber and Suzanne Sinke (eds), *Letters across Borders: The Epistolary Practices of International Migrants* (Basingstoke: Palgrave Macmillan, 2006), pp. 175–99.
39 Roberts, *Y Wladfa Gymreig*, p. 20.
40 Roberts, *Y Wladfa Gymreig*, pp. 28, 26.
41 W. Casnodyn Rhys, 'Making a New Country II', NLW MS 20549E (*c.*1919–20), p. 2.
42 Rhys, 'Making a New Country', pp. 2–3. I have recounted similar stories elsewhere: Taylor, 'Welsh-Indigenous Relationships', 148–9; Lucy Taylor, 'Global Perspectives on Welsh Patagonia: The Complexities of being both Colonizer and Colonized', *Journal of Global History*, 13 (2018), 446–68, 462.
43 Thomas, 'Dyddiadur Taith', no page numbers.
44 Rhys, 'Borderland of Civilization', p. 10. For details, see Taylor, 'Welsh-Indigenous Relationships', 153.
45 Abraham Matthews, *Hanes y Wladfa Gymreig yn Patagonia* (Aberdâr: Mills ac Evans, 1894), p. 57.
46 Casnodyn Rhys, 'Book Manuscript', p. 57.
47 T. G. Pritchard, 'Hanes fy Nhaith o Pittsburgh Pa i Patagonia' [copy – original lost], Museo Regional Gaiman (1875). See also, Taylor, 'Welsh Way of Colonization', 1082–3.
48 Pritchard, 'Hanes Fy Nhaith', p. 27.
49 Pritchard, 'Hanes Fy Nhaith', p. 30.
50 Pritchard, 'Hanes Fy Nhaith', p. 41.
51 Pritchard, 'Hanes Fy Nhaith', p. 38.
52 Pritchard, 'Hanes Fy Nhaith', p. 25.
53 Quoted in Gavirati, 'Contacto entre Galeses', 285.
54 Matthews, *Hanes y Wladfa*, p. 31.
55 Matthews, *Hanes y Wladfa*, p. 31.
56 Matthews, *Hanes y Wladfa*, pp. 31–2.
57 Mensajes Presidenciales, Dirección Servicios Legislativos, Biblioteca Nacional del Congreso, 'Dossier Legislativo, Mensajes Presidenciales', III/79 (2015),

20, *https://bcn.gob.ar/uploads/adjuntos/DOSSIER-legislativo-A3N79-Mensa jes-presidenciales-Roca.pdf* (accessed 24 August 2022).

58 Jones, *Y Wladva Gymreig*, pp. 1116–18; translated extracts taken from a full transcription in Glyn Williams, 'Welsh Settlers and Native Americans in Patagonia', *Journal of Latin American Studies*, 11/1 (1979), 41–66, 58–9.

59 Williams, 'Welsh Settlers and Native Americans', 59.

60 W. Casnodyn Rhys, 'Collection of writings by W. Casnodyn Rhys', NLW MS 16654C; M 976 (*c*.1890).

61 For example, Davies, handwritten notes, 255.

62 Captain Brent, 'Report on the Welsh Colony at Chupat. "Amethyst" at Monte Video, March 26 1885', Papurau'r Llywodraeth 1867–98 from the library of Henry Tobit Evans, NLW 20903 D.

63 Jones, *Y Wladva Gymreig*, p. 115; extracts from Williams, 'Welsh Settlers and Native Americans', 60.

64 Pilar Pérez, 'Futuros y Fuentes: las Listas de Indígenas Presos en el Campo de Concentración de Valcheta, Rio Negro (1887)', *Nuevo Mundo, Mundos Nuevos* (2015), *https://journals.openedition.org/nuevomundo/68751* (accessed 23 August 2022), p. 9.

65 Evans, *John Daniel Evans*, p. 93; capitals in original.

66 Evans, *John Daniel Evans*, p. 93.

CHAPTER SIX

Y Wladfa and Assimilation

This chapter continues our broadly chronological journey through the Welsh Patagonian experience by focusing on the period of sustained assimilation, from the mid-1870s onwards. Up until that point the Welsh had acted with relative autonomy in Y Wladfa and Indigenous groups also sustained a high level of freedom and self-governance. However, from 1875 the Chubut Valley became drawn into the orbit of the state: officials started to arrive and the military began its Conquest of the Desert, crossing the Rio Negro into southern Patagonia in 1879.[1] Both territorial conquest and political subordination to the Argentine state culminated in the appointment of Colonel Fontana as governor of the whole region in 1885. While many more expeditions and Indigenous conflicts ensued, this symbolically 'closed the frontier' in the national imaginary: Patagonia was Argentine.

The story of Welsh assimilation within Argentina is one of inevitable incorporation, but riven too with crosscurrents of resistance, given their desire for political autonomy, their awkward fit within the civilization/barbarism binary and their position in the British Empire. As a result, the chapter is divided into three sections which focus on three relationships: the Welsh and the Argentine state; the Welsh and the Indigenous after the Conquest of the Desert; and the Welsh and Britishness. Through a combination of de facto power and ideological stubbornness, these tensions were sustained right up until 1899 but eventually the dream of an autonomous Wladfa was swamped by assimilation. Processes of assimilation were thus at work not only in Wales but also in Argentina. While many Welsh people resisted assimilation in both empire-building Britain and nation-building Argentina, many also sought the benefits that association with aggrandizing state projects could offer, paying for their inclusion by giving up autonomy.

Assimilation as nation-building: the Argentine state

The project to establish Argentina as a nation began with the declaration of independence from Spain in 1816 but (following a period of turmoil) a new generation of politicians took power mid-century to build a liberal state, implementing a new constitution in 1853. This set out a federal system, steeped in the following principles: disestablishment of the Catholic church; (limited, male-only) elections; separation of powers; rule of law; individual rights; and free trade.[2] However, while Buenos Aires had all the trappings of a liberal polity, the rest of the country was regarded as a land of still-barbaric people and practices: the 'brutish' landowners with their fiefdoms; the 'idle' rural peasants (*gauchos*) of mixed heritage; the Afro-Argentines whose presence 'stained' the country's history; and the Indigenous who embodied 'primitive savagery'. This urban/rural, civilization/barbarism binary shaped (and perhaps remains) the blueprint for the nation and the pivot point for state policy.[3]

State-led assimilation, aimed to tackle this 'barbarism', focused on three planes: the demarcation of Argentine boundaries and possession of its resources; the extension of liberal citizenship to include the whole population; the embrace of Eurocentric capitalist modernity. Key to this was the possession of Indigenous land and the planting of European settlers. The 1853 constitution enshrined immigration as a social good in its preamble, offering guarantees 'to all men of the world who wish to dwell on Argentine soil' and exhorting governments to promote (explicitly) European immigration.[4] Many migrants came as part of the general exodus of the European poor to the Americas and by 1869, 13 per cent of the population was foreign born. Immigration accelerated after the 1876 Avellaneda Law was passed which created immigration offices in European cities and provided subsidized travel: this encouraged a huge 5.9 million migrants to seek their fortune in Argentina between 1870 and 1914, 80 per cent of whom were Spanish or Italian.[5] By 1893 around 26 per cent of the Argentine population were foreign born, rising to 30 per cent in 1914.[6]

Nation-building also entailed enacting a certain racialized vision of this, as yet, soft-shelled polity within which everyone should assimilate, including both original and new settlers. The geopolitics of culture identified Europeanness as a mark of racial and civilizational superiority, and for ideologue Juan Alberdi, 'the European immigrant brings to Argentina in his knapsack the living matter of industrial civilization, the working practices and the practical education grounded in his experience'.[7] Thus, what was *terra nullius* could be filled, impregnating the land (and nation) with the sensibility of European modernity and capitalist relations, wresting it not only militarily and legally but also ontologically from the 'savage Indian'.

It was this dream of a Europeanized Argentina which the Welsh were supposed to help create – and uphold. They were to act as educators and agents of European civilization: as 'planters' they were to bring the Patagonian territory within the orbit of the Argentine state; as farmers they were to assimilate the land into capitalist production; as white Europeans, they were to culturally educate the 'blackened' and barbarized people by example, teaching them the habits of the new state; and as carriers of European culture they were to boost Argentina's global standing in the Eurocentric world. To do so, they were expected to assimilate and in return would receive land, animals, food supplies and settlement goods – and citizenship. However, the Welsh did not desire inclusion but to create a new and independent homeland. Right from the start, then, they challenged Argentina's assimilationist project, creating significant political tensions.

This clash was evident right from the start. The senate debate of 1863 which discussed the establishment of a Welsh colony provides a valuable insight into Argentine concerns.[8] The proposal was led by Minister for the Interior Guillermo Rawson who argued, predictably, that the Welsh colony would 'contribute to the pacification of those regions, the security of our frontier, and expanding the civilized population of the republic'.[9] He added that it would encourage other migrants to the region, noting: 'the population of the desert is of interest to the public purse, whatever their nationality'.[10] Opposition to the proposal, though, was led by Senator Frías who expressed open prejudice: 'This country of Wales is rather exceptional in England [*sic*].

Their agriculture ... is a century behind and they have their own dialect and strange customs.'[11] He saw them as predatory protestants 'driven by the desire to capture the will of the Indigenous in order to dominate the territory that they occupy' and trojan horses for British intervention, noting that 'protection' of protestant missionaries led to British colonization of what became Honduras, Belize and Caribbean Nicaragua.[12] Other senators agreed. Madriaga argued: 'we are opening the doors of the fortress to an enemy who besieges us', while Alsina (who would become president in 1868 until 1874) said: 'There is the fact of the Islas Malvinas ... one cannot ignore such a notorious spirit as that of the British Government.'[13] Frías also noted the Welsh resistance to assimilation in Britain: 'the people are irascible and independent-minded ... for two centuries they remained without submitting to the general regime and attempted to create a sort of independent island in the country where they are situated'.[14] Senator Fragueiro agreed: 'I expect that all men [sic] who come to our country will harmonize their interests with ours. But ... when I see that this colony will just be English people I cannot give my vote to this project.' The confusion between Welshness and Englishness is evident here (in Spanish, inglés is used for both English and British). Only Senator Villafane seemed to grasp their home situation: 'It is well known that the country of Wales is against the rest of England [sic], that is, its institutions, [there is a] certain antagonism that produces unrest in that population, and it is in order to extract itself from these drawbacks that it is so ready to emigrate and come here' so they might 'rather be good allies than enemies of our nationality.'[15] Rawson agreed: 'far from allying themselves with their country of origin' he says 'they have allied themselves with the national authority in order to resist aggression.'[16] Although the bill was defeated by 21–5 on this occasion, it was amended and passed a year later. However, many of the issues raised in this debate would resurface as tensions, especially the refusal to cede political power, the desire to maintain cultural separateness and the strategic use of relations with Britain: Senator Frías was not so wrong.

The question of political autonomy clashed with the Argentine desire for their assimilation right from the start. Guillermo Rawson, the minister for the interior responsible for guiding the Welsh settlement process, worked hard to dissuade Welsh ambitions for autonomy as is evident from his letter to Lewis Jones dated shortly after they arrived in September 1865. Rawson wrote:

> I had the opportunity to explain to you, in writing and with all clarity, what the government ideally desires on this issue [autonomy], ideas that were in complete contradiction to you, and it was only after you told me that you accepted the view of the national authority that I proceeded to draw up the contract.

He adds:

> I have made you understand that the government wants the population of its territories to become Argentine citizens according to the law of the country … without consenting to the formation of isolated groups of just one nationality, to the exclusion of others.[17]

It is clear that, in the view of the government, the Welsh settlers should assimilate within Argentina and become citizens. He adds that he has explained this: 'in terms that do not allow for the smallest doubt, and I hope that you in turn have communicated these principles, as is your duty, to your leadership who need to know them in order to correct their behaviour'.[18]

For Rawson, this is not a Welsh colony (which might become autonomous) but rather a colonial settlement of individual Welsh people who are citizens of the Argentine republic. It is also a matter of cultural assimilation within a melting-pot of immigrants: 'I repeat to you that the idea of living isolated, without hearing any other language but your own, without contact with other groups of people, is an absurd idea.'[19] Although the rest of the letter is far more positive and imagines a wonderful, productive future for the colony, Rawson was very firm: assimilation was not a choice but part of the bargain.

For the first ten years, though, the Argentine state did not enforce their assimilationist view, being preoccupied with conflict in the River Plate region, internal political wrangling and nation-building projects to the north. This encouraged the Welsh to continue with their dream (and practice) of political autonomy and in many ways to create a state within a state. As Lewis Jones expressed it: 'For centuries, our people have not exercised their political talent because they did not have a land. But now we have a land so we must get serious about its politics.'[20] Even before they had embarked on the *Mimosa* the Welsh leaders had devised a constitution that expressed their dream of independence, its grand tone mimicking the constitutions of far larger states. The preamble declared: 'We, the people of the Welsh Colony, with the aim of establishing order, ensuring peace and promoting general progress, order and establish this Constitution.'[21] They did not lack ambition, nor a sense of their own dignity, even though their legislature would only meet once a month and consist of just twelve representatives.[22] This document signals a political intent that does not chime with settler colonialism, and indeed they passed two 'laws': Administration of Justice Law in 1873 and the 1875 Law of Electoral Privileges and Elections, which were also written as if they ruled a nation-state.[23] For example, the electoral 'law' details who can vote, who can stand, how the electoral system operates and ends by proclaiming: 'Approve and publish the present as a Law of the Welsh Colony of Chubut.'[24]

It was alarm at this assertive autonomy, plus the increasing flow of settlers from Wales, which prompted the appointment of the first state official, Comisario Antonio Oneto in order to promote assimilation. Oneto represented the state in both a symbolic and bureaucratic sense, and chaired two important boards: one to oversee the measurement and distribution of the land; the other to administer loans given out to the most needy.[25] Oneto was not respected, though. Abraham Matthews suggests that he wanted to 'live quietly, and leave the settlers to do the work, and for him to receive the payment', adding that the officers tolerated, rather that respected, his authority.[26] John Coslett Thomas concurred. He was Oneto's factotum who warmed his coffee, counted his hens' eggs and accompanied him on jaunts.[27] Thomas describes him as a scientist who spoke Italian (native), Spanish and English, and quickly learned a little Welsh – but also a figure of fun. He was very short-sighted, would not walk anywhere without a stick and 'he was the most easily-frightened man in whose company I have ever been.'[28] Thomas was obliged to sleep the other side of the wall from him at night so that he could knock by the headboard if he could not sleep, especially if there were sailors about 'who amused themselves by frightening him in the night before they returned to their ship'.[29] Thomas also played tricks on Oneto, one time abandoning him on the wrong side of the river with the wrong horse (he had three: Darlatong, Mustafa and Baby, 'his fancy horse').[30]

The Welsh, led by Lewis Jones, encountered more substantial resistance from the other state officers, especially the harbourmaster, Major Alejandro Vivanco and his Lieutenant Candido Charneton, who arrived in March 1879. Because the Welsh had been ruling themselves, Vivanco reports, they 'display a very unruly character', while the Indigenous are there 'for the sole purpose of spying ... [so] between the two, we need to put an end to the uncertainty'.[31] Their role was to assimilate, by force if necessary, both of these communities which required disciplining by the state, and arrived with 'a supply of arms, for the purpose of imposing respect on the authorities of the Welsh Colony'.[32] They meant business: their first act, according to Jones, was to 'imprison and enchain one of the settlers, without any proof at all'.[33] For Jones 'this was the beginning of the military oppression that would be a long nightmare for Y Wladfa' and the harsh realities of assimilation.[34]

In response, the Welsh leadership tried to transform their existing council into one of the newly developed municipalities in order to sustain their political advantage. Indeed, for Lewis Jones, the municipality was a stepping stone to expanded powers: 'Y Wladfa should ask that they manage their own roads, their irrigation, schooling, trade and security', he suggested, and be able to appoint their own magistrate, police and crime system, as well as developing a free port where British ships could dock, facilitating 'easy trade between us and the Old Country'.[35] Yet once again, the visions clashed. The Argentine authorities saw the situation through the binary lens of civilization/barbarism. For Oneto, they should become *citizens* of the Argentine republic and appealed to their racial affinity as Europeans in the settler project, arguing: 'we are brothers ... let there be a new administrative dawn, based on Argentine law'.[36] Assimilation would bring benefits, he argued – they needed a teacher, otherwise the children born here will not know the language of their own country and 'will become white Patagonian Indians, without skill and lacking noble ambition of heart and mind'.[37] Oneto, like many 'modern' men of his time, assumes that 'obscure' languages are inadequate and will only disadvantage their speakers. Predictably, Lewis Jones rejected this position: 'If we can't manage education ourselves, I would rather see the government money thrown in the river', he exclaimed, though he did agree that Welsh-speaking children should also be able to stand up for themselves in English and Spanish.[38]

Oneto's cajoling approach failed to control the Welsh, then, and he was replaced in 1881 by Juan Finoquetto, a man not afraid to enforce assimilation and, for Jones, 'a thorn in the side of Y Wladfa for years'.[39] From the get-go his actions were deliberately provocative and he certainly enraged Lewis Jones whose notebook on this period gathers newspaper articles, transcribed copies of letters and his own notes of conversations, replete with fury.[40] First, he arrested a Welshman 'arbitrarily' and then refused to accept a petition from the Welsh committee, saying that he did not recognize it as a valid entity and advised them to write only as concerned citizens.[41] That is, he refused to acknowledge their 'exceptional' group-ness – they were individual settlers, like any other. The Welsh responded to this 'strange note' by asserting their privilege: they wanted the Chaco Law of 1878 applied to Chubut in order to establish a municipality, adding that they had corresponded with Ministers Mitre and Rawson, and had worked alongside Oneto on the principle of 'respecting and continuing the jurisdiction that was'.[42] Finoquetto rejected such precedents, not just because the administrative limbo allowed him to (and, one suspects, the Buenos Aires government had instructed him), but also because he seems intensely irritated with the Welsh and their determination to reject the dominant Argentine culture. For Lewis Jones, at least, he deliberately sought to depreciate the Welsh language and culture as a way to disempower them politically and enforce cultural assimilation. Indeed, he hints at a kind of xenophobia, noting Finoquetto's 'awkward confusion of not being able to understand the people's language (and perhaps their ideas) and with that, a tendency to look at the settlers as foreigners to dominate, leading his rule to be disagreeable and tiresome'.[43]

The key battleground was the issue of schooling in Welsh. The Buenos Aires newspaper *La Nación* reported on Finoquetto's annual census, noting that 200 of the 700 children in the Chubut settlement were illiterate. It later emerged that 'these figures included all of the children, from one day old upwards!' but this was more than just incompetent accounting.[44] He wrote damningly of their learning 'just in Welsh' and condemned the textbooks as containing 'statements that should not be allowed in our midst ... [including] "We the Welsh of this colony came here to keep our language and customs."'[45] Finoquetto calls this statement 'fanatical' and suggests that pupils are coerced to remain in that school, rather than attending the 'superior' government school, because they are 'afraid to incur the resentment of their preachers'.[46] He uses such statements to argue that he should be given entire oversight of education in the colony which the Welsh naturally interpret as an aggressive attack on both their culture and political autonomy.

In response and feeling weakened, the Welsh leaders organized meetings where they resolved to push back. They would appeal to the higher authorities in Buenos Aires and aimed to 'use the yearly statistic collection as an opportunity to press the Commissioner [Finoquetto] about the misrepresentation and inaccuracy of the previous set and emphasise the need for local collaboration in collecting these'.[47] Two days later, on 20 December, 1882, Finoquetto called Lewis Jones into the office to make his statistical deposition. When he refused, Finoquetto took Jones prisoner for 'defying the authorities'.[48] The Welsh settlers then descended in large numbers on the comisario's offices and Richard Jones Berwyn asked for Jones to be released: he was imprisoned too. Finoquetto then definitively asserted his state authority. He asked the harbourmaster and his staff 'to take up arms to defend the Argentine flag' and demanded that the assembled Welsh settlers apologize of their threatening behaviour.[49] Once cowed, he then required them to sign a vague pledge of citizenship: 'to respect and follow the national authorities in the Wladfa, represented by the Comisario', which acknowledged their subordination to the state.[50] That is, he insisted on cultural and political assimilation.

Finoquetto's next task was to force the ringleaders to submit. Jones and Berwyn were released from prison after ten days but were soon taken by Finoquetto (surely an awkward journey) to Buenos Aires where he again demonstrated his power – hauling them from one office to another without a word of explanation and then to the police. There, they were imprisoned, according to Jones, in 'some filthy cells of iron bars with two bare boards to sleep on ... in the company of robbers and madmen and rats – some of which one had to grab and fling to the ground when they grasped at a bit of flesh'.[51] Jones contacted the chief constable and they were soon released on surety by an Irishman, Michael Duggan, who came from his Sunday breakfast to help them. After a month, the two were pardoned – even though there had been no inquiry nor proof – by the interior minister, Bernardo Irigoyen. They had been taught a lesson in state authority.

This incident was the culmination of an inevitable clash between the nation-building policy promoted by the Argentine state which required assimilation, and the Welsh desire to wield political power and cultural predominance in the Chubut Valley. As we have seen, this clash was evident even before they arrived in Patagonia, and the issues raised by Guillermo Rawson – their status as individual settler-citizens rather than an ethnic group, and subordination to Argentine law and authority – re-emerged in their relations with both Oneto and Finoquetto. From the Welsh perspective, their de facto autonomy came true in the first ten years, and Oneto's policy of benign lassitude fuelled this misapprehension. Although predictable, Finoquetto's policies of coercive assimilation came as an upsetting surprise but were highly effective: he demonstrated the power of the state over human life, its capacity to imprison and deal brutally with rebels, even those it identified as white European. The pardon issued to Jones and Berwyn set them free, but it also endorsed Finoquetto's actions. Assimilation was now inevitable and even the Buenos Aires Standard which served the English-speaking community urged the Welsh 'to make the best of a bad bargain', saying: 'Welshmen in Chubut should not be so exclusive; they should have their children taught Spanish and should try as far as possible to harmonize with the customs of the country'.[52] The British Embassy official, Edward Monson, agreed. He wrote in the *Liverpool Echo* that 'the rapid advance of colonization in the area will mean that before long the Welsh will come into contact with many other people' and called for 'more disposition on both sides towards assimilation and amity than, I fear, exists at this moment'.[53] Indeed, perhaps as a result of this reputation for rebellion and their dogged adherence to Welsh language and customs, Chubut was ruled from Buenos Aires until 1955 by appointed governors in order to ensure that assimilation could be complete.

This was when the dream of political autonomy, and the creation of a specific Welsh community ended: thereafter Cymraeg was a matter for home, chapel and social gathering alone.

Becoming Argentine citizens, rejecting barbarism

As we have seen, the Welsh had an ambivalent relationship to Indigenous people: on the one hand they despised their backwardness and feared sudden violence; on the other they felt gratitude for their help in the early days and cherished with pride the Welsh capacity to regulate their relationship through friendship rather than force. There is also evidence of genuine friendship as 'brothers of the desert'. In the end, though, the colonial binary and its devastating consequences for people like Katrülaf would prevail. Ambiguity was effectively wiped away by the armed state with its crude and racialized binary: colonizer/colonized. Jonathan Ceredig Davies tells of a moment when the presence of this binary became vivid for him:

> I well remember seeing passing me one day some hundreds of these unfortunate prisoners surrounded by soldiers on their march to the sea to be taken away in vessels to Buenos Aires where they were given away as servants to rich people or rather as slaves practically. I could not help shedding tears to see the poor Indians thus treated for trying to defend their own liberties.[54]

It is important to register Davies's sense of sorrow, pity and outrage, but this incident also shows just what a difference 'difference' can make. The Welshman observed this horror from the roadside, secure in his immunity from such treatment, while the Indigenous people were made radically insecure, and must walk away from their homeland and social world which was being smashed before their eyes.

The Welsh, though, were set on the settler colonial path towards full assimilation within the Argentine nation. The pivotal act was the Rifleros expedition, just after the Conquest of the Desert when twenty-nine Welsh men journeyed to the Andes in search of new land for Welsh settlers alongside the new governor of Chubut Province, Col. Luis Fontana. This famous trek created a bond, forged in adversity and adventure, between the Welsh and Fontana, and provided the whole community with a new heroic settler identity with which to embed them not only in the landscape but in Argentina as a nation.

Fontana arrived in Chubut on 28 May 1885, ready to dislike the 'difficult' Welsh.[55] John Daniel Evans says he was 'not communicative at all' and confessed, once he got to know them, that 'they had given him a terrible impression of us in Buenos Aires', thinking they were like Australian convicts.[56] However, he came to like them and admire their knowledge of the region as well as their shooting skills. Fontana had been tasked by Buenos Aires to explore the hinterland, and his stated aim: 'to study below the geographical and economic surface of the territory under my command' reveals the possessive sensibility that underpinned this mission to appropriate Patagonia.[57] His published report is replete with notes on the rocks and minerals; pasturelands and mountains; rivers, forests, lakes and animal life which he encountered along the way, noting always their potential utility for the new state – *la patria*. It had long been a Welsh desire to expand the colony towards the fertile Andes to establish new settlements attractive to migrants from Wales, so, on John Murray Thomas's suggestion, Fontana agreed to mount a joint Welsh-Argentine expedition.[58] The Welsh, led by Thomas, contributed provisions and horses to the value of 6,000 pesos to the project which eventually opened up the Andes to Welsh colonization in Esquel and Trevelin.[59] That is, both parties wanted to take possession of the land to further national and personal aims.

Both Fontana and the Welsh trekkers record with excitement the beauty and fruitfulness of the Andean foothills. Fontana reflected on the marvellous incongruity of the situation: 'one is amazed that such magnificence has remained, until today, hidden from industrious and civilized man!', adding 'with good reason the Indians resisted before abandoning areas as beautiful and so full of resources as these!'[60] The spirit of rightful possession by 'industrious and civilized man' is reinforced by the name eventually given by Fontana to the Andean settlement, Colonia 16 de Octubre: 16 October was the date in 1885 when the law creating the National Territories – the legal performance of possession – was passed by congress.[61]

The Welsh accompanied him each step, demonstrating their knowledge of the landscape and environment, with John Murray Thomas (surveyor, photographer and would-be goldminer) and John Daniel Evans (explorer and expert guide) riding alongside Fontana. The Welsh too observed the beauty and potential utility of the Andean country, viewed through the possessive gaze of the colonizer. Llwyd ap Iwan, for example, noted:

> We came to an enchanting little valley some two leagues long by two wide. It was about the finest bit of scenery yet discovered, a kind of shallow basin the bottom covered by long grass, strawberry plants and flowers and the soil a black loam and the sides of the valley covered by mountain tuft grass. There were good sized trees and two or three stretches of water running through it. Fifteen thousand sheep could graze there very well.[62]

Like a good settler, ap Iwan is appraising the landscape for what it offers to him, noting the amenities for a good life and valuing its capacity to grow mutton and wool to be shipped for cash, but also as a place to live – a potential new homeland. The echoes of colonial exploration are not lost on Thomas, who observes in his diary:

> Saturday 14th: we have our beds amongst the trees ... it is very picturesque to see the fires at night and the men sitting round by them – looking through the trees reminds me of Dr Livingstone's journeys in Africa and the backwoodsmen's tales of N. America.[63]

A key dimension to colonial possession is the naming of markers in the landscape. In a gesture that speaks volumes, Fontana named one 'forest-clad mountain... Pico Thomas' after John Murray Thomas.[64] In doing so, the governor demonstrated his own mastery of the landscape and political supremacy, as well as acknowledging his esteem for the Welsh and their rightful place as possessors of the 'new' land. The transformation of the Welsh from awkward inhabitants to Argentine citizens is also expressed by the ceremony which, when they eventually arrived in the Andes, took place to name a huge lake after their leader: Lago Fontana. Thomas, recounts that:

> a pyramid of stones was made, a hole being placed in the middle, the Argentine flag was hoisted and saluted with three charges of musketry, I then made a speech and read the act naming the lake, then the paper was signed by all in the camp and placed in a bottle placed amongst the stones. Then the governor made a speech – after which we gave him three hurrahs. I, Mayo, England, Germany and Spain and the Patria Argentina were vivaad.[65]

Both the Welsh and Governor Fontana enacted the claim to possess this Andean region in a communal act that draws together the troupe as a 'band of brothers' engaged in a common purpose to claim the land. They solidified settler possession by performing a solemn bureaucratic act (declaring possession and interring a signed paper) which legitimized their appropriation of the land.

The other side of settler possession is Indigenous dispossession and the 'elimination of the native' from the land. This journey also seemed to demonstrate the success of this erasure, and the continuation of Indigenous life only as mere remnants of a defeated world. The most graphic example of 'erasure' was encountering Cacique Foyel's camp. As we learned in Katrülaf's testimony, Foyel had been to present himself at Where the Welsh Are but he had not brought all his people. He was then sent back to bring them down, accompanied by Captain Lasciar and a small troop of soldiers, but (according to Fontana's report) had planned to overwhelm the soldiers and flee with his people. Laziar pre-empted his attack, though, and a major battle ensued – it was this camp/battleground they found on their journey. For Fontana, the scene exemplified the Argentine struggle in Patagonia:

> There, lonely and beaten by the winds, arose like phantoms in the wide desolation of the desert the tents of the Cacique Foyel who was the last bastion of barbarism demolished by the force of our victorious civilization. The abandoned tents, the broken lances, the skeletons of men and horses, the used

Remington cartridges and the mantles in tatters, *bombacha* [trousers] and grey jackets, told us that a little time ago a death tragedy had been played out.[66]

In the Welsh archives too it registers as evidence of the 'death' of Indigenous life. John Daniel Evans recalled: 'it was shocking to see the mute testimonies of the terrible battle: we found an iron stirrup, a section of cape with buttons, broken lances and skeletons of horses … hides were hung from the tents which waved in the breeze.'[67] For Evans, this sight did not speak of glory and the triumph of civilization but of death and loss.

How much more difficult must this encounter have been, though, for the Indigenous family who had been forced to guide Fontana: a man, two women and six children. After the Conquest of the Desert, Indigenous people disappear from the record as 'fierce Indians' to reappear as labour resources. In the archives, Indigenous people are now met as cattle hunters, sheep drivers, forced soldiers or desert guides. One of these guides was Martín Platero and his family, a man regarded by both Fontana and the Welsh not as a 'Brother of the Desert', nor as a 'Child of the Desert' but as an object of utility to the expedition like any other resource to be requisitioned in service of the Argentine state project.

It happened like this: the company came across some tents about halfway through the journey which belonged to Martín Platero, named for his skill in silverwork (*plata* = silver).[68] Platero's family had formerly lived under the powerful leader Sayhueke but had somehow evaded capture and now hunted and lived alone, surviving as best they could.[69] Given their experiences, this encounter must have been frightening. Evans recalls: 'Fontana surrounded the tents with ten soldiers … the galloping of the horsemen … daring and reckless, terrified them.'[70] He tried to buy trust by giving one woman his silk neckerchief and then spoke to Platero. We can observe Platero trying to both placate and evade these dangerous men: he says that he does know their destination, but not well, and yet (in Evans's careful phrasing) 'he did not refuse to be their guide.'[71] There is no mention of payment in the archives, but obviously he had very little choice and tensions were running high. Platero and family travelled slowly. When Evans went back to find them, mutual distrust was unmasked:

'his attitude was very suspicious, he had his lance half out and care-
lessly brought his horse next to mine and began to cut his lance, which
is the best position to fight on horseback'. In response, Thomas took
his Remington from its holster and pointed it at Platero's head, ordering him to march or be shot.[72] There is no sense of 'brotherhood'
here – they are on opposite sides now, with the Welsh truly allied
with the Argentine state. Later, Thomas and Fontana agreed that he
intended to escape, so they took away his lance and three knives: that
night, they considered tying him up, but thought him unlikely to flee,
given that they held his family. These, then, were the terms on which
Platero was to 'help' the expedition to the Andes – unpaid, coerced,
unarmed and his family held ransom against his good conduct. Of
course, we have no record of Martín Platero's thoughts, still less of
the women who accompanied him, but this situation must have been
deeply frightening.

At the foothills of the Andes, they left the women, children and
a few weaker horses to camp and Platero continued with the men up
to Lago Fontana. There, they begin erecting the flagpole to be used
to celebrate the Welsh and Argentine possession of the lands. This
worried Platero who asked them what it is for. One 'joker' from the
Welsh pack, Antonio Miguens, responded that: 'tomorrow, when the
sun rises, we will hang you by the neck from the top of the pole'.[73]
This, of course, was an entirely plausible explanation in Platero's eyes,
given the arbitrary brutality he had witnessed during the Conquest
of the Desert and their absolute power over him and his homelands.
So, overnight, he made a body shape in his bed, took a horse and
galloped to his family who packed hurriedly and fled for their lives.
Returning from the naming ceremony, Thomas tell us that Miguens:
'saw the blankets and thought [Platero] still asleep. He tip-toed over,
launched a wave of swearwords and kicked at the blankets where his
rear end would be'.[74] They realized then that he had gone, so Fontana
sent five men to chase him down and bring him back, but they found
only the abandoned goods and horses.

The callous treatment of Martín Platero by the whole group is
compounded by a general lack of fellow feeling. For example, Llwyd
ap Iwan's diary records it merely in passing: 'he was under the impression that we intended to hang him. The weather today is unpleasant'.[75]
This is predictable but still shocking, given the rhetoric of friendship

and 'brothers of the desert', that characterizes the memoirs and images that are still conjured today in schoolbooks and documentaries, as we will see in the following chapter.

Still yearning for autonomy

For many, then, inclusion within the Argentine state seemed both inevitable and desirable, yet others strove to resist Argentine assimilation, driven not only by the dream of autonomy but also by a sense of superiority. Indeed, despite developing happy relations with Rawson and Fontana, a strong impression emerges from the archive that the Welsh leadership (at least) considered themselves 'better' than Argentinians and their nation. They disdained Oneto as idle and dismissed Charneton, Vivano and especially Finoquetto as brutish, playing into stereotypes of Spanish colonialism as violent and brutal. As a result, some wanted to assert Welsh autonomy by a tactical use of Britishness. This might seem counterintuitive but we should recall, as we saw in chapter three, that Welsh ideologues often strategically deployed discourses of Britishness to empower their cause, a move now framed globally by the pre-eminence of the British Empire. It is certainly ironic, though, that it was the most ideological of the Welsh settlers – those who had left Britain explicitly to found an autonomous community away from the anglophone world – who would lead the astonishing demand that Britain intervene in Welsh Patagonia to prevent their assimilation into Argentina. W. Casnodyn Rhys exemplified this paradoxical Patagonian Britishness. He recalls in his memoirs the arrival of *HMS Triton* in 1866 and opens with this reflection: 'Britishers in their roamings and adventures in foreign lands are encouraged by the knowledge that the sleepless eye of John Bull is resting upon them everywhere. John has a knack of finding out a British subject in distress.'[76] The *Triton* had called by to see how the Welsh fared and gave them 'a great many pairs of seamen's boots' and 1,000 yards of flannel, leading Rhys to write: 'in gratitude the settlers can only say "DUW GADW SHON DARW" [God Bless John Bull]'.[77] Similarly, he writes of *HMS Cracker's* arrival in a chapter called 'John Bull to the Rescue', saying it was 'an Angel of Mercy' and 'won the admiration and affection of the Settlement' as 'an exhibition of the sterling character of John Bull'.[78]

The continuing Welsh claim to Britishness – and ambivalence towards assimilation in the Argentine national project – was exposed in the late 1890s, initially over the issue of military drilling. In 1895, the new governor of Chubut Eugenio Tello decided to enforce Welsh submission to central authority and issued three decrees: compliance with the order that all Argentine men 18–40 should join the National Guard; participation in military drilling on Sundays; and assertion of state jurisdiction over the irrigation canals – which had been financed, excavated and maintained entirely by the Welsh community.[79] The Welsh were appalled and immediately petitioned Buenos Aires on the matter of military drilling. They argued that Sunday was, for them, a sacred day, and though they did not refuse to drill, suggested that another day be selected. The government eventually ordered Tello to change the day, but growing tensions on the border with Chile a year later made matters more urgent and the next governor, Carlos O'Donnell, once more insisted on Sunday drilling.[80]

The Welsh elite again objected, but in terms that expressed open contempt for the Argentine army and exalted their own sense of moral superiority. They argued that they did not want their young people to lose their religious customs or 'live alongside troops made up of mestizos, Indians, negroes and the dregs of Argentine prisons' and as such emphasized their claim to 'ideals of purity in respect of their ethnic group [*raza*] and way of life'.[81] However, O'Donnell refused to change the day, arguing that this was a good way to integrate the young Welsh and Argentines, adding that it was the old complaining, and not the young.[82] The Welsh in turn called meetings in Gaiman on 22 and 29 August 1898 where they resolved to ask O'Donnell again to change the day and if this were not successful, to 'petition the National Senate asking for resolution of the case'.[83] Their sense of entitlement is all the more remarkable when we recall that, at this peak moment, the Welsh still only constituted 3,750 people, a number dwarfed by the 5.9 million migrants arriving between 1871 and 1914.[84] Given their insignificance within this human tsunami, it is astonishing that the Argentine government paid them any heed, yet from 1865 to the turn of the century they received frequent attention from government ministers and even presidents (despite the sweeping social change, ongoing military action, rocketing economic development and intense political turmoil that they were also managing during this period). Why they garnered attention is an intriguing question. One factor, surely, is precisely the Welsh capacity to act as a disciplined, coherent unit and therefore to claim – and exercise – a political autonomy that they simply did not have on paper.

It was perhaps this disproportionate clout, plus the need to secure southern Patagonia against the Chileans, which prompted newly elected President Roca (architect of the Conquest of the Desert) to resolve the matter in 1899.[85] As W. M. Hughes observes: 'he could see that the trouble of drilling ... would lead to unfortunate results and resolved ... to go there personally to bring a peaceful resolution', but this mark of great honour was also part of a skilful strategy to secure Argentina's claims, fitting nicely with meeting Chilean President Errázuriz in Punta Arenas.[86] Roca's visit proved to be a turning point in Welsh-Argentine relations, demonstrating and also deepening Welsh assimilation within the Argentine national project.

Roca was welcomed enthusiastically by crowds in both Rawson and Gaiman where, Hughes tells us, 'he shook the large, calloused hands of the Welsh farmers and said to his companions that these were the hands that would bring triumph to the Republic'.[87] Y Drafod, the Welsh-language newspaper of Y Wladfa, reported on his arrival: 'in Puerto Madryn they waved flags and there were huge demonstrations of happiness'.[88] In Trelew, after a display of target practice shooting at guanacos, the train arrived in town 'covered in flags and to the welcome of fireworks hung from the streets which exploded with a tremendous noise. Later, to the sound of music from the band ... His Excellency appeared [and] a unanimous "Viva! Viva!" exploded all around.'[89] Roca flattered the Welsh, exclaiming that he 'had not expected to find the colony so well advanced' and praised the population, saying that 'the unshowy elegance, the courtesy of the people showed that they were people of taste and of high character'.[90] In return, Y Drafod described Roca as 'a courageous soldier, an unyielding statesman of commanding reason, a strong and immutable man'.[91] He was the very epitome of hyper-masculine power. Moreover, it celebrated the president's role in the Conquest of the Desert, saying: 'after bringing civilization to the desert, [he] returned to rise triumphant'.[92] In contrast to Welsh opinion during the Conquest of the Desert, then, the Welsh people who lined the streets waving flags or wrote editorials for Y Drafod now embraced its aims and their assimilat-

ed place in the new nation. After listening to their complaints about
the military drilling Roca resolved the issue on his return to Buenos
Aires and was, in Hughes's words: 'a real friend to [the Welsh], until
the day he died.'[93]

It seems that most of the Welsh settler community were indeed
content to assimilate within Argentina.[94] However, the leadership
kept alight the flame of political autonomy, lobbied the government
at every turn and thought up schemes to defend Welsh culture, re-
focusing attention on the Britishness of the Welsh. Even in the early years of strife with Finoquetto (1882), discussions began among
the Welsh about proposing that a British vice-consul be appointed
to stimulate trade with Britain. During the drilling disputes, some
self-styled 'British citizens' sent an 'official petition' to the British secretary of state for foreign affairs, Lord Salisbury, asking him to 'desig-
nate, without delay, a British Consulate in the territory of Chubut.'[95]
We should recall now the concerns raised in the congressional debate
that Y Wladfa would become a pretext for British intervention in Patagonia, and it was not surprising that concerns began to circulate in
Buenos Aires that this 'underhandedly pro-British community could
evolve into a British Protectorate.'[96] Astonishingly, this unlikely even-
tuality almost came to pass.

The 'secret meeting behind locked doors' in Gaiman which had
petitioned for a change to the drilling day, had also resolved to: 'send
T. B. Phillips (Cilsant) to raise the matter before Minister Salisbury
and to [US] President McKinley.'[97] As well as advocating the Welsh
case in Buenos Aires, Llwyd ap Iwan and Thomas Benbow Philips
were also tasked to go to London to 'take their complaints to the government of Her Majesty and of the USA' by petitioning the British
government.[98] Indeed, Jorge Barzini reveals that 5,000 pesos from
the Welsh trading company, the Compañía Mercantil de Chubut, was
voted to fund 'Mission England', alongside some personal donations
from Welsh settlers.[99] Phillips and ap Iwan arrived on 19 December
1898 and soon began a press campaign as well as meeting Welsh MPs
from all parties to put their case. Their extensive report sent to the
minister of the colonies, Joseph Chamberlain, asserted the supposed
rights of Britain over Patagonia, claiming its effective occupation
by John Narborough in 1670 with 'the subsequent colonization by
British subjects in 1865'.[100] They suggested to Chamberlain that: 'the

lands occupied in the Chubut Valley should be organized as an independent state of Argentina, under the joint protection of Britain and the United States of America'.[101] What the congressmen had feared back in 1863 was exactly what was proposed by the two Welshmen in London.

This strategy was – and is – both astonishing and, frankly, delusional. Argentina was a key component in Britain's informal empire, a relationship that required no military defence or costly administration but which reaped huge profits – and regional strategic benefits. The British were deeply involved in trade and investment in beef refrigeration and shipping, but also provided financial services and loans, and had captured key assets like the rail network and postal/telegraph system.[102] Creating a protectorate (consisting largely of dry scrubland) for 3,750 Welsh people would jeopardize all that and put them in a costly and unjustifiable conflict with a key ally and trading partner. Moreover, as Geraint Owen observes, Foreign Secretary Lord Salisbury thought colonies 'undesirable' because of their cost and the danger of embroiling Britain in foreign disputes.[103] We might recall that the British were fighting the Boer War in defence of English settlers at this very moment. While the Welsh MPs did try to lobby on behalf of the two settlers, the idea of a protectorate was firmly rebuffed. The very foundation of the existing colony depended on Welsh recognition of Argentine sovereignty in Patagonia (otherwise how could they have been granted land?) and they had accepted goods and animals from the Argentine state. Moreover, the Crown had never shown any desire to enact sovereignty before this point and 'the colonists do not make out a rag of a case'.[104]

When the Argentine press heard of these plans they called for the expulsion of the Welsh from Patagonia. In response, Governor O'Donnell sent the police to Trelew to arrest fifteen members of the local committee, plus the chair and secretary of the municipal council, ordering them out of chapel in front of the whole congregation to demonstrate state authority.[105] They were imprisoned in Rawson and accused of high treason in a show of force, though they were released the next day.

This debacle exposed a rift in Y Wladfa's community between the ideological 'old guard' and the less politicized folk who began to speak out and disown the protectorate idea. For example, the Kenneth Skinner archive includes a transcribed telegram sent from Buenos Aires (probably to London) on 6 March 1899 which stated:

> Buenos Aires situation complicated. General Roca ... has received a ... manifesto signed by Welshmen ... [that] declare[s] that Messrs Phillips and ap Iwan have no authority to make complaints or to act upon their behalf, and that the members of the Welsh community in Patagonia are perfectly contented with their treatment by the Argentine authorities.[106]

There are other signs too that most people were backing away from the idea. Barzini tells us that Phillips's letters home complain incessantly that Llwyd ap Iwan 'is not helping him at all, not writing letters or manifestos, or accompanying him to meetings', and when O'Donnell interviewed the Welsh leaders they all replied that no one had authorized the delegates to ask for a protectorate and portrayed them as 'two eccentrics'.[107] In another source – a letter printed in *Y Drafod* – the author praises Roca and O'Donnell, and comments: 'as one local person said to me yesterday "I should like to write to the governor to thank him for his kindness only I cannot write in Spanish" and this is the feeling of almost all the people of Y Wladfa'.[108] They had gone a step too far.

This was, perhaps, the final death of Welsh autonomy as the community itself turned away from the dream of Y Wladfa to embrace life as settlers in Argentina. Though the antagonisms were not forgotten, especially concerning drilling on a Sunday, the fact of Argentine state institutions, laws and nation-building, plus the everyday demands of life and work – weather, marriage, grief, harvest, chapel, children – led most to accept Argentine power, while cherishing the language, customs and lifeways of Wales. This dynamic was reinforced when the political crisis was overtaken by an existential one: the floods of August 1899 which inundated the Chubut Valley. The loss of life, livestock, farmhouses, machinery and much of the canal system left the colony destitute, including Lewis Jones. Conflicts were set aside, and the Argentine state allocated £9,000 to help with repairs to canals and farms: the settler state proved its usefulness in adversity – and this closed the chapter on Welsh autonomy. Welsh assimilation became complete.

Conclusion

Settler colonial theory usually assumes that settlers agree with the state-led programme and are more than happy to embrace citizenship within their new nation: assimilation is not understood to be a problem. However, the Welsh case shows that in some cases, settlers might resist integration within the state and push against its authority, using the settler colonial scenario to pursue their own agenda. Key to understanding this distinction are social, economic and political relations in the origin country and the experience of assimilation as 'a kind of (cultural) death' in Wales, summed up in the phrase: 'For Wales, See England'. The Welsh colonizers had briefly enjoyed autonomy, especially between 1865 and 1875, but in the end they swapped one locus of assimilation for another.

The settlers from Wales and the Argentine state had, right from the beginning, a very different vision of the relationship between settler and state. The Welsh were searching for political autonomy and the preservation of cultural difference, based on sustaining an ethnic enclave. The imperative of Argentine nation-building, though, was to create a new society based on assimilation which demanded that, while migrants could keep their own tongue and habits at home, they must rally to the culture and flag of their new country. The price of citizenship was assimilation, and for those settlers escaping grinding poverty (Spanish and Italian) or ethnic oppression (central European Jews) this deal was unproblematic. For the Welsh leadership, though, it was a bitter bone of contention for forty years. For them, they had escaped cultural assimilation and political powerlessness in Britain (being colonized) only to experience a kind of recolonization in Argentina through processes of state-led assimilation.

Yet on the other hand, they flourished and embraced the colonizing drive. While some regretted the demise of Indigenous societies they took up the position of colonizing settler with alacrity on the trek to the Andes, a journey which entailed using and discarding Martín Platero and his family in accordance with the new norm. The fruits of Indigenous dispossession were enjoyed by the Welsh settlers – they could claim their land and use them as guides, as well as labourers on the farm. Indigenous erasure or forced inclusion within the Argentine national project was taken as natural, even while many

Welsh people resisted their own linguistic, cultural and political assimilation. This unusual situation is made more brain-twisting by the Welsh call to Britishness. Their surprising embrace of the British Empire, at the same time as seeking cultural and political autonomy in Patagonia, sits at odds with the contemporary view of Y Wladfa as a bastion of Welsh independence, especially from 'England'. They felt empowered as vicarious members of the British Empire and drew on this sense of superiority in dealings with the Argentine state, celebrating the cultural and civilizational pre-eminence of 'Britishness' to which they lay claim. In the end, they paradoxically summoned their membership of what they had once rejected – Britain – without imagining that they would be shunned by the British establishment whose view of Wales was shaped by Welsh subordination within the hierarchy of nations in Britain. In the end, good relations with Argentina were far more important to London and relations with the Welsh colony were expendable. Viewed more broadly, Y Wladfa demonstrates that the situation of settlers can be highly complex, counterintuitive, paradoxical and unresolved, and settler colonial theory might be enriched by testing its ideas through complicated cases like the Welsh in Patagonia.

Here, though, we can also note that the priorities and actions of the Welsh leadership do not necessarily represent those of the whole community, and we glimpse the attitudes of the ordinary folk who cheered for Roca on the streets of Trelew and petitioned against the foolish exploits in London. This should remind us, as I suggested in the introduction, that often we can only draw on a very skewed archive which collects and cherishes the thoughts and opinions of some, whilst losing to the dust of time the experiences of women, of working-class settlers and of those without the means or time to commit their ideas to paper. While letters are sometimes signed 'in the name of all the settlers' do they really reflect the views of everyone? Perhaps so, perhaps not, but at the very least we should resist the urge to generalize the thoughts of a few specific people to everyone. Most importantly, we can question the assumptions that are made and try to identify the myths that they lead us to. Of course, there are solid facts which underpin the fabled Welsh courage, moral action and cultural tenacity that has played an important role in sustaining pride, boosting Welsh identity and engendering political confidence up to today. But, now that Wales is in a new phase of political devolution and is embracing a more diverse understanding of Welshness, the time to unpack such stereotypes is upon us. This is the purpose of the final chapter.

Notes

1 Carolyn Larson, 'The Conquest of the Desert: the Official Story', in Carolyn Larson, *The Conquest of the Desert: Argentina's Indigenous Peoples and the Battle for History* (Albuquerque: University of New Mexico Press, 2020), pp. 17–42.

2 David Rock, *Argentina 1516–1987: From Spanish Colonization to the Falklands War and Alfonsín* (London: I. B. Taurus, 1985).

3 Alejandro Grimson, *Mitomanías Argentinas: Cómo Hablamos de Nosotros Mismos* (Buenos Aires: Siglo Veintiuno Editores, 2012).

4 Natalio Botano and Ezequiel Gallo, 'Introduction', in Natalio Botano and Ezequiel Gallo (eds), *Liberal Thought in Argentina, 1837–1940* (Indianapolis: Liberty Fund, 2013), pp. 236–44, 236.

5 Walter Nugent, *Crossings: The Great Transatlantic Migrations, 1870–1914* (Bloomington: Indiana University Press, 1995), p. 114.

6 Julia Albarracín, *Making Immigrants in Modern Argentina* (Notre Dame: University of Notre Dame Press, 2020), p. 47.

7 Botana and Gallo 'Introduction' p. xv.

8 See also Mario Emanuel Larreburo, 'Entre el "Territorio Vacío" y la "Inmigracion Deseada": Dilemas de la Construcción del Estado Nacional en un Debate Parlamentario de 1863', *Revista Tefros*, 20/1 (2022), 79–95.

9 Senado de la Nacion, 'Diario de Sesiones 17 Agosto 1863', in Clemente Dumrauf, *La Colonial Galesa del Chubut: su Lucha por el Gobierno Propio* (Buenos Aires: Editorial Dunken, 2008), pp. 88–127, 94.

10 Senado, 'Diario de Sesiones 17 Agosto 1863', pp. 100–1.

11 Senado, 'Diario de Sesiones 17 Agosto 1863', pp. 89, 91.

12 Senado, 'Diario de Sesiones 17 Agosto 1863', p. 93.

13 Senado, 'Diario de Sesiones 17 Agosto 1863', pp. 106, 107.

14 Senado, 'Diario de Sesiones 17 Agosto 1863', p. 91.

15 Senado, 'Diario de Sesiones 17 Agosto 1863', p. 115.

16 Senado, 'Diario de Sesiones 17 Agosto 1863', p. 102.

17 Guillermo Rawson, 'Carta a Lewis Jones 16 Septiembre, 1865', in a bound collection of transcribed papers, NLW Facs 402, pp. 15–17, 15.

18 Rawson, 'Carta a Lewis Jones', p. 15.

19 Rawson, 'Carta a Lewis Jones', p. 17.

20 Lewis Jones, *Y Wladva Gymreig yn Ne Amerig* (Caernarfon: W. Gwenlyn Evans, 1898), p. 102.

21 Reproduced in Clemente Dumrauf, *La Colonia Galesa del Chubut: su Lucha por el Gobierno Propio* (Buenos Aires: Dunken, 2008), pp. 131–4, 131.

22 Dumrauf, *Colonia Galesa*, p. 132.

23 Dumrauf, *Colonia Galesa*, pp. 144–7, 155–9.

24 Dumrauf, *Colonia Galesa*, pp. 155–9, 159.

25 Abraham Matthews, *Hanes y Wladfa Gymreig yn Patagonia* (Aberdâr: Mills ac Evans, 1894), p. 78.

26 Matthews, *Hanes y Wladfa*, pp. 86–7.

27 John Coslett Thomas, 'Autobiography (handwritten)', NLW FACS 919, pp. 93–4.

28 Thomas, 'Autobiography', p. 95.

29 Thomas, 'Autobiography', p. 98.

30 Thomas, 'Autobiography', p. 96.

31 Jones, *Y Wladva Gymreig*, p. 97.

32 Jones, *Y Wladva Gymreig*, p. 97.

33 Jones, *Y Wladva Gymreig*, p. 97.

34 Jones, *Y Wladva Gymreig*, p. 96.

35 Jones, *Y Wladva Gymreig*, p. 107.

36 Jones, *Y Wladva Gymreig*, p. 105.

37 Jones, *Y Wladva Gymreig*, pp. 104–5.

38 Jones, *Y Wladva Gymreig*, p. 107.

39 Jones, *Y Wladva Gymreig*, p. 109.

40 Lewis Jones, 'Y Carcharariaid a'i Ganlyniadau, Rhagfyr 10/82–Mawrth 21/83' (1882–3), NLW MS 12200A, no page numbers.

41 Jones, *Y Wladva Gymreig*, p. 129.

42 Jones, *Y Wladva Gymreig*, p. 130.

43 Jones, *Y Wladva Gymreig*, p. 138.

44 Jones, 'Y Carcharariaid'.

45 Jones, 'Y Carcharariaid'.

46 Jones, *Y Wladva Gymreig*, p. 132.

47 Jones, 'Y Carcharariaid'.

48 Jones, *Y Wladva Gymreig*, pp. 133–4.

49 Jones, *Y Wladva Gymreig*, p. 134.

50 Jones, *Y Wladva Gymreig*, p. 135.

51 Jones, *Y Wladva Gymreig*, p. 135.

52 Jones, 'Y Carcharariaid'.

53 Jones, 'Y Carcharariaid'.

54 Jonathan Ceredig Davies, 'Deunydd a Defnyddiwyd gan Jonathan Ceredig Davies yn ei "Patagonia: a Description of the Country"', notes for the book (*c.*1890), NLW MS 8545-8B, p. 285.

55 Luis Jorge Fontana, *Viaje de Exploracion en la Patagonia Austral* (London: British Library Historical Print Editions, 1886), p. 9.

56 Clery A. Evans (ed.), *John Daniel Evans 'El Molinero: una Historia entre Galeses y la Colonia 16 de Octubre* (Esquel: Grafica Alfa, 1994).

57 Fontana, *Viaje de Exploracion*, p. 72.

58 Fontana, *Viaje de Exploracion*, p. 11.

59 J. M. Thomas, 'Diary of Expedition to the Andes starting from Chubut on October 14, 1885 being 29 men all told. Returned home 3pm February 1st 1886', Kenneth Skinner Papers, Folder 15, NLW.

60 Fontana, *Viaje de Exploracion*, pp. 76 and 77.

61 Fontana, *Viaje de Exploracion*, p. 80.

62 Llwyd ap Iwan, '1st Expedition' entry for 2 January. The strawberries and diverse flora were eliminated by the settlers' grazing animals.

63 Thomas, 'Diary of an Expedition', entry for Saturday, 14th.

64 ap Iwan, '1st Expedition' entry for 2 January, p. 76.

65 Gregorio Mayo was another experienced expeditioner. Thomas, 'Diary of an Expedition'.

66 Fontana, *Viaje de Exploracion*, p. 90.

67 Evans (ed.), *John Daniel Evans*, p. 72.

68 Evans (ed.), *John Daniel Evans*, p. 71.

69 Paul Birt (ed.), *Bywyd a Gwaith John Daniel Evans, El Baqueano* (Llanrwst: Gwasg Carreg Gwalch, 2004), pp. 176–91.

70 Evans (ed.), *John Daniel Evans*, p. 71.

71 Evans (ed.), *John Daniel Evans*, p. 71.

72 Evans (ed.), *John Daniel Evans*, p. 71.

73 Evans (ed.), *John Daniel Evans*, p. 74.

74 Evans (ed.), *John Daniel Evans*, p. 74.

75 ap Iwan, '1st Expedition' entry for 2 January.

76 William Casnodyn Rhys, 'Collection of Writings by W. Casnodyn Rhys', NLW MS 16654C (*c.*1900), published as David Hall Rhys (ed.), *A Welsh Song in Patagonia: Memories of the Welsh Colonization* (Milton Keynes: Lightening Source, 2005), p. 77.

77 Rhys (ed.), *A Welsh Song*, pp. 78–9.

78 Rhys (ed.), *A Welsh Song*, p. 77.

79 Geraint Owen, *Crisis in Chubut: a Chapter in the History of the Welsh Colony in Patagonia* (Swansea: C. Davies, 1977), p. 43.

80 R. Bryn Williams, *Y Wladfa* (Caerdydd: Gwasg Prifysgol Cymru, 1962), p. 254.

81 Dumrauf, *La Colonia Galesa*, pp. 61 and 62.

82 Jorge Barzini, 'La Mision de Thomas B. Phillips y Llwyd ap Iwan a Londres', in Fundación Ameghino, Asociación Punta Cuevas, Asociación Cultural Galesa de Puerto Madryn, *Los Galeses en la Patagonia III* (Trelew: Biblioteca Popular Agustín Alvarez, 2008), pp. 119–34, 129; Dumrauf, *La Colonia Galesa*, p. 62.

83 Barzini, 'La Mision de Thomas', p. 121; Dumrauf, *La Colonia Galesa*, p. 62.

84 Williams, *Y Wladfa*, p. 321.

85 Dumrauf, *La Colonia Galesa*, p. 63.

86 William Meloch Hughes, *A'r Lannau'r Gamwy: Atgofion* (Lerpwl: Gwasg y Brython, 1927), p. 172.

87 Hughes, *A'r Lannau'r Gamwy*, p. 172.

88 'Visita la Colonia el Presidente de la Republica', *Y Drafod*, Viernes 3 de Febrero, 1899, in República Argentina, *Roca y los Galeses* (Buenos Aires: Gobierno de Argentina, c.1900), p. 16.
89 'Visita la Colonia', p. 15.
90 'Visita la Colonia', p. 16.
91 'Visita la Colonia', p. 18.
92 República Argentina, *Roca y los Galeses*, p. 12.
93 Hughes, *A'r Lannau'r Gamwy*, p. 173.
94 For analysis of the economic and social consolidation of the colony, see Glyn Williams, *The Welsh in Patagonia: The State and the Ethnic Community* (Cardiff: University of Wales Press, 1991).
95 Dumrauf, *La Colonia Galesa*, p. 52.
96 Dumrauf, *La Colonia Galesa*, p. 52.
97 Barzini, 'La Mision de Thomas', p. 121.
98 Owen, *Crisis in Chubut*, p. 46.
99 Barzini, 'La Mision de Thomas', p. 124.
100 Dumrauf, *La Colonia Galesa*, p. 63.
101 Dumrauf, *La Colonia Galesa*, p. 63.
102 David Rock, *The British in Argentina: Commerce, Settlers and Power, 1800–2000* (Houndsmills: Palgrave, 2019).
103 Owen, *Crisis in Chubut*, p. 46.
104 Owen, *Crisis in Chubut*, p. 50. Their arguments countering this position are reproduced in Barzini, 'La Misión de Thomas', pp. 125–6.
105 Barzini, 'La Misión de Thomas', p. 127; Owen, *Crisis in Chubut*, pp. 47–8.
106 Transcribed telegram, 6 March from Buenos Aires (to London?), Kenneth Skinner Research Materials, folder 15, NLW, no MS number.
107 Barzini, 'La Misión de Thomas', pp. 124, 127.
108 Notes on *Y Drafod*, no. 175, Kenneth Skinner Research Materials, folder 15, NLW, no MS number.

CHAPTER SEVEN

Y Wladfa, Assimilation and Coloniality Today

The story of Welsh Patagonia continues to have a powerful influence over Welsh culture and shapes part of the collective mythology of Wales, especially Welsh-speaking Wales. In this chapter we return to Wales and explore how Y Wladfa has been deployed to strengthen resistance to anglicizing assimilation. Its role as proof of Wales's capacity to endure as a nation, even outside Wales, has made it an emblem of pride which has strengthened the nationalist political project. This impulse led R. Bryn Williams, whose writings play a pivotal role in the revival story, to close his short book commemorating Y Wladfa's centenary with these stirring words:

> Wales can be proud that she begat such heroes, and Argentina never had better pioneers ... because of their loyalty to the language and traditions of Wales ... Our tribute will be an encouragement to thousands who continue to speak our language ... and remembering their bravery will be an inspiration to the thousands who are fighting to guard the same treasures in Wales itself.[1]

That mission, and Y Wladfa's role in it, remains a core aim for many in Wales and there is a lot at stake when unpacking the bundle of stories and ideas which constitute this icon of modern Welsh history. Indeed, there is an understandable fear that scrutinizing the Welsh-Indigenous friendship – the moral cornerstone of the colony – will weaken Welsh culture by calling into question the deeply ethical gesture of friendship with a stranger. This fear, and the threat to Welsh status, is real if we simply turn to the opposite position and argue, as a few commentators on social media have, that this settler enterprise is an object of shame.[2] Although driven by the well-meaning impulse, this turn to condemn the settlers misses the complexity of the Welsh position as colonized (at home) and colonizing (abroad) and decontextualizes the interplay of social relations in Patagonia. It is this dynamic – the tension between the fear of losing the moral power that the romantic vision endows, and the accelerating impulse to take a more critical view – that I explore in this chapter.

The chapter falls into three main sections which examine how Y Wladfa has been portrayed in popular media (especially TV, radio and film) and cultural products written for children (including novels and school materials). The sections are organized in chronological order: the period around the centenary (1965) when interest was reawakened; the mainstreaming period when Y Wladfa became embedded as a topic in popular culture (1970s–2000s); finally, the period around the 150th anniversary (2015) when celebration was tempered, by some, with critical reflection. One peculiarity of this settler colonial scenario is that the relationship between Wales and Y Wladfa is imagined as exclusive, as if somehow untouched by polluting global dynamics and linked by a 'glass corridor'. Cultural products and people seem to leap across the Atlantic with ease, untouched by geopolitics and skimming over the sweep of world history. This aura of innocence has sustained the sense of moral righteousness which is so important for Welsh identity and a powerful tool in the Welsh struggle against assimilation at home. However, at the same time, its discourse reinforces settler colonialism in Patagonia and makes Indigenous people invisible as contemporaries today.

Welsh cultural capital

The sources studied in this chapter are very different to those used previously, but they are still archival objects which render the past visible. The documentaries in particular offer snippets of oral history, albeit edited, and all TV and radio media provide a visual or aural landscape which reflects experience in the past. The narrative that they convey is equally revealing of the concerns, priorities and assumptions of those interviewed and filmed in Patagonia, which in turn generates Welsh understandings of what Y Wladfa was, shaped by the programme makers, editors and narrators who interpret its significance. Such portrayals, as well as writing for children, contribute to what Tim Edensor calls 'national structures of feeling'.[3] Drawing on Raymond Williams's interpretation of culture (which links tangible cultural motifs with personal emotions), Edensor sees 'the national [as] constituted and reproduced, contested and reaffirmed in everyday life' a process in which popular culture plays a key role.[4] These 'national structures of feeling' work hard to forge bonds of groupness which not only make sense of the group's subject position, but can be mobilized for political ends. Their impact is particularly potent where the nation lacks governmental power or economic resources and so relies on cultural capital as its main source of structural coherence and power, as was the case in Wales up until 1998. In this context, portrayals of national empowerment and social pride in popular culture are an invaluable political asset.

The widespread availability of broadcast media in Wales from the 1950s onwards and its well-documented impact on social narratives makes this an obvious site of study.[5] Often, the media play a pivotal role in disempowering subordinate nations by promoting assimilation within the dominant society, reinforced by the economic and political structures of hegemonic media environments.[6] Yet the media can also be a vehicle for resistance to assimilation and social mobilization. Indeed, David Barlow observes that there is 'ample evidence of the media being instrumental in the process of developing a sense of nation' and building Wales as an 'imagined community', energizing Welsh nationalism.'[7] Moreover, TV and radio media in Wales were explicitly politicized through the struggle for Welsh-language services: Saunders Lewis's famous speech calling for the active defence of the Welsh language, *Tynged yr Iaith*, was broadcast on radio, while Gwynfor Evans went on hunger strike to demand that the Welsh-language channel, S4C, be created.[8]

Another key medium of cultural content are materials produced for children, given that schools are a primary site of authoritative knowledge production and dissemination. As Peter Hunt suggests, children's books engineer society in contestable ways: 'Adults write,

children read and this means that ... adults are exercising power
and children are either being manipulated or resisting manipulation
... Children's books are inevitably didactic in some way.[9] Indeed,
schools are a core medium for nation-building and the diffusion of
cultural capital, as teachers not only present 'facts' but interpret them
too.[10] Even in 1976, Bud Khleif argued that Welsh-medium schools
'are agencies for building self-confidence and ... increas[ing] awareness of ... cultural heritage', noting that teachers 'have a sense of mission' to 'get the slurs and distortions out of their history textbooks'.[11] It
is through interpretation that pupils absorb the dominant narrative,
and its retelling to family and friends reinforces the established myths
more broadly in society.[12] This is especially true in Welsh-speaking
Wales where the teaching profession is highly valued in society, not
only for the knowledge they impart, but also for their role in promoting and sustaining the Welsh language and its core cultural assets.
Teaching pupils about Y Wladfa – a success story of Welsh courage,
ingenuity and moral strength – thus contributed by counteracting the
negative discourse of Welsh inadequacy. In turn, the narrative likely
shaped dominant cultural interpretations in film, TV, art, theatre, etc.
whose authors could themselves be highly influenced by what they
learned at school.[13]

   Children's literature plays a pivotal role in teaching pride in national identity, then, and in Wales this was first promoted by O. M.
Edwards who developed *Cymru'r Plant* (Children's Wales) in the
1890s and much of children's literature – including publications
about Y Wladfa – follows this lead.[14] As Siwan Rosser explains, Edwards aimed 'to foster a collective national identity for Wales' and 'in-
still[ed] in children a collective sense of belonging'.[15] Moreover, *Cymru'r Plant* both reflected and shaped Welsh political concerns. It was
published during a surge of nationalism, just as Welsh Liberal MPs
were advocating Home Rule, and was a 'call to arms' for Welsh youth.
Rosser explains: 'his many real readers responded enthusiastically to
his call' which resonated beyond the classroom, as: 'the warmth ...
is evidence of how readily many Welsh children, parents and teachers welcomed [*Cymru'r Plant*]'.[16] As we will see shortly, R. Bryn Williams's writing about Y Wladfa, especially his children's novel *Bandit
yr Andes*, played a similar role in the 1960s political resurgence, an-
choring national pride to Wales's Patagonian colony.

Reviving Y Wladfa 1950–70

It seems that Y Wladfa faded from public consciousness in Wales for the first half of the twentieth century, linked to the passing of the original settlers and the gradual assimilation of the Welsh within the Argentine model of citizenship. Interest was rekindled, though, during the 1950s and gained momentum in the run-up to the centenary in 1965 which offered an opportunity to celebrate the feat at a time of uncertainty for the Welsh language and culture at home.

Some of the first outputs were made by W. R. Owen, an influential radio producer who, in 1962, created a landmark programme for BBC television, *The Desert and the Dream*, narrated by Hywel Davies with research by R. Bryn Williams.[17] It opens with nostalgic music, which sets a Welsh air to the Spanish guitar, to create an atmosphere of wistful nostalgia for a fading world, mingled with pride. It starts with footage of cattle wrangling and introduces us to an array of gauchos with 'unlikely names' like 'the best bronco rider in the whole valley, Handel Jones', men who 'speak Spanish, and Welsh'. In a melancholy celebration of the pioneer spirit, Davies tells how 'their great grandfathers opened up some of the toughest country in South America' but infers that they, and their dream, are a relic of the past. He goes on to chart the decline of Welsh culture – no Welsh-speaking minsters for the chapels, St David's Hall now an athletics club and the pampas grass creeping over the graves of Lewis Jones and Abraham Matthews. Twice he states that 'the Welsh language is dying in Patagonia' and, by inference, the Welsh themselves.

Other documentaries of the era adopt a similar uneasy tone, as though they are unsure of the mostly assimilated Argentines they find. In *Patagonia 68*, John Ormond films men sitting around an *asado* (Argentine barbecue) wearing gaucho clothing and sipping mate, yet also singing 'Oes Gafr Eto?', an odd performance of Welshness.[18] Is their hybridity a cause to celebrate Welsh endurance, or a source of sadness that the Welsh way of life is so vulnerable to assimilation? Certainly, the achievements are celebrated (especially the irrigation system) and the resilience of Welsh culture is gladly showcased via interviews with Irma Jones de Hughes about *Y Drafod* (Welsh-language newspaper) and Tegai Roberts's radio programmes. But Ormond closes by reflecting backwards to the glories of the past and the feat of survival, saying: 'Miracle, miracle in the way that the first visitors conquered the difficulties in all directions. As is their love for Wales, their interest in the language, in Wales and her traditions.'[19]

These outputs were perhaps influenced by the wider cultural context in Wales which was similarly characterized by both the fear of cultural collapse and a desire to seek stories and contemporary actions that engendered pride. This was the period of Saunders Lewis's *Tynged yr Iaith*, the Welsh-language TV licence strike and the founding of the language campaigning movement, Cymdeithas yr Iaith Gymraeg.[20] The centenary of Y Wladfa in 1965 fitted into this wave of mobilization and added an international dimension to the broader campaign for language rights and cultural dignity.

It is in this context that R. Bryn Williams's books for children and adults played a vital role in shaping Welsh understanding of Y Wladfa as a heroic enterprise, building robust cultural capital. Indeed, as Esther Whitfield suggests, his outputs 'prepare the ground' for the rise of Welsh nationalism, political resistance and cultural reassertion in the 1960s.[21] He began by sharing popular stories he heard growing up in Y Wladfa in *Straeon Patagonia* but *Bandit yr Andes*, a book for 8–12-year-olds (analysed below), is his best-known fictional work.[22] Like *Cymru'r Plant*, it celebrated the goodness of the *gwerin* (rural folk), inspired Welsh society at a time when it seemed under threat and enabled cultural resistance by imagining a flourishing future for Wales, embodied by children.[23] *Bandit yr Andes* had already won a prize at the 1950 National Eisteddfod in Caerphilly and was then transmitted on the Welsh-language BBC children's hour slot, *Awr y Plant*.[24] The book was a favourite of town and school libraries (my own copy is stamped as belonging to the 'Secondary Modern School, Llanrwst') and is often recalled with nostalgia by those who read it at school. Two children's authors today – Siân Lewis and Siân Northey – both cite *Bandit yr Andes* as a stand-out book from their childhood, while E. Wyn James calls it a touchstone of Welsh media and cultural production.[25] In addition, R. Bryn Williams was an academic historian who wrote the first and still influential history of Welsh Patagonia: *Y Wladfa*.[26] This too was available in school libraries for older children (my copy belonged to the 'Senior School, Gwaun-Cae-Curwen').

One way to begin decolonial discussions is to ask how Indigenous people are portrayed in these cultural products. In some documentaries, Indigenous people are scarcely mentioned, and then just appear as characters in the past, a form of narration which naturalizes settler colonialism and renders their contemporary presence invisible. For example, in *Desert and the Dream*, Davies narrates only that, 'Patagonia was Indian territory ... [where] the forefathers of these Indians hunted and rode to war.'[27] This is important because, as discussed in the theory section, relegating Indigeneity to the past is a way of declaring that colonialism is over and that the 'elimination of the native' is complete. In another example, Nan Davies's *Y Gymru Bell* (also from 1962), Indigenous people are made visible in the present, yet their only relevance is as emblems of the past.[28] Thus, while she conducts lively interviews with Welsh-speaking farmers about sheep breeding, alfalfa crops and their families, she brings an Indigenous child on screen merely to refer to his grandfather as: 'the head of a tribe of nomadic Indians'. She mobilizes his presence on the streets of Gaiman today to serve Welsh interests by using it as a hook to reflect on the myth of friendship and celebrate 'religious heritage of the old Welsh settlers'.[29] While we would not expect her to do otherwise at this time, the portrayal signals that Indigenous people are 'of the past' and 'backwards' even if they stand next to us on the street. A critical view today helps to identify how media representations can reflect and recreate persistent tropes which empower the Welsh and disempower the 'Indian boy'. In doing so, these portrayals both endorse and naturalize the settler colonial order.

We can see how the discourse of legitimate, indeed moral, settlement works by examining the children's novel *Bandit yr Andes* which celebrates the Welsh-Indigenous friendship within 'benevolent', patriarchal settler colonialism. The story begins when three Welsh Patagonian children – Dei, Glyn and Morfydd – become lost in the *paith* after playing truant from school. They stumble across a gang led by Bandido Diego who take them by force to their hide-out – a secret valley accessed only by a cave – where they discover they are not bandits, but freedom fighters. There, Diego's sister, Ramona, suggests that they make friends with the 'Indians', led by Tiwel. Ramona explains: 'Diego learned of this valley from Chief Saweti because he had been a friend to the Indians', adding, 'they and we are safe from the Army here'.[30] This short exchange establishes the story's moral economy which pivots around relations with the 'Indians', even though they are absent in this discussion. We realize that the 'dangerous' bandits are morally good, not only due to Ramona's kindness but also because they are friends with the 'Indians'. *Bandit yr Andes* thus deploys the 'myth of friendship' to signal moral virtue – and also links immorality to Argentine military persecution (the Conquest of the Desert).

The children's first encounter endorses the truth of Welsh-Indigenous friendship which, as I argued in chapter five, in turn confirms Welsh virtue and the cultural capital that it imparts. The children ride to the 'Indian Camp' and go to greet the 'Chief' in Welsh: 'Welcome children, friends of the Indians … I have been down to Y Wladfa and learned Welsh in School of the Welsh.'[31] The 'proof' that the 'Indians' love the Welsh is sealed by Cacique Tiwel's trust of the Welsh and appreciation of the language (though of course as a 'savage' he must speak it clumsily).

The story also, perhaps unsurprisingly, reinforces a gendered and racialized 'natural order of things'. Diego's benevolent settler masculinity is demonstrated by his paternalistic agency as a European who intervenes to save, as a father might, the defenceless and pitiable Indians from the vicious army captain, Miranda. This contrasts with the passivity of their leader, Chief Saweti who says, 'I will leave everything to the friends of the Indians', a move which diminishes Saweti's masculinity and reinforces Diego's benevolent authority.[32]

In stark contrast to Diego is Officer Miranda whose villainous character is confirmed by his treatment of the Indigenous Patagonians. He explains to his troops:

> As you know the Indians are a plague and a disgrace in our country and it is our responsibility to catch them and drive them to the Capital. Around a hundred of them have been caught in the Andes. We will go to fetch them. There is no need to treat them with care at all because they are no better than animals. Truly, these horses are worth more than them.[33]

However, Williams lets us know that Miranda is a 'bad apple', and it was people like him, not the Argentine government, who were responsible for the violent repression of Indigenous Patagonians during the Conquest of the Desert. In a speech to a Welsh chapel congregation later on, Diego explains:

As you know, Miranda and his soldiers are collecting [Indians] on the pampas on the orders of the government. But the government did not want them to be abused. After all, the Indians were in this country before us. The aim of the government is to collect them in special places of the country in order to educate them in the benefits of our civilization. But what happened? Miranda collected them all up, abused them on the way down from the Andes and drove them to the Capital. Why? To sell them as slaves ... which is against the law. My only aim is to save the poor Indians from falling into his hands.[34]

This speech solidifies the binary between good and evil, but also distances the Argentine government from responsibility for the Conquest of the Desert, rewriting history. Perhaps this should not be surprising given that, by the 1950s, the Welsh settlers had adopted Argentine identity and felt loyal to their adopted nation and its civilizing mission. It also demonstrates Diego's paternalism and celebrates the superiority of European ways of life, expressed through 'our civilization'. This civilization entails 'developing' the 'primitive' Indians. Later, when Glyn reflects that the 'Indians' cannot sustain their former hunting ways in the enclosed valley, Ramona explains this change not as a devastating loss of their way of life but as an opportunity to develop European lifeways, saying:

we taught them how to farm. There are hundreds of milking cows here. And we have fields of wheat to have bread. There are also plenty of pigs and chickens. Plenty of fruit on the trees, and fish in the river. We could live well here for years.[35]

The book thus celebrates Indigenous assimilation (and the erasure of their way of life) through Diego's paternalistic generosity. It suggests that effective colonization could be best accomplished not through coercion or violence but by an act of Christian love, in a reiteration of familiar motifs from the nineteenth-century trove of Welsh stories and ideas, as we saw in chapter five.

Williams does portray one scene where Indigenous people take centre stage. They hold a ceremony with song, dance and speeches which conveys a sense of Indigenous concerns and spirituality. Saweti speaks in the 'Indian language' of 'the courage of their ancestors … their right to the vast lands of Patagonia and of how the Christians or bad Spanish stole it from them … their persecution and the suffering that their people endured.'[36] Yet this portrayal confirms that glory is in the past and today the Indigenous are subjugated, not only by the army but by the white settler class. Saweti is merely a device to reflect settler powerfulness as Williams makes his final words all about the Welsh and Diego: 'He raised his eyes towards the rising sun and thanked Pilan for sending the Welsh to Y Wladfa … And to bless the work of the Indian's friends.'[37]

The book ends with a scene of happy settler colonialism which is portrayed as moral, effective and a cause for celebration. At a Christmas gathering, the Welsh schoolteacher states that: 'The Welsh are called the "Friends of the Indians" … We vehemently appealed on behalf of the poor Indians at the government's door, but in vain … It is good to welcome Chief Saweti too … Without his help we would have starved when we first came.'[38] Thus Williams reminds us of the well-known stories that anchor the novel in Y Wladfa's history, strengthening the seeming veracity of both. Then the children call on Chief Saweti to speak: 'Pilan did well … sent Diego and other men to save Indians. We do not forget. Welsh are very fine too. We now live in Indian Valley … We come to trade skins and feathers for bread … We happy now. Welsh too live happy.'[39] These declarations of friendship endorse settler colonialism and celebrate the Welsh way of colonization. It is this message that enables Y Wladfa to be held aloft as a source of pride and mobilization in Wales during the campaigns for cultural resurgence in the 1960s.

Mainstreaming Y Wladfa: 1970–2000

The centenary celebrations in 1965 generated renewed interest in Y Wladfa and it became a standard topic in the Welsh cultural landscape, especially for Welsh speakers. Academic interest in Y Wladfa grew in a cultural climate which began to focus on reinterpreting Welsh history, concentrating on labour movements and identity which resonated with a growing confidence and new focus on culture in wider society.[40] The landmark text *The Desert and the Dream* by Glyn Williams (R. Bryn Williams's son) emerged in the same intellectual spirit, providing detailed facts and a rigorous academic analysis of the economy and political relationships in Welsh Patagonia. During the upsurge of pride and engagement in Welsh culture, Y Wladfa was drawn into the mainstream of Welsh life and became a fairly frequent feature of TV and radio, following on from the early documentaries. For example, Dai Jones Llanilar recorded *Cefn Gwlad* in Patagonia, Selwyn Roderick filmed *Plant y Paith* in the early 1980s, and returned in the late 1990s to make the documentary *Patagonia: Yno o Hyd*.[41] All were repeated quite often. Usually, programmes revolved around interviews with older people who reflected on their family stories, as a form of oral history. One example is *Oes yn y Wladfa* (1985) in which Gareth Owen interviews Garmon Owen who went to Patagonia in 1910.[42] Programmes such as *Patagonia Heddiw* (2008) with Huw Meredydd Roberts feature a number of shorter interviews with Welsh speakers, including many of the same personalities.[43] Similarly, the four programmes of *Cof Patagonia* (2002) trace the history of Y Wladfa from 1902 to 2002 through the reflections of current Welsh descendants, matched with evocative images of family photographs.[44] All of these programmes are quite repetitive, largely through necessity because the place and pool of interesting Welsh speakers is small. The themes are similar too – and indeed echo these of the earlier series: the history and importance of the irrigation system, farming practices, chapel life, Welsh culture (radio, museum, eisteddfod); Argentine culture (gauchos, asado, mate); and the gradual decline of Welsh values and the language. Indigenous people rarely feature in such programmes, appearing only as stories of the old past, or as haunting images. In this way, Y Wladfa and the outline of its story became familiar to the wider Welsh public, building on the childhood tales and normalizing the settler colonial environment, with Original Peoples a distant memory.

Y Wladfa also became a mainstream topic in schools. The Education Reform Act of 1988 created a separate statutory body for Education in Wales, and enabled the development in 1993 of the Curriculum Cymreig which aimed explicitly to promote Welsh culture and heritage.[45] This initiative developed from educational activists in Wales already teaching Welsh historical achievements, as well as

organizing cultural events like eisteddfodau. This 'cultural restorationism' was, in Wales, a reaction against Thatcherism but also reflected a shift in history teaching away from 'great men of England'
to the celebration of everyday historical actors, an approach better
suited to Welsh historical experience.[46] The explicit adoption of the
Curriculum Cymreig spurred these trends and led to the creation of
history textbooks, some of which are in use today, that now included
Y Wladfa in the panoply of Welsh heroic feats. For example, in book
4 of *Cymru Ddoe a Heddiw* published in 1990, Geraint Jenkins introduced Y Wladfa within a section on the Welsh language, alongside a
discussion of scientist Thomas Gee, the Eisteddfod, the Urdd (youth
organization) and Cymdeithas yr Iaith Gymraeg (Welsh Language
Society). He framed Y Wladfa as 'one of the most courageous and
romantic chapters in Welsh history' and emphasized the Welsh desire for a righteous settlement, saying 'their hope was ... to establish
their own chapels and schools and to live peacefully in freedom'.[47]
Indigenous people are only mentioned once in the text: 'The Indians
showed them how to hunt', and are thus made fleetingly present in
order to signal the 'myth of friendship'.[48]

Similarly, *Storïau Hanes Cymru*, another Key Stage One textbook,
celebrates Y Wladfa alongside Llewelyn (last 'true' prince of Wales),
Betsi Cadwaladr (pioneering nurse), Hedd Wyn (First World War
poet) and Laura Ashley (fashion designer).[49] Pupils learn by reading a
short novel *Daniel Evans* while the teacher's workbook provides notes
and materials.[50] The reader learns about Edwyn Roberts's lecture in
Wales; the *Mimosa* journey; settler life (farm, school, chapel and
eisteddfod) and ends with a vision of the successful settlement. Indigenous Patagonians appear in this tale in a description of the 'first
encounter', accompanied by an illustration, which reads: 'Daniel's
aunt, Ann, fell in love with Edwyn. On their wedding day, Indians
suddenly arrived. Daniel was afraid. He had never seen Indians before but they all soon became good friends.'[51] This event makes Indigenous people visible in the story, yet the text portrays them as Other:
they arrive 'suddenly' and instil fear, disrupting a moment of love and
unity in the Welsh community, but then fear is resolved through the
myth of friendship. Its message is ambiguous. On the one hand it suggests that Daniel's fears were unfounded and he should not misjudge
Othered people, yet it also portrays Y Wladfa as unproblematic and

settler colonialism seems 'natural' while Indigenous people (without being given names or families, a past nor a future in the text) simply appear in order to add, and then resolve, the jeopardy of Otherness. The teacher's notes which accompany the story do not refer to the 'Indians' at all. This leaves both children and teacher to interpret this element of the story as they will – to ignore it, misrepresent or even problematize it, yet without guidance.

The purpose of such textbooks was to introduce children to key characters and events in Welsh history which have been ignored or demeaned previously. It was part of a social and political movement to strengthen Welsh culture in accordance with the Curriculum Cymreig which aimed to 'help pupils to understand and celebrate … living and learning in Wales … to identify their own sense of Welshness… and to foster … an understanding of an outward-looking and international Wales'.[52] However, this nationalist agenda with anti-assimilationist goals, was predicated on interpreting Y Wladfa as an unproblematic enterprise and Indigenous people as caricatures whose presence serves only to illustrate Welsh goodness. Thus, the colonial relationships which characterized nineteenth-century Patagonia were reproduced in textbooks, without filter, in twentieth- (and indeed twenty-first) century schoolrooms.

A core motif of this period is the 'glass corridor' between Wales and Patagonia. Many of the TV programmes open with a map and dotted line which literally draws an exclusive pathway across the Atlantic. Similarly, the story book *Daniel Evans* opens with two children, one in Wales and one in Patagonia, who share his ancestry and are linked by holding two copies of the same photograph. This search for a twin image of Welshness in Patagonia is pursued by documentary makers. For example, the TV programme *Pobl y Wladfa* (1991) sees Glyn Llewelyn visit the Trelew Eisteddfod and follows a familiar format.[53] It opens with chapel singing and pans across the open *paith*, Llewelyn interviews notable Welsh speakers (Mair Davies in the Christian bookshop, Luned Gonzales at Lewis Jones's graveside), he visits the Welsh school and a Welsh learner's class, and finally films a packed eisteddfod hall which shows that 'there is still a bustling Welshness [*bwrlwm Gymreig*] here'. However, while the motifs mirror life in Wales, the Welshness feels like a thin performance, especially when he interviews young competitors in awkward Welsh, and even thinner when the two old brothers at Hyde Park Farm explain that they are Argentine 'it is just that we speak Welsh'. Llewelyn may have opened with the phrase 'Welcome to distant Patagonia, a country that surely means something to every one of us', but quite what it means beyond the performance of Welshness is neither clear, nor explored.

This sense of a glass corridor and the search for an elusive 'authentic' Welshness is a key theme in film star Matthew Rhys's 2006 TV programme *O'r Môr i'r Mynydd*.[54] The documentary follows an annual horse-back re-enactment of the Rifleros journey with Colonel Fontana to 'discover' Cwm Hyfryd in 1885. It is still recalled today partly, I suspect, because of its star narrator, but also because of the bilingual coffee table book it generated.[55] The film is evocative and beautifully shot, fuelled by a romantic and heroic understanding of Y Wladfa in which Welsh men (and this is a very masculinist enterprise) are the chief protagonists. The Welsh gauchos are quiet and tenacious, tough and emotional, and deliver a vision of the past that owes more to nostalgia than reality. Indeed, there is often a sense in TV portrayals that Wales is searching for a glimpse of its own past in this 'backwards' Patagonian location and emphasizes a desired history rather than historical fact. For example, while it was Colonel Fontana who led the expedition, he is mentioned just once and only after twenty minutes of the half-hour programme. Moreover, Argentina's nation-building military project and the Conquest of the Desert is absent from the story. I discussed the journey of Fontana and the Rifleros in chapter six, based on the diaries of John Murray Thomas, John Daniel Evans and Luis Jorge Fontana. A key moment in those accounts was encountering the ruins of Foyel's camp with its obvious signs of battle and death. Rhys does not mention this, nor does he Martín Platero, the Indigenous man forced to guide them to the mountains whose traumatic experiences were noted in all three diaries. By making the trip about Welsh pioneers, rather than Argentine colonization/nation-building, the TV programme can ignore these vivid encounters with violence. By contrast, Rhys does spend time at the monument at the Valley of the Martyrs and recalls the Malacara story, saying 'the Welsh were murdered by three Indigenous (*brodorion*)' and this time does cite an entry from John Murray Thomas's diary: 'we put stones over the graves of the men that were assassinated by the Indians'. Then, while the film shows a mural with Indigenous faces in raised cement, he explains that the fourth Welshman 'escaped from the attackers by galloping his horse across a precipice'. Rhys thus portrays Indigenous people as both savage and in the past, existing today only as images, no more and celebrates this highly masculinized settler venture. The film is a perceptive and evocative portrayal of this band of men, but it presents a version of the original journey which serves a very partial truth, in both senses of the word.

Same old story? The 150th commemoration

The run-up to the 150th anniversary in 2015 coincided with a period of growing confidence in the capacity of Wales to sustain a distinctive political and cultural profile and an opening-up of Welsh history.[56] Also being questioned in wider public fora was the British colonial legacy, while the decolonial agenda in universities was gathering pace, as well as international movements such as the Native American Idle No More (2012) and Black Lives Matter (2013) campaigns.[57] A tentative climate for reassessing Y Wladfa was growing, and two films contributed to this reappraisal: the mainstream movie *Patagonia* (2010) and the indie film, *Seperado* (2010).

Patagonia did much to renew interest in Y Wladfa in the run-up to the 150th anniversary of the *Mimosa*'s arrival. Although the reviews and analysis focused on the novel plotline (two stories running in parallel) and the complex lives of the female characters, it also marked a step-change in thinking by presenting a more nuanced and reflective discussion about the colony and Welshness.[58] To my eyes, the film expresses conflicted feelings about Welsh identity and the performance of the 'same old tropes' which are tested in the crucible of Patagonia. For example, we first meet the Welsh protagonist Gwen while she works as a guide at St Fagan's Museum of Welsh Life. Dressed in a 'typical' black hat and shawl, her performance of classic Welshness is disrupted by her speaking on her mobile phone. This dissonance between a cherished yet performed Welsh stereotype is echoed by the project which takes Rhys, her partner, to Patagonia to photograph the Welsh chapels. He sets up elaborate time-lapse systems to catch repeated images of empty buildings standing alone in the *paith*, representing a spiritual past, flooded with ghosts. 'Arwrol [heroic]' he says to Matteo, their Welsh Patagonian guide, who just pulls a face (though he later agrees). Matteo makes money by showing Welsh tourists the sights, the fantasy Wladfa: his friend Diego says 'he sells dreams to tourists – takes them out on horseback'.[59] While Rhys seeks out the well-worn Welsh story, the lived reality of Welsh Patagonia disrupts his assumptions. He meets a Welsh-speaking veteran of the Falklands/Malvinas war (on the Argentine side), Martín Corazón Jones ('corazón' means 'heart'): he is drunken and sentimental, they play pool and listen to ZZ Top, he pulls a knife and steals the camera equipment, he rages and cries over his dog, yet he is a friend. Rhys's plans are also scuppered when the small Indigenous boy Pablito steals and unravels his roll of film; meanwhile his wife escapes with Matteo, searching for, but soon discarding, life on his run-down farm. The parallel story of a teenager (brilliantly played by Nahuel Pérez Bizcayart) and his elderly neighbour coming to Wales in search of her home farm, has less to say about Welsh culture but it reminds us that the settlers were more than caricatures – they were people, including women, with complex back stories and mixed emotions.

The film leaves us with a sense of unease because it opens a series of questions: what is the significance of Y Wladfa? Why do we venerate chapels or dress up in costumes? What is the past for? It rejects many of the stereotypes portrayed in television programmes and books, and it thus contributes significantly to opening more mature conversations about Welsh identity, viewed through the lens of this icon within the Welsh cultural repertoire, Patagonia. Yet still the film is, really, all about the Welsh and while it does challenge Welshness, it keeps the 'old stories' about Welsh-Indigenous relations alive. In the (trilingual) text introduction before the film starts, Patagonia is described as a *terra nullius*, 'a far off territory inhabited only by nomadic tribes of Tehuelches … [where they] worked hard to irrigate the land and, helped by the Tehuelche, they finally conquered the stony plains'.[60] Moreover, in an interview on the DVD version, Marc Evans enthuses about the project, reflecting on 'the unique adventure, partly because of the fantastic relationship between the Welsh colony and the Indigenous Indians at the time when Argentina was forming'.[61] Given that he grew up with such stories, it is unsurprising that Evans reiterates the 'myth of friendship' discourse. While he does not bring these stereotypes directly into the story, they still underpin his approach to the movie, and the Welsh Patagonian enterprise.

Seperado, though, calls for a far more radical reassessment because it sees the whole place (not just selected Welsh excerpts) as it is today.[62] Made by Gruff Rhys of the Super Furry Animals, this brilliant, anarchic (and sometimes very funny) movie challenges stereotypes about Y Wladfa, whilst never losing its Welshness. The film is often factually flawed but Rhys eyes Y Wladfa with a critical gaze not encountered elsewhere. He calls out the 'Welsh media gang-bang, people like me falling over themselves to *cyrraedd* [find] this crazy, romantic place and … It's got tea houses, it's got chapels, daffodils, you name it.' Unusually, he discusses the impact of the last military dictatorship (1976–83) and the capturing and assassination of young people who tried to resist it.

Most importantly, he spends around ten minutes discussing the situation of Indigenous people today. He drives (to the soundtrack 'Gyrru, Gyrru, Gyrru') to Paso de Indios where he stops and films young Indigenous people riding bikes on the street. His film makes space for sociologist Santiago Farina and human rights lawyer Gustavo Macayo to provide nuanced critical analysis. Farina calls the 'peaceful relationship' a 'legend' and undermines its claim to be unique in the Americas. He highlights the horror of the Indigenous genocide in Patagonia, and shows the statue of General Roca in Buenos Aires covered in graffiti which makes visually present Indigenous political resistance today. Macayo charts the human rights abuses they continue to endure, saying 'they have been systematically segregated and separated from state structures and marginalized from society. Yes, there is racism, not just the Welsh descendants – it is generalized.' Indeed, Macayo frames his analysis within the sweep of global capitalist expansion and settler colonialism, thus shattering the glass corridor, saying 'the Welsh weren't directly responsible for the genocide but they did benefit and … this allowed the Argentine state to say that Patagonia is Argentine, because this was the first foothold of colonization.' *Seperado* makes space to tell the 'Other' story of the Chubut Valley lived today and invests film time to present important critiques of settler colonialism, a commitment which is impressive and also unique: it has never been repeated in the mainstream media. Yet it does not take that final step to actually include the voices,

thoughts and concerns of Indigenous Patagonians themselves. Tehuelche and Mapuche people remain silent – they are politicized and
spoken about, but not given centre stage in their own story.
Despite Rhys's efforts, the wider discourse did not shift. Indeed,
as the 2015 deadline neared, this critical phase began to close and
analysis retreated into the familiar stories and stereotypes as critique
made way for celebration. One high-profile example of this trend
was the discussion of Indigenous-Welsh relations in *Patagonia with
Huw Edwards* (a former senior BBC newsreader).[63] Mostly, the programme sustained the usual narrative – this is a 'story of courage,
enterprise and dedication which ignites one's imagination' and 'one of
the greatest adventures of Welsh history'. However, in a step forwards,
this colonial context is portrayed as having losers, not just winners:
'it is ironic the Welsh had occupied land that was home to a power-
less minority on another continent. We should be careful when we
talk of a close relationship between the Welsh and Indigenous people.
There's been a tendency to sentimentalize everything'. Yet the discussion goes no further and unpacking the settlement project per se is
avoided. The documentary frames the Malacara incident in the Conquest of the Desert ('nobody should be surprised that this extreme
mistreatment had created an urge to take revenge on the new settlers') but colonialism is placed firmly in the past. Thus, Indigenous
people and injustice are made visible, but the logics of possession,
barbarization and assimilation, of which the Welsh were an integral
part, are not discussed. Moreover, there is no mention of Indigenous
communities today, their struggle for land rights or the continuities
of settler capitalism and racism.

Of course, these limitations are not surprising, given the powerfulness of the myth of friendship in Welsh culture and society, and
the nature of the programme. Moreover, the atmosphere around
the 150th anniversary was one of celebration and inter-Welsh cultural exchange, reinforcing the sensation of a 'glass corridor', which
discussions of colonialism would have disrupted. A wide range of
cultural products flooded the media.[64] Jon Gower's book *Gwalia Patagonia* became a bestseller and well-loved presenters such as Beti
George made radio programmes featuring the quirky personalities
and stories drawn from the Welsh-speaking communities of Patagonia, while journalist Dylan Iorwerth made a three-part series for

BBC Wales, *Patagonia 150*.[65] There was even a radio sitcom about the *Mimosa* and the founding years called *Somewhere Else*.[66] Beyond the media, activities were supported by the Arts Council of Wales, including visits by Welsh artists like Luned Rhys Parri, jewellery maker Steph Davies and poet Mererid Hopwood.[67] Harpist Catrin Finch and the BBC National Orchestra of Wales also went to Patagonia, giving two concerts and playing with local musicians, schools and community groups.[68] Some musicians went in the opposite direction, such as Nicolas Avila who joined the band Brigyn with his bandoneon on a tour of Wales, playing at the Llangollen International Festival and the official ceremony in Cardiff.[69] All of the activities were focused on celebrating cultural links between Wales and Patagonia and, given the spirit of celebration, none of the coverage in the press or websites seems to have thought critically about the colonial venture, or made connections with Indigenous communities.

Indeed, the activities around the anniversary served to backtrack and re-adopt the 'heroic feat' and 'myth of friendship' narratives, glossing over colonialism and making any critique of Y Wladfa very difficult. Of course, for the descendants of the settlers this was a chance to honour the memory of their forebears and to share stories of their courage, fortitude, setbacks and survival. On a personal level it is understandable that they should enjoy public recognition and approbation of their ancestors' undoubted bravery and hard work. One example of this dynamic is the coffee-table book of photographs edited by Eirionedd Baskerville, a knowledgeable and assiduous researcher, which charts the 'pioneers' who 'rolled up their sleeves and set about taming the wilderness'.[70] As expected, the notes which accompany the photographs celebrate the Welsh settlers as key protagonists. For example, a photograph of the statue above Puerto Madryn which depicts an 'Indian' looking out to sea is annotated 'as if he could see the approaching Mimosa'.[71] This places the Welsh as agents at the centre of the Indigenous story, as if they are incomplete without their Welsh settler compatriots. By contrast, the earlier book *Una Frontera Lejana*, which reprints photographs by John Murray Thomas, Henry Bowman and Carlos Foresti, is far less celebratory and emotively charged.[72]

It was in this spirit of Welsh heroism that a plaque was unveiled on Liverpool's Princess Dock in May 2015 to commemorate the *Mimosa*'s

departure. There, Dr Ben Rees of the Merseyside Welsh Heritage Society spoke of the 'heroic first settlers' and hinted at the tenacity of
Welshness when saluting 'the Argentinian Welsh community for
keeping their heritage alive'.[73] Also in attendance were Carwyn Jones,
then first minister of Wales, the lord mayor of Liverpool, a descendant
of Edwyn Roberts as well as the Argentine ambassador to the UK,
Dr Alicia Castro. The anniversary was also a political showcase, then.

The Welsh government was obviously involved in the commemoration, and sponsored the cultural exchanges of artists and musicians,
capitalizing on the reflected heroism of the early settlers. The visit of
the Argentine ambassador to Wales and the first minister's reciprocal
visit to Chubut raised the visibility of the government's activities and
developed its international profile, strengthening the institution in
Welsh eyes. The first minister launched proceedings on 1 February
2015 in Cardiff with Ambassador Castro, saying 'as a nation, we are
very proud of the strong links that we share with the settlements in
Patagonia', while Lord Dafydd Wigley, lifelong Welsh politician and
honorary chair of the Welsh Celebrations Coordinating Committee,
expressed the hope that these events would bring the governments
of Argentina and the UK closer together.[74] Similarly, the first minister's visit to Chubut (26–8 July) was hailed as 'a diplomatic success',
not least because no British official of the first minister's rank had
visited Argentina for ten years.[75] Jones's itinerary in Chubut mingled
political formalities with a succession of 'typical' Welsh activities: he
met with Governor Martín Buzzi and prominent cabinet ministers
Aníbal Fernández and Mario Das Neves, but also visited Welsh-language schools and museums, laid a wreath on Lewis Jones's grave and
had tea at Capel Seion in Bryn Gwyn.[76] The effect of this activity was
to raise Wales's profile as an international actor respected by a major G20 power, and whose role in foreign policy was taken seriously.
This contrasts with the scant attention paid by Westminster and the
London-centric media to these events, confining its impact to the key
constituency of Welsh voters.

Argentina also used these events to promote the incumbent Per-
onist government's political agenda. As ever, this was built on the
'myth of friendship' discourse. First, they deployed it to strengthen
the Malvinas claim (an issue that always plays well to Argentina's do-
mestic audience). Buzzi argued 'the Welsh settlement in our lands

belies the idea held by some [Malvinas/Falkland] Islanders that under the Argentine flag they would not be respected'.[77] This argument was reiterated by Alicia Castro, who claimed Argentine credit for the endurance of Welsh culture: 'the establishment of Welsh settlers in Argentina, that preserved their traditions, language and cultural identity, is a fine example of the respect, friendship and opportunities that our county offers to British descendants'.[78] (She also provocatively gave Carwyn Jones a book called *Malvinas Matters: Notes from the Embassy of Argentina in London.*)

Secondly, the 'myth of friendship' was used to strengthen Argentina's multicultural agenda which, alongside a very progressive LGBTQ+ platform, burnished its credentials as a Westernized country, thus elevating its regional and global position. Indigenous people had won recognition of their 'prior occupancy' of Argentine soil during the rewriting of the constitution in 1994 which opened space for Indigenous communities to make land claims over their former territories.[79] Alicia Castro was aligned with the Kirchner governments of the 2000s which facilitated these claims, and also developed an 'intercultural education programme' which introduced the teaching of Indigenous languages and cultures (patchily) to the primary school curriculum.[80] For the Argentine state, the Welsh-Indigenous 'friendship' was something to celebrate, because it exemplified both a happy colonial past (diverting attention from the Conquest of the Desert) and a happy settler society in the present. Martín Buzzi also made some political capital from the myth, using it to advocate for 'the need to pull the Mapuche and Tehuelche people from invisibility' which, in turn, acted as a hook for him to mention provincial initiatives.[81] These included the restitution of human remains from museums to be buried 'with dignity and all human rights', programmes to promote the teaching of Mapuche and Tehuelche in schools, and the restitution of '350,000 hectares to 55 Mapuche-Tehuleche communities'.[82] These positive developments were only won after exhausting work on the part of the Indigenous communities themselves – often struggling against obstructive state agencies – but in this forum, and enveloped in the myth of friendship, Buzzi claimed credit for his administration.[83]

The myth of friendship was even appropriated by director of the Argentine National Library, Horacio González, to gloss over the

Conquest of the Desert and the violent oppression endured by Ka-trülaf and his Peoples. In the coffee-table book of photographs com-missioned by the Argentine government, González suggests that 'co-lonialism' entails 'dishonourable methods of forced occupation' and contrasts with 'settlers … [who] establish a way of life by extending their own and who are prepared to be respectful towards the people they encounter'.[84] He lauds the Welsh colony, arguing that 'this epic … purges colonialism of its most dangerous element – subjugation – bringing to the fore instead curiosity about human diversity and the idea of territory as a complex adventure of cultures'.[85] Given his powerful position in the production and dissemination of knowledge in Argentina, this rewriting of history is deeply disturbing as it enables a vision of multicultural Argentina where difference is confined to the harmless realm of culture and all can live in social and political har-mony, deleting memories – and lived realities – of violent subjugation.

The desire to scrub out the violence of forced dispossession and attempted erasure is central to the settler colonial logic which aims to 'eliminate the native' but also to eliminate the stain of shame at the heart of the settler state by reconfiguring history or relegating coloni-alism to the past. As Mariano Nagy explains, the issue of Indigenous rights challenges the usual story of the Conquest of the Desert (that it necessary to forge Argentina – and anyhow a long time ago), so that 'questioning this process equals questioning who we are [as Argen-tines]'.[86] Indigenous people are 'acceptable' he argues so long as they are poor and dispossessed because they fit with the state narrative. Yet this 'tolerable Indian' is counterposed to the 'fake Indian' [indio trucho] who defies the stereotype by acting politically, asserting their rights and refusing to stay in, or of, the past. Such 'Indians' are not celebrated as the quiescent, helpful folk of the 'myth of friendship', rewritten for today, but reconfigured as dangerous subversives, even terrorists. In turn this justifies state intervention, especially if they threaten the 'powerful interests linked to extractivism … agriculture or tourism' by demanding their right to lands that were stolen from them.[87] This results in 'racial name-calling, house invasions, land dis-possession [and] killing by the security forces'.[88] So much for multi-culturalism, which is limited only to the 'tolerable Indian'.

The 2015 commemorations included not only a celebration of the 'friendly Indians' of the past, then, but also their counterpart, the 'tolerable Indians' of the present. Carwyn Jones, for example, witnessed the fictional encounter between Welsh and Indigenous acted out each year on the shores of Puerto Madryn in which bread and water is exchanged and shared. This 'tradition', began during the nation-affirming commemorations of the republic's bicentennial in 2010 and portrays Indigenous and Welsh as equals whilst ignoring the global hierarchies of power and wealth which surrounded that meeting in 1866 – and today.[89]

Similar images of the 'happy settler family' were performed at the opening event in which Silvia Ñanco performed a sacred song or 'Tail' and Lonko (Cacique) Ángel Ñanco of the Tehuelche community, greeted his Mapuche counterparts from Nahuelpán. Perhaps using this strategically as a platform to promote his own community's interests, he praised the efforts of Martín Buzzi and his culture secretary Claudio Dalcó, who had facilitated their efforts to return the remains of Cacique Inakayal stolen in 1880 and stored in La Plata Museum. This was, after all, an opportunity for everyone to strengthen their own political standing and concerns. What is left unsaid in the news reports is that the Centro Indígena Tehuelche Mapuche first began claiming Inakayal's remains in 1989.[90] These were partially returned in 1991, but further remains were found in 2006 which were only returned in 2014 after a long bureaucratic process. During that year Gladys Ñanco of the Pu Fotun Mapú organized a cultural event around this return, with talks and an exhibition, 'demonstrating and promoting understanding of our culture, so that people can see we are a community which still exists and persists in our territories'.[91] The problem of Indigenous invisibility-in-plain-sight which makes Indigenous political impact so difficult is sustained in part by the dominant 'myth of friendship' which 'sees' the Indigenous in the past and thus colludes with the fallacy that Indigenous communities were eliminated in the Conquest of the Desert and exist today only as 'a few remnants' of a dying breed. Simply advertising presence ('persistence') is thus a statement of resistance. She also hints at the institutional obstacles the communities face:

> 'this is the first time in 17 years that the authorities have visited us … we always had to beg for a place … uncertain if they would lend us a venue … It is now [on the eve of 150

commemorations], that the Oceanographic Museum has found a time and space for us so that we could make this event happen.[92]

The portrayal of Indigenous people in Welsh media and school materials echoes these themes, even today, of the desirable 'Indian' as a 'tolerable' Other who is helpful, peaceful and very firmly of the past. As such, it intervenes, albeit indirectly, in racial relationships in Patagonia, working to disempower Indigenous people by supporting the stereotype of acceptable Indigeneity and making their presence and political struggles invisible, both in Wales and in the image of Y Wladfa more broadly. These portrayals have not changed in recent schoolbooks. For example, in *Cymeriadau: Yr Hen Fordd Gymreig*, they are shown as helpful ('teach them how to hunt'), violent (the graphic shows spear-wielding 'Indians') but also weak and pitiable ('today, there are not many Tehuelche Indians at all').[93] A different form of erasure-through-presence is taught in *Dewch i Deithio: Patagonia* where two children, Min and Mei, listen to Tehuelche music which carries them off in a trance 'to somewhere else in Chubut ... to the middle of nowhere'.[94] This makes Indigenous people other-worldly, distant in time and space, and reiterates the *terra nullius* trope in a fresh guise. Most troubling, though, is Indigenous Patagonian portrayal on the much-used *Twinkl* teacher-resources website. The text is highly racializing and borrows the nineteenth-century fallacy of Tehuelche tallness, saying: 'they were very tall with dark skin, long hair and paint on their skin'.[95] They are made relevant only as exotic actors in the past and excluded from the present, warranting no mention in the final section 'Life Today'. This resource is a real anomaly in the current anti-racist agenda in Wales, yet its presence is a symptom of the way that the narrative of Y Wladfa is both constantly reiterated (and therefore 'everyday knowledge') and has been overlooked in discussions about decolonizing the curriculum – and Wales. Of course, it is hard for authors to explain complex political situations and social relationships simply and briefly. But Welsh educators should ask: what work are the images doing and who benefits from this portrayal?

Conclusion

This chapter has analysed how Y Wladfa has been portrayed in popular culture since the 1960s and assessed its role in strengthening Welsh identity by demonstrating cultural tenacity and engendering political pride. It was not the only such emblem in the pantheon of Welsh heroic feats to play a role in Wales's cultural resurgence, but had a special appeal because it added an international dimension and fed the exotic, romantic imagination. Y Wladfa was thus a cultural tool in the fight against further assimilation within the British state and tapped into anti-colonial sentiments (even though labelling Wales as colonized today is problematic). However, doing so depended on reiterating time and again the myth of friendship which, as we have seen from previous chapters, is not only complex and one-sided, but also serves to seal in aspic a romantic vision of Y Wladfa which, while it serves to empower the Welsh, has a detrimental impact on Indigenous people within the settler colonial scenario. The myth relegates Indigenous people to the past which feeds the pernicious dominant narrative in Argentina that 'there are no Indians, they killed them all' in the Conquest of the Desert. This makes the portrayal of Indigenous presence today invisible and silences and disempowers Indigenous people in their struggle for land, dignity and the remains of their loved ones. While I am confident that none of the cultural producers mentioned here aimed to do so, the dominant story told in cultural products for the last sixty years has celebrated and reinforced settler colonial power and marginalized and caricatured Indigenous people, compounding their exclusion from cultural dignity and land rights in Argentina.

My aim here has not been to condemn the cultural producers, but rather to demonstrate how seemingly 'natural' stories are produced and reproduced in popular culture. They have been at work, shaping commonplace ideas and building stories of the past which are cherished because they fortify Welsh culture against the buffeting winds of anglophone assimilation, institutional subordination and sheer prejudice. However, in this new climate of strengthening cultural confidence and the promotion of anti-racism in public life, the time has come to look again, as Gruff Rhys did, with fresh, critical eyes at the 'myth of friendship'. In the concluding chapter, then, we will introduce some Indigenous experiences today, and suggest ways in which we might begin to form a new and meaningful Welsh-Indigenous 'friendship' in the future.

Notes

1   R. Bryn Williams, *Gwladfa Patagonia, 1865–2000* (Llanrwst: Gwasg Carreg Gwalch, 2000), p. 97. This edition has an added Spanish translation.

2   For example, an episode of *Hansh*, '"Cymru a Phatagonia: Rhamantus neu Ormesol?" gan Tegwen', June 2020, *https://www.youtube.com/watch?v=nHN-pm7ylPvc* (accessed 18 December 2023). See also Huw Williams, 'Heb ei Fai, Heb ei Eni: "Disgwrs" a Moeseg y Wladfa', *Gwerddon*, 36/hydref (2023), 55–72.

3   Tim Edensor, *National Identity, Popular Culture and Everyday Life* (Oxford: Berg, 2002), p. 20.

4   Edensor, *National Identity*, p. 20.

5   With many thanks to the team at the Screen and Sound Archive and Broadcast Archive, National Library of Wales, for their invaluable help.

6   David Barlow, Philip Mitchell and Tom O'Malley (eds), *The Media in Wales: Voices of a Small Nation* (Cardiff: University of Wales Press, 2005); Jamie Medhurst, '"Nation shall speak Peace unto Nation"? The BBC and the Nations', *Critical Studies in Television*, 17/1 (2022), 8–23.

7   David Barlow, 'What's in the "Post"? Mass Media as a Site of Struggle', in Jane Aaron and Chris Williams (eds), *Postcolonial Wales* (Cardiff: University of Wales Press, 2005), pp. 193–214, 200.

8   Colin Williams, 'Non-Violence and the Development of the Welsh Language Society, 1962–c.1974', *Welsh History Review*, 8 (1976), 426–55; Elain Price, *Broadcasting for Wales: The Early Years of S4C* (Cardiff: University of Wales Press, 2022).

9   Peter Hunt, '"Instruction and Delight" in Children's Literature: Approaches and Territories', in Janet Maybin and Nicola Watson (eds), *Routledge Companion to Children's Literature and Culture* (Basingstoke: Palgrave, 2009), pp. 14–26, 14.

10 Alison Murphy, 'Charting the Emergence of National Identity in Children in Wales', *Children and Society*, 32 (2018), 301–13.

11 Bud Khleif, 'Cultural Regeneration and the School: An Anthropological Study of Welsh Medium Schools in Wales', *International Review of Education*, 22/2 (1976), 177–92.

12 Jonathan Scourfield, Bella Dicks, Mark Drakeford and Andrew James, *Children, Place and Identity: Nation and Locality in Middle Childhood* (London: Routledge, 2006).

13 Robert Phillips, 'History Teaching, Cultural Restorationism and National Identity in England and Wales', *Curriculum Studies*, 4/3 (1996), 385–99.

14 Siwan Rosser, 'Language, Culture and Identity in Welsh Children's Literature: O. M. Edwards and *Cymru'r Plant*, 1892–1920', in Riona Nic Congáil (ed.), *Codladh Céad Bliain: Cnuasach Aistí ar Litríocht na nÓg* (Baile Átha Cliath: Leabhair, 2012), pp. 223–52.

15 Rosser, 'Language, Culture', p. 224.

16 Rosser, 'Language, Culture', p. 227.

17 W. R. Owen, *The Desert and the Dream* (BBC, National Library of Wales, Clip Cymru, 1962).

18 John Ormond, *Patagonia 68* (BBC Wales, National Library of Wales, 1968), MMS 993444495602419.

19 Ormond, *Patagonia 68*.

20 Gwyn A. Williams, *When Was Wales?* (London: Penguin, 1991), pp. 261–95.

21 Esther Whitfield, 'Welsh-Patagonian Fiction: Language and the Novel of Transnational Ethnicity', *Diaspora*, 14, 2/3 (2005), 333–48, 335.

22 R. Bryn Williams, *Straeon Patagonia* (Llandysul: Gwasg Gomer, 1946); *Bandit yr Andes* (Caerdydd: Hughes a'i Fab, 1951). His other books for older children and adults were also popular: *Y March Coch* (Bala: Gwasg y Bala, 1954); and *Croesi'r Paith* (Llandybïe: Llyfrau'r Dryw, 1958).

23 Rosser, 'Language, Culture', pp. 228–30.

24 Williams, *Bandit yr Andes*. Notes on pages two and four refer to its provenance. He also won the National Eisteddfod chair for his epic poem on y Wladfa in 1964.

25 E. Wyn James, 'Identity, Migration and Assimilation: The Case of the Welsh Settlement in Patagonia', *Transactions of the Honourable Society of Cymmrodorion*, 25 (2018), 76–87, 78; Bethan Gwanas 'Yn Mwydro am Lyfrau', *https://gwanas.wordpress.com/tag/bandit-yr-andes/* (accessed 8 June 2023).

26 R. Bryn Williams, *Y Wladfa* (Caerdydd: Gwasg Prifysgol Cymru, 1962).

27 Owen, *Desert and the Dream*.

28 Nan Davies (BBC), *Y Gymru Bell* (National Library of Wales, Clip Cymru, 1962).

29 Davies, *Y Gymru Bell*.

30 Williams, *Bandit yr Andes*, p. 56.

31 Williams, *Bandit yr Andes*, p. 57.

32 Williams, *Bandit yr Andes*, pp. 67, 71.

33 Williams, *Bandit yr Andes*, p. 97.

34 Williams, *Bandit yr Andes*, p. 109.

35 Williams, *Bandit yr Andes*, p. 56.

36 Williams, *Bandit yr Andes*, p. 123.

37 Williams, *Bandit yr Andes*, p. 123.

38 Williams, *Bandit yr Andes*, p. 137.

39 Williams, *Bandit yr Andes*, pp. 137–8.

40 For example, the journal *Llafur* was founded in 1970–1 to 'promote and popularise the knowledge and study of all aspects of people's history in Wales', *https://www.llafur.org/about-us/*. Gwyn A. Williams wrote his

groundbreaking history *When was Wales?* in 1985 (London: Pelican) and Raymond Williams developed his influential theories of culture by reflecting on the liminality of life on the Welsh Marches, see Raymond Williams, *Who Speaks for Wales? Nation, Culture, Identity*, ed. Daniel Williams (Cardiff: University of Wales Press, 2003).

41   Dai Jones Llanilar, *Cefn Gwlad Patagonia* (2000), *https://www.bbc.co.uk/programmes/p03c0nbp* (accessed 5 August 2024); Selwyn Roderick, *Plant y Paith* (National Library of Wales, Clic Cymru, 1980); Selwyn Roderick, *Patagonia: Yno o Hyd* (National Library of Wales, Clic Cymru, 1998).

42   Gareth Owen, *Oes yn y Wladfa* (HTV Wales, Porth, Coleg Cymraeg Cenedlaethol, 1985).

43   *Patagonia Heddiw* (National Library of Wales, Clic Cymru, 2008).

44   Cynhyrchiad Taliesyn, *Cof Patagonia* (Porth, Coleg Cymraeg Cenedlaethol, 2002).

45   Kevin Smith, *Curriculum, Culture and Citizenship Education in Wales* (Houndsmills: Palgrave, 2016), pp. 35–7.

46   Robert Phillips, 'History Teaching, Cultural Restorationism and National Identity in England and Wales', *Curriculum Studies*, 4/3 (1996), 385–99.

47   Geraint H. Jenkins, 'Patagonia', in *Darganfod Hanes Cymru: Llyfr 4L: Cymru, Ddoe a Heddiw* (Rhydychen: Gwasg Prifysgol Rhydychen, 1990), pp. 26–7, 26.

48   Jenkins, 'Patagonia', p. 27.

49   John Evans, *Storïau Hanes Cymru CA1, Canllaw Athrawon* (Caerdydd: Dref Wen, 1996), pp. 31–2.

50   John Evans, *Daniel Evans in Patagonia* (Cardiff: Dref Wen, 1996).

51   Evans, *Daniel Evans*, pp. 14–15.

52   Welsh Government (2003), cited in Smith, *Curriculum, Culture*, p. 39.

53   Glyn Llewelyn, *Pobl y Wladfa* (Cwmni Hel Straeon, 1991).

54   Matthew Rhys, *O'r Môr i'r Mynydd* (S4C, 2006).

55   Matthew Rhys, *Patagonia: Crossing the Plain/Croesi'r Paith* (Llandysul: Gwasg Gomer, 2010).

56   For example, Jasmine Donahaye *Whose People? Wales, Israel, Palestine* (Cardiff: University of Wales Press, 2012), and Charlotte Williams, Neil Evans and Paul O'Leary (eds), *A Tolerant Nation? Revisiting Ethnic Diversity in a Devolved Wales* (Cardiff: University of Wales Press, 2015).

57   Gurminder Bhambra, Dalial Gebrial and Kerem Nişancioğlu (eds), *Decolonizing the University* (London: Pluto Press, 2018); Christopher Lebron, *The Making of Black Lives Matter: Brief History of an Idea* (Oxford: Oxford University Press, 2023).

58   For example, 'Marc Evans' road trip adventure in Patagonia', *Wales Online*, 25 February 2011, *https://www.walesonline.co.uk/lifestyle/showbiz/marc-evans-road-trip-adventure-1854928* (accessed 5 August 2024); Jennifer Wood, 'Signifying the Nation: (In)communication, Absence and Rational (Be)longing in Marc Evans' *Patagonia* (2010)', in Brigitte le Juez and Bill Richardson (eds), *Spaces of Longing and Belonging: Territoriality, Ideology and Creative Identity in Literature and Film* (Leiden: Brill Rodopi, 2019), pp. 210–32.

59 Marc Evans, *Patagonia* (Verve Pictures, 2020).

60 Evans, *Patagonia*.

61 Evans, 'Interview', *Patagonia* (DVD).

62 Gruff Rhys, *Seperado* (ie ie, 2010).

63 Marc Edwards, *Patagonia with Huw Edwards* (BBC Four, 2015).

64 A flavour of the TV offerings can be found on this S4C press release: *https://www.s4c.cymru/en/press/post/28165/s4c-announces-a-special-week-of-patagonia-programmes/* (accessed 18 December 2023).

65 Jon Gower, *Gwalia Patagonia* (Llandysul: Gwasg Gomer, 2015); Dylan Iorwerth, *Patagonia 150* (BBC Wales, 2015).

66 *Somewhere Else* (BBC Cymru Wales, December 2015).

67 *Patagonia 150: Dathlu 2015* (Welsh Arts International, 2015).

68 'On the Road to Patagonia with BBC National Orchestra of Wales', *Wales Online*, 20 October 2015, *https://www.walesonline.co.uk/whats-on/arts-culture-news/road-patagonia-bbc-national-orchestra-10298460* (accessed 5 August 2024).

69 Brigyn, 'Patagonia 150', *http://www.brigyn.com/patagonia150/index.html* (accessed 5 August 2024).

70 Eirionedd Baskerville, *Patagonia 150: Yma i Aros – Here to Stay – Aquí para Quedarse* (Talybont: Y Lolfa, 2015), p. 8.

71 Baskerville, *Patagonia 150*, p. 16.

72 Luis Priamo, *Una Frontera Lejana: La Colonización Galesa del Chubut* (Buenos Aires: Ediciones Fundacón Antorchas, 2003).

73 'Mimosa Patagonia sailing ceremony marks 150 years since settlers departed', *Daily Post*, 31 May 2015, *https://www.dailypost.co.uk/news/north-wales-news/mimosa-patagonia-sailing-ceremony-marks-9361972* (accessed 5 August 2024).

74 'Celebrations for 150th anniversary of Welsh settlements in Argentine Patagonia', *Merco Press*, 1 February 2015, *https://en.mercopress.com/2015/02/01/celebrations-for-150th-anniversary-of-welsh-settlements-in-argentine-patagonia/comments* (accessed 5 August 2024).

75 '"A Diplomatic Success" the presence of Wales First Minister Carwyn Jones', *Merco Press*, 28 July 2015, *https://en.mercopress.com/2015/07/28/a-diplomatic-success-the-presence-of-wales-first-minister-carwyn-jones* (accessed 5 August 2024).

76 'A Diplomatic Success'.

77 'Carwyn's host links Welsh in Patagonia to Falklands', ITV News, 28 July 2015, *https://www.itv.com/news/wales/update/2015-07-27/carwyns-host-links-welsh-in-patagonia-to-falklands/* (accessed 5 August 2024).

78 'Celebrations for 150th'.

79 Morita Carrasco, *Los Derechos de los Pueblos Indigenas en Argentina*, IWGIA, Asociación Comunitaria de Aborígenes (Argentina, 2000). For a discussion of the ensuing tensions, see Carolina Crespo, '"Que Pertenece a Quién": Procesos de Patrimonialización y Pueblos Originarios en Patagonia', *Cuadernos de Antropología Social*, 21 (2005), 133–49.

80   Raúl Diaz and Jorgelina Villarreal, 'Extender la Interculturalidad a Toda la Sociedad: Reflexiones y Propuestas desde el Sur Argentina', *Cuadernos Interculturales*, 7/13 (2009), 15–26.

81   'Emotivo Homenaje por los 150 Años de la Llegada de los Colonos Galeses a Madryn', *El Chubut (edicion digital)*, 28 Julio 2015, *https://www.elchubut.com.ar/puerto-madryn/2015-7-28-emotivo-homenaje-por-los-150-anos-de-la-llegada-de-los-colonos-galeses-a-madryn* (accessed 5 August 2024).

82   'Emotivo Homenaje'.

83   See, for example, Lof Sacamata-Liempichun, 'La Historia del Lof Sacamata-Liempichun (Paraje Payaniyeo, Alto Rio Senguer, Chubut): El Reclamo y el Pedido de Restitución de Nuestro Ancestro' (GEMAS Grupo de Estudios sobre Memorias Alterizadas y Subordinadas, 2020), *https://gemasmemoria.com/2020/07/03/la-historia-de-la-lof-sacamata-liempichun-paraje-payaniyeo-alto-rio-senguer-chubut-el-reclamo-y-el-pedido-de-restitucion-de-nuestro-ancestro/* (accessed 5 August 2024).

84   Embassy of Argentina, *Y Wladfa* (Buenos Aires: Gobierno de Argentina, 2015), p. 10.

85   Embassy of Argentina, *Y Wladfa*, p. 13.

86   Mariano Nagy, 'Violencia contra los Pueblos Originarios: Estructura y de Coyuntura', *El Puan/Óptico* (2020), 58–64, 60, *https://ri.conicet.gov.ar/handle/11336/170398* (accessed 5 August 2024).

87   Nagy, 'Violencia contra los Pueblos Originarios', 63.

88   Nagy, 'Violencia contra los Pueblos Originarios', 58. For examples in English, see Geraldine Lublin's discussion of the Santiago Maldonado case, 'Adjusting the Focus: looking at Patagonia and the Wider Argentine State through the Lens of Settler Colonial Theory', *Settler Colonial Studies*, 11/3 (2021), 386–409; Cristian Aliaga, 'The "Land Wars" in Twenty First Century Patagonia', *Journal of Latin American Cultural Studies*, 28/10 (2018), 139–51.

89   Geraldine Lublin, 'La Identidad en la Encrucijada: la Comunidad Galesa del Chubut y las Conmemoraciones del Centenario y Bicentenario de la Revolución de Mayo', *Identidades*, 5/3 (2013), 115–30.

90   'Charla sobre la Restitución de los Restos de Icayal', *Diario Jornada*, 2 December 2014.

91   'Amplia Convocatoria a Charlas Organizadas por el Gobierno y la Comunidad Mapuche-Tehuelche de Madryn', *Secretaría de Medios e Información Pública*, 27 July 2014.

92   'Amplia Convocatoria'.

93   Catrin Stevens, *Cymeriadau: Yr Hen Ffordd Gymreig* (Aberystwyth: Cynllun Adnoddau Addysgu, 2008).

94   Anni Llŷn a Sioned Hughes, *Dewch i Deithio: Patagonia* (Aberystwyth: Canolfan Peniarth, 2021), p. 12.

95   Twinkl, 'Patagonia Worksheet', *https://www.twinkl.co.uk/resource/differentiated-reading-comprehension-the-colony-patagonia-wl-l-1567* (accessed 5 August 2024), 1.

CHAPTER 8

Conclusion – and Ways Forwards

I began this book in an unorthodox way by introducing you to Katrülaf and his story. I did this in order to shake up conventional thinking about Y Wladfa by starting with a narrative that draws from experiences, lifeways and relations to the state that are very different from those of the Welsh. Yet one is also struck by the similarities between the communities – family love, daily tasks, the excitement of travel and mixed emotions when encountering a stranger. This humanization of Katrülaf and his people is important because it helps us to recognize his other experiences: the horror of deception, violence, intimidation, dispossession and social catastrophe. This too is the story of Patagonia, and one long hidden from sight in Wales: bringing it into view is necessary to build a tolerant, diverse and anti-racist society.

The first step on any decolonial journey is to look beyond the stereotypes so vital to 'Othering' to find the complex people behind it all: to tackle dehumanization we must humanize, not only Indigenous people but also Welsh Patagonians. For some in Wales, Y Wladfa is a part of their family history and for many it is a cherished emblem of Welsh tenacity, courage and ingenuity. My aim is not to discard this truth, but to dismantle the stereotype (which is wearing very thin) and reveal the human experiences at play. For this reason, I began my research in the archives before I read the standard histories so as to 'meet' the key protagonists for myself in their letters, journals, diaries and memoirs. I found their character and humour, their intense worry, rivalries, romances, grief, confusion and sheer hard graft. It is these fresh impressions that help to reset our assumptions about Welsh Patagonia, alongside foregrounding Indigenous experience.

Reading their memoirs, I understood their fearfulness of this alien landscape, its unmilkable cows and its racialized others. It is unremarkable that Welsh-Indigenous relations were interpreted through a racial hierarchy at this period, shaped by religious paternalism, but I appreciate their decision to resist using physical violence and to see Indigenous Patagonians as people – to sometimes make real friends – even though they never doubted their own civilizational superiority. Yet at the same time, the settlers were integral instruments in Argentina's national project and were part of the wider frame of violences in both Patagonia and across the world: in the end, it was they, not the Indigenous people of the Chubut Valley, who benefitted from the Patagonian enterprise. Ultimately, I urge the reader to recognize this ambivalence and find a way to embrace it, learning to live with the tension between the hero/villain binary, to accept complexity and the difficult, muddled dynamics based on sympathy yet complicity.

Seeing this complex reality enables us to take the second decolonial step: accepting responsibility. Acknowledging the impact of Welsh colonization in Patagonia on Indigenous people, plus the complicated motives and cultural norms behind it, could promote understanding instead of blame and ease the urge to leap to the defensive. As Huw Williams notes, discussions about Welsh Patagonia in Wales often generate a polarized and binary position which turns the topic into an emblem of Welsh cultural pride versus progressive agendas.[1] Much of this is framed by Wales's own experiences of poverty, political domination by England, the suppression of the Welsh language and cultural disparagement. While there is therefore a lot at stake in such debates, the divide is a false and damaging choice, and although adopting accusatory and defensive positions is understandable, it is very unhelpful if we wish to build a genuine friendship, today, between the people of Wales and Indigenous Patagonians.

The book itself takes on and explores this tension and the ambivalent reality. The introduction sets the decolonial tone by placing Indigenous experience at its forefront and heart. The theory chapter introduces the coloniality of power as a lens of analysis and identifies three conceptual tools which are deployed throughout the book: possession, racialization/barbarization and assimilation. Wales's condition as both colonized and colonizing is established in the third chapter, discussing earlier historical examples as well as the period before and during the creation of Y Wladfa. The following three chapters explore the Welsh Patagonian settlement itself using the theoretical themes, following a roughly chronological format. 'Possession' charts the acquisition and early settlement of the Chubut Valley; 'racialization/barbarization' examines Welsh-Indigenous relations and the 'myth of friendship' during the settlement's heyday, 1865–84; and 'assimilation' analyses the tension between Welsh autonomy and incorporation into the Argentine state. The final chapter explores the meaning of Y Wladfa in Wales today, and its role as a key political cypher of Welsh cultural nationalism. It ends by suggesting that, in an era of greater political power and cultural confidence, the time has come to reassess Y Wladfa and recognize, with mature discussion, its impact on those at the receiving end of colonization.

The purpose of this book is to undertake these two steps: to humanize the dehumanized by revealing their hidden stories; and to show how Y Wladfa was entangled in meta-processes of settler colonialism which are today being held to account around the world. The third stage of decolonization is action – considering what can we do and how can we do it in a decolonial way. This is the focus of my future research, but I want to end by setting out the principles that might guide practical action and suggest ideas for future projects.

Decolonization and the origin country

The central relationship of settler colonialism, and focus for settler colonial theory, is between the original inhabitants of the land and the regime which enacts settlement – in this case, the Mapuche, Tehuelche and Pampa Peoples, and the Argentine state. It was they who claimed the territory, enacted the Conquest of the Desert and enforced the institutions and laws developed in Buenos Aires. It remains the Argentine state which owns and sells vast areas of land, authorizes oil and gas exploration, determines citizenship status and enacts Indigenous policies. However, the people who arrived to enact this strategy, like the Welsh, are generally overlooked by this framework. Their previous lives are not thought relevant and they are often framed as empty stereotypes – brutal, racist and acquisitive. Instead, settler stories, often framed by poverty or persecution, and their moral, political and cultural worlds, are discussed through the lens of migration, an approach which downplays the presence of structural inequality in settler colonialism. My analysis, though, has bridged settler studies and migration studies: it is embedded in a critique of settler colonialism yet directs our attention to the origin country, as well as the settler site. Doing so enriches our understanding by adding an important layer of detail, facts and ideas which help us to better understand the relationship between Indigenous and settlers, apart from the regime. Moreover, it reveals that not all settlements and settlers are the same – while many are eager to assimilate within their new identity and institutional regime, others resist its pull and seek to promote their own agendas. Digging down into the settlers' background helps to unpack simplistic and homogenizing assumptions about them. This is important because, while we might justifiably condemn the actions of a state, nurturing decolonial relationships on the ground, between people, requires listening, dialogue and compromise between all those who now live on what was once Indigenous land. Seeing settlers as complex actors is vital to this task, not only in Welsh Patagonia but also in Wales itself.

Welsh Patagonia has a wider significance for settler colonial studies too because it brings into sharp focus the question: what is the role of origin countries in promoting decolonization? So far, the responsibility of origin countries to redress social injustice has been sidestepped. Clearly, origin nations cannot intervene in what are now sovereign states, like Argentina, but that does not diminish their responsibility: how should origin countries acknowledge their deep structural role in creating settler colonies, and what sort of actions might they feasibly undertake? These questions are acute for Wales precisely because Y Wladfa has not been a topic of shame; rather it has generated pride, strengthened identity and contributed to Wales's own efforts to secure cultural dignity and a degree of political autonomy back home. It is also highly pertinent, as the Welsh government has committed all public institutions and schools to promoting an anti-racist agenda. While this has focused mostly on Black and South Asian experience in Wales, reckoning with colonial legacies abroad should also be part of this, especially Welsh Patagonia as it was an entirely Welsh enterprise: the buck stops with Cymru.

How might decolonial action begin?

Although Wales has limited institutional power and a meagre budget, it also has a strong moral drive and a rich cultural heritage, and it is upon these assets that we might build practical, feasible actions, both here in Wales and in Patagonia. As Huw Williams suggests: 'we need to use our creative energies, not to accuse and condemn, but to search for imaginative ways in which Welsh civic society can support efforts in Y Wladfa to promote the cause of [the Indigenous] today'.[2] It is important, though, that we avoid falling into a paternalistic, Wales-knows-best mindset: any action must be done not *for* but *with* Indigenous communities today. That is, we must pay attention to the foundations of the relationship, asking how Welsh institutions might go about developing projects and how they relate to contemporary Mapuche-Tehuelche communities. Getting these foundations right is essential to ensuring that any actions that follow do not reiterate colonial relations but promote decolonial action. This is necessary if we aspire to build a genuine 'friendship' today.

The principle of allyship might be helpful here. First Nations scholar-activists Jackson Smith, Casandra Puckett and Wendy Simon set out the principles of allyship in a useful how-to guide. For them, allyship entails actively working to support Indigenous interests (even when that means ceding power or benefits) and developing meaningful relationships which build-in accountability.[3] Creating a meaningful, accountable relationship must come prior to setting out any priorities, decisions or policies because in order for them to be truly emancipatory, they must emerge from a dialogue between equals. This in turn depends on a willingness to listen ('with an open mind and an open heart') before speaking, and to learn about Indigenous communities, their modes of knowing, lifeways and cultures, as well as their experiences of oppression, struggle and dignity, plus their everyday campaigns, concerns and needs.[4] This learning requires that the structural and systemic operation of both oppression and privilege be recognized, including an acknowledgement of one's own role, however unwitting, in those patterns of inequality.

Revealing the operation of these systemic forces has been a key task of this book, especially recognizing the history of the land (in this case, the Chubut Valley) and the acts of dispossession (to which the Welsh were crucial, albeit indirectly).[5] This kind of relationship work requires effort and, most importantly, the status of ally can only be conferred by the Indigenous community: if things go wrong, it can be withdrawn at any time. Building this relationship – establishing the terms of engagement to create equal dialogue between structurally unequal partners – must be an ongoing process which entails learning not just about the other group but about oneself through vigilant self-reflection to guard against slipping into a paternalistic or domineering approach, or creating a tick-box exercise.[6] Eve Tuck and Wayne Yang also warn against the strategic use of solidarity as a 'move to innocence' – an absolution of responsibility or guilt by paying lip-service to reparation in order to draw a line under the past.[7] For this reason, understanding allyship or solidarity as a process which needs ongoing attention and self-checking is vital to keeping the meaningfulness of the relationship alive and the friendship genuine.

This all sounds like a tall order: when done properly, allyship (rightly) requires a deep and demanding commitment, and while some individuals or solidarity groups might wish to follow this path, it is less feasible for most. Building decolonial momentum in Welsh society more generally requires that we readjust Wales's relationship with Patagonia slowly and with care, especially because the 'myth of friendship' has been both cherished and politically important. Moreover, the scope for action by the Welsh government is limited, the budget constraints are real, party politics requires compromise, and good, workable relations must be maintained with the Argentine state. Nevertheless, public bodies can adopt the key principles of allyship: learning in order to better understand Indigenous lifeways and concerns; open respectful dialogue based on listening; acknowledgement of global inequalities and self-checking; and coming together to decide feasible, useful actions with a decolonizing impact. These initiatives will inevitably be imperfect or limited but we should note the final essential quality of an ally that Smith, Puckett and Simon identify: an ally must act using their position of relative privilege to make a change today.[8]

Action points

The most obvious and feasible area for action in Wales is school education. We saw in the final chapter how skewed the story of Y Wladfa is in the textbooks and novels available to Welsh children and noted that the curriculum has already been targeted as a key arena for change, especially given that education is a matter devolved to the Welsh government. As I demonstrated, Indigenous Patagonians are made visible in textbooks but always as people who lived in the past and who 'proved' Welsh goodness by being their friends. Addressing this absence in the present is vitally important, as is enriching the story of the past by demonstrating the agency and character, lifeways and society of Indigenous Patagonians alongside the Welsh settlers.

The growth of Indigenous language learning in Patagonia (not only Mapuzugun but also the Tehuelche language) and the development of intercultural bilingual education initiatives in Argentina has generated resources suitable for schoolchildren which celebrate Indigenous culture.[9] Working with the Mapuche-Tehuelche communities today, Welsh public bodies such as the Welsh Books Council might facilitate the translation of existing materials into Welsh and English, creating a resource that would help teachers to decolonize their practice, enrich learning for pupils and enable engagement from the wider public in Wales – and far beyond. For example, the book *Mapuche Kimün/Saber Mapuche – Awkantün/Los Juegos* (Knowing Mapuche – the Games) celebrates Mapuche sports, and could be translated and integrated within the physical education curriculum for Key Stage Two. In another example, Mapuche poetry, such as the book *Traéme un arcoíris/Küpalelen kiñe relmu* (Bring me a Rainbow) might find a place in the early literacy curriculum of Key Stage One.[10] Investment in teacher training and resources would be vital, of course, but the infrastructure and initiatives being rolled out in relation to the new Curriculum for Wales, which foregrounds Black and Minority Ethnic Welsh experience, via the excellent DAR-PL scheme could be extended to include Y Wladfa.[11] Arts funders might also consider earmarking grants to promote Indigenous-Welsh collaboration to develop new schools resources, perhaps building on the existing exchange programme which sees Welsh teachers placed in the Welsh-language schools in Gaiman, Trelew and Trevelin, already partly supported by the Welsh government/British Council.[12] Developing these linkages would also connect action in Wales with the existing (though limited) decolonial initiatives in these schools.

Cultural products are an important vehicle for education more broadly and have the capacity to present fresh perspectives, make different actors visible and set new agendas. Given that Welshness existed only as a cultural formation between the Acts of Union and devolution, this is a powerful arena for social change, especially because artistic expression is widely practised and celebrated, most notably via eisteddfodau and Wales's thriving cultural landscape of theatres, writing, film, TV and art. All this makes culture a key arena for not only making visible but engaging, debating and rethinking about – and with – Indigenous Patagonia.

As we already saw with *Seperado*, film can be influential in presenting new thinking about Patagonia, and Daf Palfrey's docu-feature *Poncho Mamgu* (2008) takes this a step further. The film is remarkable, not least because it tells the story of a woman when female voices are absent from the Welsh Patagonian archive, but mainly because it engages directly with contemporary Indigenous people today. It follows the story of Hannah Davies (Daf's great, great-grandmother) and her young daughter Nel. In the film, Nel is left alone with her young brother when their mother dies in childbirth and is treated with great kindness by the 'Indians' when they come to call. Nel's daughter-in-law, Margaid, relates the family story: 'Their chief ... got off his horse, took off his poncho and put it round her shoulders and said: I'll be your friend as long as I live. If you ever need me, I'll come and help you.'[13] The film then follows Nel's eventful life, including sexual harassment in Buenos Aires, her stint as the family spinster and her eventual happy marriage back in Wales where she keeps the poncho and the memory of Indigenous kindness. *Poncho Mamgu* charts the family's trip to Patagonia to meet the descendants of the 'chief', Cacique Galats, creating a bridge between past and present and the two communities. The encounter between the two families of Nel and Galats is very moving: I wrote in my notes that Pedro, the family head, handles the poncho 'with great love, cherishing it, kissing it'. A female relative says: 'I caress this poncho and hear what happened between the Cacique Galats and Nel – I feel very happy but also emotional'. She holds it as if it is her ancestor, her own great-grandfather who lived through the Conquest of the Desert, like Katrülaf, and says: 'the kiss comes from my heart'.[14] Daf Palfrey's film is unique in portraying Indigenous people today not as exotic caricatures or remnants of the past, but as people who know grief and love. Both families reach across the cultural gap to feel their common humanity, each touching, through the poncho, their loved ones who are long gone. *Poncho Mamgu* breaks through the 'myth of friendship' to portray genuine feelings of care and gratitude, heartache and family love, and exemplifies the spirit with which we might begin to build a genuine bond of friendship today, between Indigenous and Welsh communities. It should act as a source of inspiration but also practical, human-sized care, building trust and finding common ground on the basis of shared experience.

The film raises issues about material artefacts, though. Generally, it was common in the nineteenth century for Indigenous items to be seized as souvenirs or sold to museums, and a counter-movement is growing to reclaim Indigenous ownership over these items. This is a key issue for Patagonia too – we noted the long-awaited return of Cacique Inakayal's remains, for example, and are reminded that Katrülaf's memoirs were buried in a German library archive. Of course, families who hold Indigenous artefacts of sentimental significance must decide for themselves what should be done with them (and it is not a simple issue), but public institutions are a different matter. While Welsh institutions have ordered an inventory of items in their collection linked to slavery, as yet they have not prioritized Indigenous artefacts (written or material) in their possession and this is clearly pending.[15] In a spirit of decolonial engagement, they should fully involve Indigenous historians in the process of identification and discussion about next steps, developing dialogue before acting. Welsh institutions might consider a range of options. For example, they could offer research travel grants for Indigenous historians to consult the Welsh archives; they might learn about the significance of items and use Indigenous understandings in their interpretation for public view, share curation knowledge or equipment, lend objects to museums in Patagonia or even repatriate artefacts. The National Library of Wales will soon begin engaging with Indigenous Patagonian critiques of the 'Welsh feat'. For example by hosting a website that features poetry, oral history, photography and video testimony created as part of an Argentine-Welsh collaboration between academics and Indigenous communities in Nahuelpan, near Esquel.[16] It is in situations such as these that the principles of allyship (learning by listening; respectful dialogue; acknowledgement of privilege; self-critique) must guide interaction, discussion and action.

The potential for decolonial learning through cultural interaction is significant and it seems that there is an appetite on the part of some cultural producers to develop this work. For example, in an interview with Cefyn Burgess, a textile artist based in Rhuthun, he reflected on the desirability of cultural exchange.[17] Burgess visited Patagonia as part of the 2015 commemorations and met Indigenous textile weavers, dyers and makers. They asked: why was it always Welsh people who visited Patagonia, and when could they come to Wales to show off their pieces? He was keen to implement the idea of a reciprocal visit but it did not transpire in the end. Although funding streams do exist via the British Council and Arts Council Wales, they often rely on match-funding from Argentine sources which creates obstacles given Argentina's recurring economic difficulties. Nevertheless, there is great potential to develop interaction, especially through investment to promote networks in both Wales and Patagonia to finance collaborative projects or visiting residencies for Indigenous artists. Creating an artistic exchange programme which would bring Indigenous makers to Wales, with the associated workshops and exhibitions, would provide a platform to demonstrate the presence and creative agency of contemporary Indigenous cultural producers. It might also be a vehicle for political work in raising awareness of social injustice and Indigenous political concerns, giving the lie to images of Indigenous extinction and passive victimhood.

Engaging directly with Indigenous communities in the settler location might also be a fruitful avenue of work. However, this site is more complex because it is embedded in Argentina, another sovereign state, and any activities would need to be endorsed by the local municipalities and the Chubut provincial government. Moreover, while some Indigenous organizations work alongside the state, many are in direct conflict with it over land-claims and expanding extractive industries, issues that would place the Welsh government in an awkward, probably unviable, position.[18] Still, the area of community renewal, for example investing in cultural centres, might be feasible, most obviously focusing funding in the issue of common concern: language revitalization. For both Mapuche-Tehuelche communities and the Welsh in both Patagonia and Wales, language is recognized as the key to generating identity and pride, and a vital tool in preserving knowledge and lifeways which are precious to communities subject to linguistic assimilation. This confluence of concern offers a bridging point between very different communities where they might meet on equal terms and pursue their shared aim – to strengthen their community by sustaining the language. Potentially there is much to learn from one another in terms of strategies and techniques, and recognizing that this is a shared goal might build solidarity. It could also open a shared space in which to learn about the oppressions, struggles and triumphs that each have faced, to acknowledge difficult histories and build empathy. It is precisely by finding workable, practical common goals that practices of solidarity can be created, so long as the principles of decolonial engagement form the foundation of the relationship.[19] If such interaction can follow the principles of allyship (learning by listening; respectful dialogue; acknowledgement of privilege; self-critique), then language-work might build the kind of understanding and trust necessary to build a bridge between communities that turns the myth of friendship into a reality today.[20]

The next phase of my research will raise awareness of the political and social struggles of Indigenous Patagonians today and explore the feasibility of the practical suggestions set out here. Undertaking such work will not be easy: it is hard to give up cherished myths which empower, especially if we are speaking of people's forebears, friends and families. That is why we need to humanize the protagonists, as I have done in this book, and understand that they were, like us today, embedded in wider processes (colonialism, capitalist expansion) and logics (racism, European superiority) which shaped their actions. We cannot change the past, but we can – and I think should – change the terms of engagement between Wales and Indigenous Patagonia in the future. Wales's position as both colonized and colonizing, and its contemporary concern to promote anti-racist policies, make it an important and potentially influential example through which to explore how an authentic reckoning with colonialism might be possible more broadly. As such it has a great deal to teach those who analyse and wish to decolonize settler colonialism in locations around the world.

Notes

1 Huw Williams, 'Heb ei Fai, Heb ei Eni: "Disgwrs" a Moeseg y Wladfa', *Gwerddon*, 36/hydref (2023), 55–72.
2 Williams 'Heb ei Fai', 72.

3   Jackson Smith, Casandra Puckett and Wendy Simon, *Indigenous Allyship: An Overview* (Ontario: Office of Aboriginal Initiatives, Wildfred Laurier University, 2016), p. 6.

4   Smith, Puckett and Simon, *Indigenous Allyship*, pp. 13–14, 16.

5   Smith, Puckett and Simon, *Indigenous Allyship*, pp. 13–16.

6   Jenalee Kluttz, Jude Walker and Pierre Walter, 'Unsettling Allyship, Unlearning and Learning towards Decolonizing Solidarity', *Studies in the Education of Adults*, 52/1 (2020), 49–66.

7   Eve Tuck and K. Wayne Yang, 'Decolonization is not a Metaphor', *Decolonization: Indigeneity, Education and Society*, 1/1 (2012), 1–40.

8   Smith, Puckett and Simon, *Indigenous Allyship*, p. 17.

9   Dário Luis Banegas, 'Ethnic Equity, Mapudugun and CLIL: a case study from southern Argentina', *AILA Review*, 35/2 (2020), 275–96; Javier Domingo, 'Where the Language Appears, we also Appear: Tehuelche language reclamation in Patagonia', in Netta Avineri and Jesse Harasta (eds), *Metalinguistic Communities: Case Studies of Agency, Ideology and Symbolic uses of Languages* (Houndsmills: Palgrave, 2021), pp. 119–39.

10   Collective authorship, *Mapuche Kimün/Saber Mapuche – Awkantün/Los Juegos* (Rawson: Ministerio de la Educación de la Provincia de Chubut, 2013); Jaime Huenún and Camila Peñeipil, *Traéme un Arcoíris. Poemas Mapuche para Niños y Niñas/Küpalelen Kiñe Relmu. Mapuche Küme Ülkantun pu Püchikeche Ngealü* (Santiago: Lom Ediciones, 2023).

11   'Diversity and Anti-Racist Professional Learning', *https://darpl.org/* (accessed 2 January 2021).

12   'Welsh Language Project', British Council, *https://wales.britishcouncil. org/en/programmes/education/welsh-language-project* (accessed 2 January 2024).

13   Daf Palfrey, *Poncho Mamgu* (2008).

14   Palfrey, *Poncho Mamgu*.

15   Welsh government, 'The Slave Trade and the British Empire: an Audit of Commemoration in Wales' (2020), *https://www.gov.wales/slave-trade-and-british-empire-audit-commemoration-wales* (accessed 3 January 2024). It appears that there are no Indigenous Patagonian artefacts held by Welsh museums, though this comment still holds true for materials originating from other Indigenous Peoples.

16   Geraldine Lublin, Mariela Eva Rodríguez, Carolina Crespo, Ayelén Fiori, Julieta Magallanes, Ana Margarita Ramos, Kaia Santisteban, Valentina Stella y María Marcela Tomas, 'Problematizando la Historia' https://www.library.wales/discover-learn/external-exhibitions/problematizando-la-historia/lof-nahuelpan (accessed 3 October 2024).

17   Interview with Cefyn Burgess, Rhuthun, 1 August 2019.

18   Alejandra Gaitán-Barrera and Govand Khalid Azeez, 'Beyond Recognition: Autonomy, the State and the Mapuche Coordinadora Arauco Malleco', *Latin American and Caribbean Ethnic Studies*, 13/2 (2018), 113–34; Ana Margarita Ramos, 'La Organization de Comunidades Mapuche y Tehuelche 11 de

Octobre', in Pedro Canales Tapia and Sebastião Vargas (eds), *Pensamiento Indígena en Nuestramérica* (Santiago: Ariadna Ediciones, 2018), pp. 159–89.

19   As argued in the insightful dialogue by Corey Snelgrove, Rita Kaur Dhamon and Jeff Corntassel, 'Unsettling Settler Colonialism: The Discourse and Politics of Settlers and Solidarity with Indigenous Nations', *Decolonization: Indigeneity, Education and Society*, 3/2 (2014), 1–32.

20   I am inspired here by Raban Ghazoul's suggestion that we 'build a bridge whilst walking over it', in Darren Chetty, Grug Muse, Hanan Issa and Iestyn Tyne (eds), *Welsh Plural: Essays on the Future of Wales* (London: Repeater Books, 2022), pp. 241–54, 247.

Bibliography

Aaron, Jane and Chris Williams (eds), *Postcolonial Wales* (Cardiff: University of Wales Press, 2005).

Albarracín, Julia, *Making Immigrants in Modern Argentina* (Notre Dame: University of Notre Dame Press, 2020).

Alberdi, Juan, *Argentina: Bases y Puntos de Partida para la Organización Política de la República Argentina* (1852; Barcelona: Linkgua Editores, 2006).

Alberto, Paulina and Eduardo Elena (eds), *Rethinking Race in Modern Argentina* (Cambridge: Cambridge University Press, 2016).

Alfred, Taiaiake and Jeff Corntassel, 'Being Indigenous: Resurgences against Contemporary Colonialism', *Government and Opposition*, 40/4 (2005), 597–614.

Aliaga, Cristian, 'The "Land Wars" in Twenty First Century Patagonia', *Journal of Latin American Cultural Studies*, 28/10 (2018), 139–51.

Allen, Richard, 'In Search of New Jerusalem: A Preliminary Investigation into the Causes and Impact of Welsh Quaker Emigration to Pennsylvania, *c*.1600–1750', *Quaker Studies*, 9/1 (2004), 31–51.

Ashcroft, Bill, Gareth Griffiths and Helen Tiffin, *The Empire Writes Back* (Abingdon: Routledge, 1989).

Banegas, Dário Luis, 'Ethnic Equity, Mapudugun and CLIL: a case study from southern Argentina', *AILA Review*, 35/2 (2020), 275–96.

Barlow, David, 'What's in the "Post"? Mass Media as a Site of Struggle', in Jane Aaron and Chris Williams (eds), *Postcolonial Wales* (Cardiff: University of Wales Press, 2005), pp. 193–214.

Barlow, David, Phillip Mitchell and Tom O'Malley (eds), *The Media in Wales: Voices of a Small Nation* (Cardiff: University of Wales Press, 2005).

Barzini, Jorge, 'La Mision de Thomas B. Phillips y Llwyd ap Iwan a Londres', in Fundación Ameghino, Asociación Punta Cuevas, Asociación Cultural Galesa de Puerto Madryn, *Los Galeses en la Patagonia III* (Trelew: Biblioteca Popular Agustín Alvarez, 2008), pp. 119–34.

Baskerville, Eirionedd, *Companion to the Welsh Settlement in Patagonia* (Cymdeithas Cymru-Ariannin, 2014), *http://www.cymru-ariannin.com/uploads/companion_to_the_welsh_settlement_in_patagonia.pdf* (accessed 15 November 2022).

Baskerville, Eirionedd, *Patagonia 150: Yma i Aros – Here to Stay – Aquí para Quedarse* (Talybont: Y Lolfa, 2015).

Berwyn, Richard Jones, 'Gyda'r Gwladvawrwyr yn Nyfryn y Camwy, Patagonia: Gweled Brodorion Anwar', *Cyfaill yr Aelwyd*, VII/2 (Tachwedd 1886), 40–2.

Bhambra, Gurminder, Dalial Gebrial and Kerem Nişancioğlu (eds), *Decolonizing the University* (London: Pluto Press, 2018).

Birt, Paul (ed.), *Bywyd a Gwaith John Daniel Evans, El Baqueano* (Llanrwst: Gwasg Carreg Gwalch, 2004).

Bohata, Kirsti, *Postcolonialism Revisited: Writing Wales in English* (Cardiff: University of Wales Press, 2004).

Bowen, Lloyd, 'Representations of Wales and the Welsh during the Civil Wars and Interregnum', *Historical Research*, 77/197 (2004) 358–76.

Botano, Natalio and Ezequiel Gallo (eds), *Liberal Thought in Argentina, 1837–1940* (Indianapolis: Liberty Fund, 2013).

Briones, Claudia, 'Construcciones de Aboriginalidad en Argentina', *Société Suisses des Américanistes Bulletin*, 68 (2004), 73–90.

Brooks, Simon, *Why Wales Never Was: The Failure of Welsh Nationalism* (Cardiff: University of Wales Press, 2017).

Byrd, Jodi, *Transit of Empire: Indigenous Critiques of Colonialism* (Minneapolis: University of Minnesota Press, 2011).

Calloway, Colin, *White People, Indians and Highlanders: Tribal Peoples and Colonial Encounters in Scotland and America* (Oxford: Oxford University Press, 2008).

Canio Llanquinao, Margarita and Gabriel Pozo Menares (eds), *Historia y Conocimiento Oral Mapuche: Sobrevivientes de la 'Campaña del Desierto' y 'Ocupación de la Araucanía' (1899–1926)* (Santiago: Ediciones LOM, 2013).

Carrasco, Morita, *Los Derechos de los Pueblos Indígenas en Argentina* (Buenos Aires: IWGIA As. Comm. Aborígenes de Argentina, 2000).

Carrasco, Morita, 'El Movimiento Indígena Anterior a la Reforma Constitucional y su Organización en el Programa de Partícipación de Pueblos Indígenas', Visiting Resource Professor Papers: LLILAS (University of Texas at Austin, 2002), *http://www.utexas.edu/cola/insts/llilas* (accessed 7 August 2024).

Castro, Analía, 'Estrategías de Apropiación Territorial en la Cartografía Histórica de la Provincia de Chubut, Patagonia, Argentina a Finales del Siglo XIX', *Anales del Museo de América*, 19 (2011), 101–21.

Crenshaw, Kimberlé, 'Mapping the Margins: Intersectionality, Identity Politics, and Violence against Women of Color', *Stanford Law Review*, 43/6 (1991), 1241–99.

Crespo, Carolina, '"Que Pertenece a Quién": Procesos de Patrimonialización y Pueblos Originarios en Patagonia', *Cuadernos de Antropología Social*, 21 (2005), 133–49.

Connolly, S. J., 'Settler Colonialism in Ireland from the English Conquest to the Nineteenth Century', in Edward Cavanagh and Lorenzo Veracini (eds), *Routledge Handbook of Settler Colonialism* (London: Routledge, 2017), pp. 49–64.

Chakrabarty, Dipesh, *Provincializing Europe: Postcolonial Thought and Historical Difference* (Princeton: Princeton University Press, 2000).

Claraz, Georges, *Viaje al Rio Chubut: Aspectos Naturalisticos y Etnologicos (1865–1866)*, ed. Rodolfo Casamiquela (Buenos Aires: Ediciones Continente, 2008).

Coulthard, Glen, *Red Skin, White Masks: Rejecting the Colonial Politics of Recognition* (Minneapolis: University of Minnesota Press, 2014).

Davies, R. R., *The Age of Conquest, Wales 1063–1415* (Oxford: Oxford University Press, 1987).

Davies, Russell, '"Hen Wlad y Menig Gwynion": Profiad Sir Gaerfyrddin', in Geraint H. Jenkins (ed.), *Cof Cenedl VI: Ysgrifau ar Hanes Cymru* (Llandysul: Gwasg Gomer, 1991), pp. 135–59.

Delrio, Walter, *Memorias de Expropriación: Sometimiento e Incorporación Indígena en la Patagonia, 1872–1943* (Buenos Aires: Universidad Nacional de Quilmes, 2005).

Diaz, Raúl and Jorgelina Villarreal, 'Extender la Interculturalidad a Toda la Sociedad: Reflexiones y Propuestas desde el Sur Argentina', *Cuadernos Interculturales*, 7/13 (2009), 15–26.

Domingo, Javier, 'Where the Language Appears, we also Appear: Tehuelche Language Reclamation in Patagonia', in Netta Avineri and Jesse Harasta (eds), *Metalinguistic Communities: Case Studies of Agency, Ideology and Symbolic uses of Languages* (Houndsmills: Palgrave, 2021), pp. 119–39.

Donahaye, Jasmine, *Whose People? Wales, Israel, Palestine* (Cardiff: University of Wales Press, 2012).

Duffy, Seán, 'The 1169 Invasion as a Turning-point in Irish-Welsh Relations', in Brendan Smith (ed.), *Britain and Ireland 900–1300: Insular Responses to Medieval European Change* (Cambridge: Cambridge University Press, 1999), pp. 98–113.

Dumrauf, Clemente, *La Colonial Galesa del Chubut: su Lucha por el Gobierno Propio* (Buenos Aires: Editorial Dunken, 2008).

Dunaway, Wayland, 'Early Welsh Settlers of Pennsylvania', *Pennsylvania History*, 12/4 (1945), 251–69.

Edensor, Tim, *National Identity, Popular Culture and Everyday Life* (Oxford: Berg, 2002).

Embassy of Argentina, *Y Wladfa* (Buenos Aires: Gobierno de Argentina, 2015).

Escolar, Diego, *Los Dones Etnicos de la Nación* (Buenos Aires: Prometeo, 2007).

Evans, Clery (ed.), *John Daniel Evans, el Molinero: una Historia entre Gales y la Colonia 16 de Octubre* (Esquel: Gráfica Alfa, 1994).

Evans, Neil, 'Writing Wales into Empire: Rhetoric, Fragments – and Beyond?', in H. V. Bowen (ed.), *Wales and the British Overseas Empire: Interactions and Influences 1650–1830* (Manchester: Manchester University Press, 2011), pp. 15–39.

Fabian, Johannes, *Time and the Other: How Anthropology makes its Other* (1983; New York: Columbia University Press, 2002).

Fontana, Luis Jorge, *Viaje de Exploración en la Patagonia Austral* (London: British Library Historical Print Editions, 1886).

Frigerio, Alejandro, 'De la "Desaparición" de los Negros a la "Reaparición de los Afrodescendientes: Comprendiendo al Política de las Identidades Negras, las Clasificaciones Raciales y de su Estudio en la Argentina', in Gladys Lechini (ed.), *Los Estudios Afroamericanos y Africanos en América Latina* (Buenos Aires: CLACSO, 2008), pp. 117–44.

Gaitán-Barrera, Alejandra and Govand Khalid Azeez, 'Beyond Recognition: Autonomy, the State and the Mapuche Coordinadora Arauco Malleco', *Latin American and Caribbean Ethnic Studies*, 13/2 (2018), 113–34.

Garguin, Enrique, '"Los Argentinos Descendemos de los Barcos": The Racial Articulation of Middle Class Identity in Argentina (1920–1960)', *Latin American and Caribbean Ethnic Studies*, 2/2 (2002), 161–84.

Garner, Steve and Saher Selod, 'The Racialization of Muslims: Empirical Studies of Islamophobia', *Critical Sociology*, 4/1 (2015), 9–19.

Gavirati, Marcelo, 'El Contacto entre Galeses, Pampas y Tehuelches: la Conformación de un Modelo de Convivencia Pacífica en la Patagonia Central (1865–1885)' (Doctorado Interuniversitario en Historia, Universidad del Centro de la Provincia de Buenos Aires, 2012).

Ghalzoul, Raban, 'Words that Scatter / How are We to Heal', in Darren Chetty, Grug Muse, Hanan Issa and Iestyn Tyne (eds), *Welsh Plural: Essays on the Future of Wales* (London: Repeater Books, 2022), pp. 241–54.

Gilbert, Stephanie, 'Living with the Past: the Creation of the Stolen Generation Positionality', *AlterNative* (2019), *https://journals.sagepub.com/doi/full/10.1177/1177180119869373*(accessed 20 February 2024).

Gonzalez-Sobrino, Bianca and Devon Goss, 'Exploring the Mechanisms of Racialization beyond the Black-White Binary', *Ethnic and Racial Studies*, 42/4 (2019), 505–10.

Gotkowitz, Laura (ed.), *Histories of Race and Racism: The Andes and Mesoamerica from Colonial Times to the Present* (Durham: Duke University Press, 2011).

Gower, John, *Gwalia Patagonia* (Llandysul: Gwasg Gomer, 2015).

Grimson, Alejandro, *Mitomanías Argentinas: Cómo Hablamos de Nosotros Mismos* (Buenos Aires: Siglo Veintiuno Editores, 2012).

Guano, Emanuela, 'A Color for the Modern Nation: The Discourse on Class, Race and Education in the Porteño Middle Classes', *Journal of Latin American Anthropology*, 8/1 (2002), 148–71.

Guha, Ranajit, *Elementary Aspects of Peasant Insurgency in Colonial India* (Delhi: Oxford University Press, 1983).

Hale, Charles, 'Rethinking Indigenous Politics in the Era of the "Indio Permitido"', *NACLA Report on the Americas*, 38/2 (2004), 16–21.

Hall Rhys, David (ed.), *A Welsh Song in Patagonia: Memories of the Welsh Colonization* (Milton Keynes: Lightening Source, 2005).

Hammer, Paul, 'A Welshman Abroad: Captain Peter Wynn of Jamestown', *Parergon*, 16/1 (1998), 59–92.

Harper, Marjory and Stephen Constantine, *Migration and Empire* (Oxford: Oxford University Press, 2010).

Hazlewood, Nick, *Savage: Survival, Revenge and the Theory of Evolution* (Chatham: Sceptre Books, 2000).

Hechter, Michael, *Internal Colonialism: The Celtic Fringe in British National Development* (London: Routledge, 1999).

Heng, Geraldine, *The Invention of Race in the European Middle Ages* (Cambridge: Cambridge University Press, 2018).

Hill Collins, Patricia and Sirma Bilge, *Intersectionality* (Cambridge: Polity Press, 2016).

Hooker, Juliet, *Theorizing Race in the Americas: Douglass, Sarmiento, Du Bois and Vasconcelos* (Oxford: Oxford University Press, 2017).

Hopwood, Mererid and Karen Owen, *Glaniad: Cerddi Dwy wrth Groesi Paith Patagonia* (Llanrwst: Gwasg Carreg Gwalch, 2015).

Hughes, Hugh, *Llawlyfyr y Wladychfa Gymreig* (Liverpool: L. Jones, 1862).

Hughes, William Meloch, *A'r Lannau'r Gamwy: Atgofion* (Lerpwl: Gwasg y Brython, 1927).

Hunt, E. F., 'Aaron Jenkins: the Man who Saved the Welsh Colony, Patagonia', *The Welsh Outlook*, 16/12 (1929), 371–3.

Hunt, Peter, '"Instruction and Delight" in Children's Literature: Approaches and Territories', in Janet Maybin and Nicola Watson (eds), *Routledge Companion to Children's Literature and Culture* (Basingstoke: Palgrave, 2009), pp. 14–26.

Inayatullah, Naeem and David Blaney, *International Relations and the Problem of Difference* (London: Routledge, 2004).

James, E. Wyn and Bill Jones, *Michael D. Jones a'i Wladfa Gymreig* (Llanrwst: Gwasg Carreg Gwalch, 2009).

James, E. Wyn, 'Identity, Migration and Assimilation: The Case of the Welsh Settlement in Patagonia', *Transactions of the Honourable Society of Cymmrodorion*, 25 (2018), 76–87.

Johnson, Lyman, *Workshop of Revolution: Plebeian Buenos Aires and the Atlantic World, 1776–1819* (Durham: Duke University Press, 2011).

Jenkins, Geraint H., '"A Rank Republican [and] a Leveller": William Jones, Llangadfan', *Welsh History Review*, 17/3 (1995), 365–86.

Jenkins, Geraint H. (ed.), *The Welsh Language and its Social Domains, 1801–1911* (Cardiff: University of Wales Press, 2000).

Johnston, Anna and Alan Lawson, 'Settler Colonies', in Henry Schwartz and Sangeeta Ray (eds), *A Companion to Postcolonial Studies* (Oxford: Blackwell, 2005), pp. 360–76.

Jones, Aled and Bill Jones, 'The Welsh World and the British Empire, c.1851–1939: An Exploration', *Journal of Imperial and Commonwealth History*, 31/2 (2010), 57–81.

Jones, J. R., *Prydeindod* (Llandybïe: Christopher Davies, 1966).

Jones, Lewis, *Hanes y Wladfa Gymreig yn Ne Amerig* (Caerdydd: Gwasg Genedlaethol Gymraeg, 1898).

Jones, Michael D., *Gwladychfa Gymreig* (Liverpool: J. Lloyd, 1860).

Jones, Thomas, *Historia de los Comienzos de la Colonia en la Patagonia* (1926; Trelew: Biblioteca Popular 'Agustín Alvarez', 2000).

Jones, William D., '"Going into Print": Published Immigrant Letters, Webs of Personal Relations, and the Emergence of the Welsh Public Sphere', in Bruce Elliott, David Gerber and Suzanne Sinke (eds), *Letters across Borders: The Epistolary Practices of International Migrants* (Basingstoke: Palgrave Macmillan, 2006), pp. 175–99.

Joseph, Galen, 'Taking Race Seriously: Whiteness in Argentina's National and Transnational Imaginary', *Identities*, 7/3 (2000), 333–71.

Kauanui, J. Kēhaulani, 'False Dilemmas and Settler Colonial Studies: Response to Lorenzo Veracini "Is Settler Colonial Studies Even Useful"', *Postcolonial Studies*, 24/2 (2020), 290–6.

Khleif, Bud, 'Cultural Regeneration and the School: An Anthropological Study of Welsh Medium Schools in Wales', *International Review of Education*, 22/2 (1976), 177–92.

Kluttz, Jenalee, Jude Walker and Pierre Walter, 'Unsettling Allyship, Unlearning and Learning towards Decolonizing Solidarity', *Studies in the Education of Adults*, 52/1 (2020), 49–66.

Knowles, Anne Kelly, *Calvinists Incorporated: Welsh Immigrants on Ohio's Industrial Frontier* (Chicago: University of Chicago Press, 1997).

Kradolfer Morales, Sabine, 'Ser Mapuche en Argentina en el Umbral del Tercer Milenio', *Revista del CESLA*, 10 (2007), 37–51.

Lakhani, Nina, *Who Killed Berta Cáceres? Dams, Death Squads and an Indigenous Defenders' Battle for the Planet* (London: Verso, 2020).

Laporte, Nadine, 'Gamechangers: the Women who made Y Wladfa Possible' conference paper, *Y Wladfa Gymreig Patagonia, 1865–2015*, Cardiff University, 6–7 July 2015.

Larreburo, Mario Emanuel, 'Entre el "Territorio Vacío" y la "Inmigracion Deseada": Dilemas de la Construcción del Estado Nacional en un Debate Parlamentario de 1863', *Revista Tefros*, 20/1 (2022), 79–95.

Larsson, Carolyn, *Our Indigenous Ancestors: a Cultural History of Museums, Science and Identity in Argentina, 1877–1943* (Pennsylvania: Penn State University Press, 2015).

Larsson, Carolyn (ed.), *The Conquest of the Desert: Argentina's Indigenous Peoples and the Battle for History* (Albuquerque: University of New Mexico Press, 2020).

Lazzari, Axel, 'Aboriginal Recognition, Freedom and Phantoms: The Vanishing Ranquel and the Return of the Rankülche in La Pampa', *Journal of Latin American Anthropology*, 8/3 (2003), 59–83.

Lebron, Christopher, *The Making of Black Lives Matter: Brief History of an Idea* (Oxford: Oxford University Press, 2023).

Lof Sacamata-Liempichun, 'La Historia del Lof Sacamata-Liempichun (Paraje Payaniyeo, Alto Rio Senguer, Chubut): El Reclamo y el Pedido de Restitución de Nuestro Ancestro' (GEMAS Grupo de Estudios sobre Memorias Alterizadas y Subordinadas, 2020), *https://gemasmemoria.com/2020/07/03/la-historia-de-la-lof-sacamata-liempichun-paraje-payaniyeo-alto-rio-senguer-chubut-el-reclamo-y-el-pedido-de-restitucion-de-nuestro-ancestro/* (accessed 5 August 2024).

López, Susana, *Representaciones de la Patagonia: Colonos, Científicos y Políticos, 1870–1914* (La Plata: Ediciones al Margen, 2003).

Lublin, Geraldine, 'The War of the Tea Houses, or How Welsh Heritage in Patagonia became a Valuable Commodity', *e-Keltoi*, 1/1 (2009), 69–92.

Lublin, Geraldine, 'La Identidad en la Encrucijada: la Comunidad Galesa del Chubut y las Conmemoraciones del Centenario y Bicentenario de la Revolución de Mayo', *Identidades*, 5/3 (2013), 115–30.

Lublin, Geraldine, *Memoir and Identity in Welsh Patagonia: Voices from a Settler Community in Argentina* (Cardiff: University of Wales Press, 2017).

Lublin, Geraldine, 'Adjusting the Focus: Looking at Patagonia and the Wider Argentine State through the Lens of Settler Colonial Theory', *Settler Colonial Studies*, 11/3 (2021), 386–409.

Lublin, Geraldine, Mariela Eva Rodríguez, Carolina Crespo, Ayelén Fiori, Julieta Magallanes, Ana Margarita Ramos, Kaia Santisteban, Valentina Stella y María Marcela Tomas, 'Problematizando la Historia', *https://www.library. wales/discover-learn/external-exhibitions/problematizando-la-historia/ lof-nahuelpan* (accessed 3 October 2024).

Lumbley, Coral, 'The "Dark Welsh": Color, Race and Alterity in the Matter of Medieval Wales', *Literature Compass*, 16 (2019), 1–19.

McClintock, Anne, *Imperial Leather: Race, Gender and Sexuality in the Colonial Contest* (London: Routledge, 1995).

Malcoun, Alissa and Elizabeth Strakosh, 'The Ethical Demands of Settler Colonial Theory', *Settler Colonial Studies*, 3/3–4 (2013), 426–43.

Martínez Sarasola, Carlos, 'The Conquest of the Desert and the Free Indigenous Communities of the Argentine Plains', in Nicola Foote and René Harder Horst (eds), *Military Struggle and Identity Formation in Latin America* (Gainesville: University Press of Florida, 2010), pp. 204–23.

Matthews, Abraham, *Hanes y Wladfa Gymreig yn Patagonia* (Aberdâr: Mills ac Evans, 1894).

Medhurst, Jamie, '"Nation shall speak Peace unto Nation"? The BBC and the Nations', *Critical Studies in Television*, 17/1 (2022), 8–23.

Morgan, Rhys, 'From Soldier to Settler: The Welsh in Ireland 1558–1641' (unpublished PhD thesis, Cardiff University, 2011).

Montaño, John Patrick, '"Dychenyg and Hegeying": The Material Culture of the Tudor Plantations in Ireland', in Fiona Bateman and Lionel Pilkington (eds), *Studies in Settler Colonialism: Politics, Identity and Culture* (Houndsmills: Palgrave, 2011), pp. 47–62.

Mendoza, Breny, 'Decolonial Theories in Comparison', *Journal of World Philosophies*, 5 (2020), 43–60.

Mignolo, Walter, *Darker Side of the Renaissance: Literacy, Territoriality and Colonization* (Ann Arbor: University of Michigan Press, 1995).

Mignolo, Walter, *Coloniality, Subaltern Knowledges and Border Thinking: Local Histories/Global Designs* (Princeton: Princeton University Press, 2000).

Mignolo, Walter, *Idea of Latin America* (Oxford: Blackwell, 2005).

Mignolo, Walter, *The Darker Side of Western Modernity* (Durham: Duke University Press, 2011).

Moreton-Robinson, Aileen, *White Possessive: Property, Power and Indigenous Sovereignty* (Minneapolis: University of Minnesota Press, 2020).

Morgan, Eluned, *Dringo'r Andes a Gwymon y Môr* (1904, 1909; Talybont: Honno/Y Lolfa, 2001).

Morgan, Prys, *Brad y Llyfrau Gleision* (Llandysul: Gwasg Gomer, 1991).

Murphy, Alison, 'Charting the Emergence of National Identity in Children in Wales', *Children and Society*, 32 (2018), 301–13.

Musters, George, *At Home with the Patagonians* (1871; Stroud: Nonsuch Publishers, 2005).

Nagy, Mariano, 'Violencia contra los Pueblos Originarios: Estructura y de Coyuntura', *El Puan/Óptico* (2020), 58–64, *https://ri.conicet.gov.ar/handle/11336/170398* (accessed 5 August 2024).

Nandy, Ashis, *The Loss and Recovery of the Self under Colonialism*, 2nd edn (Delhi: Oxford University Press, 2009).

Nugent, Walter, *Crossings: The Great Transatlantic Migrations, 1870–1914* (Bloomington: Indiana University Press, 1995).

Omi, Michael and Howard Winant, *Racial Formation in the United States* (New York: Routledge, 1986).

Owen, Geraint, *Crisis in Chubut: A Chapter in the History of the Welsh Colony in Patagonia* (Swansea: C. Davies, 1977).

Papazian, Alexis and Mariano Nagy, 'Prácticas de Disciplinamiento Indígena en la Isla Martín García hacia Fines del Siglo XIX', *Revista TEFROS*, 8 (December 2010), 1–17.

Parker, Mike, *Neighbours from Hell? English Attitudes to the Welsh* (Talybont: Y Lolfa, 2007).

Pateman, Carole, 'The Settler Contract', in Carole Pateman and Charles Mills, *Contract and Domination* (Cambridge: Polity Press, 2007), pp. 35–78.

Pávez Ojeda, Jorge, *Cartas Mapuches Siglo XIX* (Santiago: CoLibris/Ocho Libros, 2008).

Pérez, Pilar, 'Futuros y Fuentes: las Listas de Indígenas Presos en el Campo de Concentración de Valcheta, Rio Negro (1887)', *Nuevo Mundo Mundos Nuevos* (2015), *https://journals.openedition.org/nuevomundo/68751* (accessed 23 August 2022).

Phillips, Robert, 'History Teaching, Cultural Restorationism and National Identity in England and Wales', *Curriculum Studies*, 4/3 (1996), 385–99.

Preston, David, *The Texture of Contact: European and Indian Settler Communities on the Frontiers of Iroquoia, 1667–1783* (Indiana: University of Nebraska Press, 2009).

Priamo, Luis, *Una Frontera Lejana: La Colonización Galesa del Chubut* (Buenos Aires: Ediciones Fundacón Antorchas, 2003).

Price, Elain, *Broadcasting for Wales: The Early Years of S4C* (Cardiff: University of Wales Press, 2022).

Pritchard, Annette and Nigel Morgan, 'Culture, Identity and Tourism Representation: Marketing Cymru or Wales?', *Tourism Management*, 22 (2001), 167–79.

Pritchard, Annette and Nigel Morgan, 'Representations of "Ethnographic Knowledge": Early Comic Postcards of Wales', in Annette Pritchard and Adam Jaworski (eds), *Discourse Communications and Tourism: Multilingual Matters* (Bristol: Channel View Publications, 2016), pp. 53–75.

Querejazu, Amaya, 'Water Governance', *New Perspectives*, 30/2 (2021), 180–8.

Quijada, Mónica, 'La Ciudadanización del "Indio Bárbaro": Políticas Oficiales y Oficiosos hacia la Población Indígena de la Pampa y la Patagonia, 1870–1920', *Revista de Indias*, 59/217 (1999), 675–704.

Quijada, Mónica, '"Hijos de los Barcos" o Diversidad Invisibilizada? La Articulación de la Población Indígena en la Construcción Nacional Argentina', *Historia Mexicana*, 53/2 (2003), 489–90.

Quijano, Aníbal, 'Coloniality of Power and Eurocentrism in Latin America', *International Sociology*, 15/2 (2000), 215–32.

Ramos, Ana Margarita, 'La Organization de Comunidades Mapuche y Tehuelche 11 de Octobre', in Pedro Canales Tapia and Sebastião Vargas (eds), *Pensamiento Indígena en Nuestramérica* (Santiago: Ariadna Ediciones, 2018), pp. 159–89.

Reid Andrews, George, *The Afro-Argentines of Buenos Aires, 1800–1900* (Madison: University of Wisconsin Press, 1980).

Rhys, Matthew, *Patagonia: Crossing the Plain/Croesi'r Paith* (Llandysul: Gwasg Gomer, 2010).

Rifkin, Mark, 'Settler Common Sense', *Settler Colonial Studies*, 3/3–4 (2013), 322–40.

Rock, David, *Argentina 1516–1987: From Spanish Colonization to the Falklands War and Alfonsín* (London: I. B. Taurus, 1985).

Rock, David, *The British in Argentina: Commerce, Settlers and Power, 1800–2000* (Houndsmills: Palgrave, 2019).

Rosser, Siwan, 'Language, Culture and Identity in Welsh Children's Literature: O. M. Edwards and *Cymru'r Plant*, 1892–1920', in Riona Nic Congáil (ed.), *Codladh Céad Bliain: Cnuasach Aistí ar Litríocht na nÓg* (Baile Átha Cliath: Leabhair, 2012), pp. 223–52.

Salter, Mark, *Barbarians and Civilization in International Relations* (London: Pluto Press, 2002).

Said, Edward, *Orientalism* (London: Routledge and Kegan Paul, 1978).

Sanders, Vivienne, *Wales, the Welsh and the Making of America* (Cardiff: University of Wales Press, 2021).

Sarmiento, Domingo, *Facundo or, Civilization and Barbarism* (1845; London: Penguin, 1998).

Savino, Lucas, *Decolonizing Patagonia: Mapuche Peoples and State Formation in Argentina* (Boulder: Lexington Books, 2022).

Schlenther, Boyd Stanley, '"The English is Swallowing up their Language": Welsh Ethnic Ambivalence in Colonial Pennsylvania and the Experience of David Evans', *Pennsylvania Magazine of History and Biography*, 114/2 (1990), 201–28.

Scourfield, Jonathan, Bella Dicks, Mark Drakeford and Andrew James, *Children, Place and Identity: Nation and Locality in Middle Childhood* (London: Routledge, 2006).

Simpson, Audra, *Mohawk Interruptus: Political Life across the Borders of Settler States* (Durham: Duke University Press, 2014).

Solomianski, Alejandro, *Identidades Secretas: La Negritud Argentina* (Buenos Aires: Beatriz Viterbo Editora, 2003).

Smith, Jackson, Casandra Puckett and Wendy Simon, *Indigenous Allyship: an Overview* (Ontario: Office of Aboriginal Initiatives, Wildfred Laurier University, 2016).

Smith, Kevin, *Curriculum, Culture and Citizenship Education in Wales* (Houndsmills: Palgrave, 2016).

Snelgrove, Corey, Rita Kaur Dhamon and Jeff Corntassel, 'Unsettling Settler Colonialism: The Discourse and Politics of Settlers and Solidarity with Indigenous Nations', *Decolonization: Indigeneity, Education and Society*, 3/2 (2014), 1–32.

Spivak, Gayatri Chakravorty, *Toward a History of the Vanishing Present* (Cambridge, Mass.: Harvard University Press, 1999).

Stevens, Matthew and Teresa Phipps, 'Towards a Characterization of "Race Law" in Medieval Wales', *Journal of Legal History*, 41/3 (2020), 290–331.

Sutton, Barbara, 'Contesting Racism: Democratic Citizenship, Human Rights and Antiracist Politics in Argentina', *Latin American Perspectives*, 163/35 (2009), 106–21.

Taylor, Lucy, 'Decolonizing Citizenship: Reflections on the Coloniality of Power in Argentina', *Citizenship Studies*, 17/5 (2012), 596–610.

Taylor, Lucy, 'Welsh-Indigenous Relationships in Nineteenth Century Patagonia: "Friendship" and the Coloniality of Power', *Journal of Latin American Studies*, 49 (2017), 143–68.

Taylor, Lucy, 'Global Perspectives on Welsh Patagonia: the Complexities of being both Colonizer and Colonized', *Journal of Global History*, 13 (2018), 446–68.

Taylor, Lucy, 'The Welsh Way of Colonization in Patagonia: The International Politics of Moral Superiority', *Journal of Imperial and Commonwealth History*, 47/6 (2019), 1069–99.

Taylor, Lucy, 'Four Foundations of Settler Colonial Theory: Four Insights from Argentina', *Settler Colonial Studies*, 3 (2021), 344–65.

Todorov, Tzvetan, *The Fear of Barbarians* (Cambridge: Polity Press, 2011).

Trotter, Lucy, 'Performing Welshness in the Chubut Province of Patagonia, Argentina' (unpublished PhD thesis, The London School of Economics and Political Science, 2020).

Tuck, Eve and Wayne K. Yang, 'Decolonization is not a Metaphor', *Decolonization: Indigeneity, Education and Society*, 1/1 (2012), 1–40.

Tudur, Dafydd, 'The Life, Work and Thoughts of Michael D. Jones (1822–1898)' (unpublished PhD thesis, University of Wales, Bangor, 2006).

Tyson Roberts, Gwyneth, *Language of the Blue Books: Wales and Colonial Prejudice* (Cardiff: University of Wales Press, 1998).

Valverde, Sebastián, 'De la Invisibilización a la Construcción como Sujetos Sociales: el Pueblo Indígena Mapuche y sus Movimientos en Patagonia, Argentina', *Anuário Antropológico*, 1 (2012–13), 139–66.

Veracini, Lorenzo, *The Settler Colonial Present* (Houndsmills: Palgrave, 2015).

Wade, Peter, *Race and Ethnicity in Latin America* (London: Pluto Press, 1997).

Weber, David, *Bárbaros: Spaniards and their Savages in the Age of Enlightenment* (New Haven: Yale University Press, 2005).

White, Richard, *The Middle Ground: Indians, Empires and Republics in the Great Lakes Region, 1650–1815* (Cambridge: Cambridge University Press, 1991).

White, Sophie, *Wild Frenchmen and Frenchified Indians: Material Culture and Race in Colonial Louisiana* (Philadelphia: University of Pennsylvania Press, 2014).

Whitfield, Esther, 'Welsh-Patagonian Fiction: Language and the Novel of Transnational Ethnicity', *Diaspora*, 14, 2/3 (2005), 333–48.

Williams, Charlotte, Neil Evans and Paul O'Leary (eds), *A Tolerant Nation? Revisiting Ethnic Diversity in a Devolved Wales*, 2nd edn (Cardiff: University of Wales Press, 2015).

Williams, Colin, 'Non-Violence and the Development of the Welsh Language Society, 1962–c.1974', *Welsh History Review*, 8 (1976), 426–55.

Williams, Fernando, *Entre el Desierto y el Jardín: Viaje Literatura y Paisaje en la Colonia Galesa de la Patagonia* (Buenos Aires: Prometeo, 2010).

Williams, Glyn, *The Desert and the Dream: A Study of Welsh Colonization in Chubut, 1986–1915* (Cardiff: University of Wales Press, 1975).

Williams, Glyn, 'Welsh Settlers and Native Americans in Patagonia', *Journal of Latin American Studies*, 11/1 (1979), 41–66.

Williams, Glyn, *The Welsh in Patagonia: The State and Ethnic Community* (Cardiff: University of Wales Press, 1991).

Williams, Gwyn A., *Madog: The Making of a Myth* (London: Eyre Methuen, 1979).

Williams, Gwyn A., *The Search for Beulah Land* (London: Croom Helm, 1980).

Williams, Gwyn A., *When was Wales?* (London: Penguin, 1985).

Williams, Huw, 'Heb ei Fai, Heb ei Eni: "Disgwrs" a Moeseg y Wladfa', *Gwerddon*, 36/hydref (2023), 55–72.

Williams, R. Bryn, *Straeon Patagonia* (Llandysul: Gwasg Gomer, 1946).

Williams, R. Bryn, *Bandit yr Andes* (Caerdydd: Hughes a'i Fab, 1951).

Williams, R. Bryn, *Y March Coch* (Bala: Gwasg y Bala, 1954).

Williams, R. Bryn, *Croesi'r Paith* (Llandybïe: Llyfrau'r Dryw, 1958).

Williams, R. Bryn, *Y Wladfa* (Caerdydd: Gwasg Prifysgol Cymru, 1962).

Williams, Raymond, *Who Speaks for Wales? Nation, Culture, Identity*, ed. Daniel Williams (Cardiff: University of Wales Press, 2003).

Wolfe, Patrick, 'Settler Colonialism and the Elimination of the Native', *Journal of Genocide Research*, 8/4 (2006), 387–409.

Wood, Jennifer, 'Signifying the Nation: (In)communication, Absence and Rational (Be)longing in Marc Evans' *Patagonia* (2010)', in Brigitte le Juez and

Bill Richardson (eds), *Spaces of Longing and Belonging: Territoriality, Ideology and Creative Identity in Literature and Film* (Leiden: Brill Rodopi, 2019), pp. 210–32.

Wysote, Travis and Erin Morton, '"The Depth of the Plough": White Settler Tautologies and Pioneer Lies', *Settler Colonial Studies*, 9/4 (2019), 479–504.

Zhang, Yongjin, 'Barbarism and Civilization', in Mlada Bukovanski, Edward Keene, Christian Reus-Schmidt and Maja Spanu (eds), *Oxford Handbook of History and International Relations* (Oxford: Oxford University Press, 2023), pp. 218–32.

Index